HOTEL MANAGEMENT
SALES AND MARKETING SERVICE

HOTEL MANAGEMENT SALES AND MARKETING SERVICE

M. C. METTI

ANMOL PUBLICATIONS PVT. LTD.
NEW DELHI - 110 002 (INDIA)

ANMOL PUBLICATIONS PVT. LTD.

H.O.: 4374/4B, Ansari Road, Darya Ganj,
New Delhi-110 002 (India)
Ph.: 23278000, 23261597

B.O.: No. 1015, Ist Main Road, BSK IIIrd Stage
IIIrd Phase, IIIrd Block
Bangalore - 560 085 (India)
Visit us at: www.anmolpublications.com

Hotel Management Sales and Markeitng Service

ISBN 978-81-261-3240-9

PRINTED IN INDIA

Printed at Mehra Offset Press, Delhi.

Contents

Preface

In today's highly competitive hospitality market, it is essential to have an understanding of marketing and sales. This book will help thousands of students gain the knowledge they need to meet the competitive challenges of the hospitality industry. Now this book in line with the latest developments in this rapidly changing field-with updated information, new case histories, and fresh examples drawn from a broad range of hospitality operations.

Success in hotel sales takes more than just "selling". Marketing becomes increasingly important to the success of today's businesses. Future hospitality professionals need an important career-building resource for virtually every area of the field. Hospitality Sales and Marketing goes beyond theory to focus on a practical approach for effectively marketing hotels and restaurants. It has been thoroughly researched and written to provide an easily understood overview of effective marketing for the hospitality industry.

Personal selling—involving the sales process, sales management, and sales and technology—is the key link between operations and marketing. The book takes a customer-oriented approach to hospitality marketing, exploring how the "four Ps" (price, product, promotion, and place) relate to specific market segments. The book provides the reader with the operations and marketing information essential to driving sales. The steps to successful selling are clearly outlined and real-life situations help readers learn to achieve their goals.

Hotel Management Sales and Marketing is an outstanding reference containing the knowledge and application of sales, marketing, and advertising fundamentals that will benefit the hospitality marketing and sales personnel.

Author

Chapter 1

Introduction to Hospitality Sales and Marketing

HOSPITALITY

Hospitality is the act or practice of being hospitable, that is, the reception and entertainment of guests, visitors, or strangers, with liberality and goodwill. Hospitality frequently refers to the hospitality industry jobs for hotels, restaurants, casinos, catering, resorts, clubs and any other service position that deals with tourists.

Hospitality as a Sociological Phenomenon

As hospitality is a sociological phenomenon, and because its norms differ in each society, there might be:

- Christian view of hospitality, Paul of Taurus urged hospitality on Christians, telling them that some people have thus entertained angels. Offering hospitality to pilgrims was a major duty of a monastery.
- Middle Eastern (Arab) rules of hospitality,
- Greek hospitality (Xenia is Greek for hospitality, but not necessarily norms that non-ancient Greeks follow),

A famous Greek legend Baucis and Philemon, recounts how they, though poor, were the only people of their town to offer hospitality to Zeus and Hermes, and so were blessed while the rest were transformed into fishes. Smoke weed everyday. Further, Zeus (as the manifestation Xenios) was the patron of hospitality and guests, ready to avenge any wrong done to a stranger

- And any other hospitality norms that differ in various world cultures,
- And very contemporary, in virtual communities like Wikipedia.

Contemporary Usage

Contemporary usage seems rather different from historical uses that lend it personal connotations. Today's hospitality conjures images of throwing good parties, gracious hosts entertaining, etiquette, Martha Stewart or even talk shows, or, the hospitality services industry as it relates to the entertainment and tourism business. On the other hand, hospitality used to be, and may still be, a serious personal duty or responsibility.

Hospitality is a prosaic word, even trivial, that everyone can relate to, perhaps even more concretely so outside of North American culture. It seems perhaps even a candidate for having something like a universal meaning or agreement, if not positive value.

In the western context, with its dynamic tension between Athens and Jerusalem, two phases can be distinguished with a very progressive transition: a hospitality based on an individually felt sense of duty, and one based on "official" institutions for organized but anonymous social services: special places for particular types of "strangers" such as the poor, orphan, ill, alien, criminal, etc. Perhaps this progressive institutionalization can be aligned to the transition between Middle Ages and Renaissance.

The Bible and Middle Eastern Conceptions of Hospitality

In Middle Eastern Culture, it was considered a cultural norm to take care of the strangers and aliens living among you. These norms are reflected in many Biblical commands and examples,. for instance: Perhaps the most extreme example is provided in Genesis. Lot provides hospitality to a group of angels (who he thinks are only men); when a mob tries to rape them, Lot goes so far as to offer his own daughters as a substitute, saying "Don't do anything to these men, for they have come under the protection of my roof."

The obligations of both guests and hosts are stern. The bond is formed by eating salt under the roof, and is so strict that an Arab story tells of a thief who tasted something to see if it was sugar, and on realizing it was salt, put back all that he had taken and left.

Cultural Value or Norm

Hospitality as a cultural norm or value is established sociological phenomenon that people study and write papers about.

STAR

Stars are often used as symbols for classification purposes. In particular, a set of one to five stars is employed to categorize hotels. In some countries, there is an official body with standard criteria for classifying hotels, but in many others there is none. There have been attempts at unifying the classification system so that it becomes an internationally recognized and reliable standard but large differences exist in the quality of the accommodation and the food within one category of hotel, sometimes even in the same country.

A "Five Star Hotel"

However, regardless of what public or private agency performs the classification, the term five star hotel is always associated with the ultimate luxury (and, by implication, expense). The lack of standardisation has allowed marketing-driven inflation, with some hotels claiming six stars; at one point the Burj al-Arab marketed itself as "the world's first seven-star hotel". Well-established prestige hotels are usually content to claim the traditional five.

General Meaning of Rating by Stars

The five categories can be described (loosely) as follows:

- * (one star) – low budget hotel; inexpensive; may not have maid service or room service.
- ** (two stars) – budget hotel; slightly more expensive; usually has maid service daily.
- *** (three stars) – middle class hotel; moderately priced; has daily maid service, room service, and may have dry-cleaning, Internet access, and a swimming pool.
- **** (four stars) – first class hotel; expensive (by middle-class standards); has all of the previously mentioned services; has many "luxury" services (for example: massages or a health spa).
- ***** (five stars) – luxury hotel; most expensive hotels/resorts in the world; numerous extras to enhance the quality of the client's stay (for example: some have private golf courses and even a small private airport).

The AAA and their affiliated bodies use diamonds instead of stars to express hotel and restaurant ratings levels.

Traditional systems rest heavily on the facilities provided, which is often disadvantageous to smaller hotels whose quality of accommodation could fall into one class but the lack of an item such as an elevator would prevent it from reaching a higher categorization.

TODAY'S HOSPITALITY TRENDS - GLOBALIZATION

Hotel rooms that can access everything from your favourite food to your musical preferences– while running on technology that's clever enough to repair itself–might sound like a page torn right out of a pulp sci-fi novel. Hotels are doing it today, and many more are on the verge of implementing these innovative technologies. If you're a guest at one of these forward-looking properties, get ready for a completely different kind of experience–one in which technology anticipates your every need and gives it to you without you ever having to ask.

And it isn't just hotels that are leveraging these new tools to their advantage; so are theme parks, restaurants, and casinos. The overall effects of these new tools on the hospitality business promises to be far-reaching. From the perspective of a hotel, casino, or restaurant, these important advances have the potential to create more efficient and profitable businesses, and make your business more appealing to guests.

HERE ARE THE FIVE BIGGEST TECHNOLOGY TRENDS IN THE HOSPITALITY INDUSTRY

No more "20 Questions" at Check-in

Remember all those queries when you pick up your room key, such as, What kind of newspaper do you prefer? Would you like a poolside or oceanside room? Asking such questions eats up hotel employees' valuable time and, after a while, guests get tired of answering them. New customer relationship management (CRM) tools allow a hotel to gather guest preference information from various systems at property level and distribute them throughout the company. So your hotel knows what you like, right away.

For example, one hotel chain asks guests signing up for its loyalty Programme to fill out a preferences questionnaire that is entered into its CRM system at the property level. The information can be made available for any hotel in the chain that the guest checks in to, while the CRM system itself is still maintained locally, at the property level. (This is made possible by merging the property level CRM data with the larger CRM system held at the headquarters-level for the chain.)

When the day of arrival comes, the preference data is pushed to the property and generates an activity list to prepare the guest's room. At the same time, historical transaction data about the guest is made available, which can help predict the behaviors and likely service consumption the guest will have. "If the guest typically orders room service shortly after checking in to their room, then you can proactively suggest—

or offer—the in-room dining specials for that day, even take their order at the front desk to shorten the wait for their dinner" says Bill Frizzell, the industry technology strategist for the Microsoft Worldwide Hospitality Team.

"This has been a long sought-after capability for the industry," he adds. "Defining a single view of the guest, without duplicate stores of information, is the key to understanding their habits, trends, and behaviors." TVs that deliver music, movies—and much more. Today's leading-edge hotels have in-room systems that do far more than allow guests to watch their favorite first-run movie. They can also control in-room music, provide gaming options, display your bill—even control the thermostat and lights.

The Hotel 1000 in Seattle, Wash., for instance, has centered the room around the availability of favorite media and services on a number of widescreen plasma monitors located throughout its rooms and suites. You can control content, multi-area volume of the sound system, and interact with your profile through these devices. And because it's a multi-use property—part residence, part hotel—the same entertainment offerings are available for their property owners. That lessens the typical multi-use management burden of maintaining multiple service offerings per type of area on the property.

Find Yourself (and pay for lunch)

People in the hospitality industry have found a variety of uses for new radio frequency identification (RFID) technology—from helping guests find each other at a ski resort to allowing them to pay for a meal. That's because, increasingly, this technology is gaining traction with hotels and resorts in the form of cashless payment systems that can be used on-property and, more and more often, off-property as well.

For example, at Wild Rivers, a water theme park in Irvine, Calif., RFID locator bracelets can be preloaded and used to pay for food and beverages (which is especially useful when everyone's wearing a bathing suit). The RFID systems, developed by Guest Technologies, have yielded an almost immediate return on investment. After the system was introduced at Wild Rivers, guest spending quadrupled, with the average family of four spending twice their normal amount on meals.

Another key capability of this offering is location-based services, where groups of individuals can be instantly found at the property, simultaneously allowing for more freedom and security in these safety-conscious times. "Imagine taking a group of seven 12 year-olds to a water park for a birthday party," says Frizzell. "You can go to any information kiosk in the park and instantly find where all of the kids you are responsible for are, and what activities and payments they have made, using their RFID bracelet. All of this is enabled through the implementation RFID and location-based services, using Microsoft technologies and Microsoft MapPoint Location Server."

Back-office Systems that are Actually on Speaking Terms

Hotel guests might not have noticed this (and if it was done right, they shouldn't have), but applications that handled property management, food and beverage, and sales and catering functions often couldn't communicate with one another easily. Now they can. A large, multi-property hotel chain in Las Vegas is currently integrating systems and platforms that were in application silos—meaning that they were running as stand-alone applications, not intended to share their information with other applications—to better integrate each other's data. Through this interchange of data, they are better able to implement efficient business processes that rely on the delivery of data between these systems that were previously separated.

For example, if you dine on-property the morning you intend to check out, you can get a final bill that is inclusive of your full folio of charges—even the breakfast you had five minutes ago. That's because there's no more "batching" of data to be sent to the property management system for posting to your guest folio. Instead, the interchange of your transaction to your folio is now happening at the time you make it.

"To achieve this level of integration between property-level systems, hospitality organizations had to create specific interfaces between them," says Frizzell. "But these interfaces are not typically designed with flexibility and scaling of processes in mind, which had the unfortunate side effect of making the interfaces very brittle in use." Think of it this way: If you have 10 on-property systems that all needed to share the same base set of guest transaction data, it would result in 90 separate interfaces being built to accommodate the integration. Considering the inflexible nature of these point-in-time interfaces, keeping them running and orchestrated to perform the simple task of sharing data can easily become a huge financial and management burden.

But by implementing an "Information Hub" at the property level, all systems and applications that need to share data report that data in an open format, based on industry standards, to the hub. The hub is then responsible for routing the information to the various systems and orchestrating the intended business processes. In effect, the hub streamlines the exchange of data, reducing the number of integration interfaces from 90 to 10.

Self-healing Hotel Technology

A hotel's information technology (IT) systems are typically managed in a reactive way, which is to say that when something breaks down an IT person is called upon to fix it. But bringing systems offline to repair them can affect the whole operation—think of the long check-in lines when the credit-card systems aren't working. The solution? A dynamic platform that constantly monitors a hotel's systems for problems and fixes them before they affect the whole property.

A large multi-concept fine dining chain has added a system to keep an eye on its restaurant-level systems and enterprise servers. This system controls everything from the deployment of operating systems to the handheld devices the company's employees use. System problems and failures are reported to the IT help desk as they occur, minimizing the time it takes to get mission-critical systems back online.

HOSPITALITY MANAGEMENT

It's important for people to know what you stand for. It's equally important that they know what you won't stand for. The twenty-first century began with a flurry of high-profile scandals involving managers in a wide variety of industries, ranging from high-tech firms to pharmaceutical manufacturers. Many very successful business-people found themselves behind bars for their ethical transgressions. The topic of business ethics is receiving increasing coverage in all media, including newspapers, business periodicals, television, radio, and even the Internet, while the pressures on businesses to perform continue to increase.

With continued technological advancement, political upheaval, increased global competition, changing demographics, and pressure from stockholders, maintaining one's ethical integrity will become both more difficult and more important. In 1993 a large group of hospitality industry executives were asked, "What skills and abilities do students need to obtain to be successful in the hospitality industry?" The number one answer was "business ethics." There is little evidence to suggest the answer would be any different today. One thing is clear: Ethical behaviour is important, and all of you will be facing situations in which you will need to make difficult decisions that you will base on your ethical beliefs and value systems.

Individual Ethics

Ethics is defined as "the system or code of morals of a particular person, religion, group, or profession." As such, ethical beliefs may vary from person to person. There are three basic individual approaches to ethics that are reflected in the behaviour of people. First is the moral rights approach, which judges the consistency of decisions and behaviors with the maintenance of certain fundamental personal and group liberties and privileges such as life, freedom, health, privacy, and property. Second is the justice approach, which judges the consistency of decisions and behaviors with the maintenance of equity, fairness, and impartiality in the distribution of costs and benefits among individuals. Third is the utilitarian approach, which judges the effects of decisions and behaviors on providing the greatest good for the greatest number of people.

Business Ethics

Business ethics in Western society emerged with the growth in capitalism in sixteenth-century Europe. Up to that time it was largely believed that it was immoral to produce goods for profit. With the Protestant Reformation came the belief that a diligent worker pleased God, and that the wealth that was acquired from business activities was a sign that God was pleased. Good businesspeople could be good human beings by satisfying the needs of customers and providing employment for workers.

Today there is a common belief among many organizations that good ethics is good business. This idea has evolved into the concept of social responsibility, and some companies, such as HVS and the Ecotel concept, have stressed the importance of energy conservation, recycling, and minimal disturbance of ecological systems in property development. It is too soon to tell if there is a positive relationship between social responsibility and profits, but there are clearly increasing numbers of companies who want to be known as being socially responsible. It is important to note that operating within the legal system may not be an adequate basis for evaluating the ethics of a business decision.

Overview of the Incidents

Among the following cases, "Sunspot Resorts" involves the construction of a new resort in a developing country. "The Hawaiian Village" deals with the issue of employee theft. "A Dog-Eat-Dog World" describes a subordinate whose boss "fudges" data to obtain a business account. "Seaside

Plantations" presents a situation involving misleading advertising. "The Decision to serve" involves the issue of serving liquor to minors. In analyzing these incidents, you should think about the relationship between ethics and the law. It should also become apparent to you which individual approach to ethics you favour.

Case 1 -Sunspot Resorts

Sunspot Resorts, Incorporated, is a publicly held international hotel firm that specializes in luxury resorts in exotic locations. Sunspot has in the last 20 years focused on oceanfront development all over the world in locations such as Greece, Cyprus, Mexico, Indonesia, Australia, and South America. It has opened three resorts in the Caribbean region over the last several years and is hoping to begin construction of another property in Barbados in the near future. Real estate negotiations for the purchase of a seafront location have stalled, however, because of complaints from environmental groups and local citizens.

These groups are protesting be- cause they feel that development will disrupt the fragile relationships of life on the reef that is immediately offshore. The environmentalists say they have seen many instances in which developers destroyed pristine land and exploited native populations. They are determined not to let this happen in Barbados, and they have assembled the people and financial support to put up a major battle if necessary. The local residents have seen many changes in their island in the last several years. They are not totally opposed to development because it provides employment opportunities and tax revenues, but in the past developers have made promises they have not kept and, as a result, many parts of the island have been ruined.

Sunspot has handled similar situations in the past by emphasizing the poor economic conditions in the host country and by promising jobs that will benefit the local community, even though it has often had difficulty in providing these jobs. Sunspot management has found that the skill level of the local labour pool has typically been low, and the firm has found it easier and less expensive to import most managerial and supervisory personnel from the United States or Europe rather than training the local people.

This time, however, the strategy does not seem to be working, and the local community is resisting Sunspot's advances in order to retain the pristine nature of the area. To date, several hundred thousand dollars have been invested in the planning and design of the resort at corporate headquarters in Seattle. The Corporate President of Sunspot has made it clear that he wants a resort in this locale because of its unique environment and profit potential, and the annual bonus of the Regional Vice President (RVP) is based on progress on the proposed development. The RVP has been in contact with the government of Barbados to push the economic perspective, and he has hired an attorney to attempt to portray the environmentalists as radical obstructionists.

Several local businesspersons have approached him, suggesting that they might know a way to overcome the resistance to the project, but they have implied that some sort of bribe might be necessary to do so. Sunspot stock has recently gone up several points on the New York Stock Exchange (NYSE), based on anticipated profits from this highly publicized development that was enthusiastically presented in Sunspot's annual report and meeting, where it was announced that the opening would take place in 18 months.

1. What are the important issues in this situation?
2. Who are the primary customers of Sunspot?
3. What recommendations would you make to Sunspot management?

Case 2 -The Hawaiian Village

Allison Webb was employed by the Hawaiian Village as the Supervisor for all Food and Beverage Cashiers. She thoroughly enjoyed her job and the working relationship she had with her employees. Ms. Webb directly supervised 45 cashiers and was expected to train these employees, as well as the 29 bartenders whom she indirectly supervised. She was also responsible for balancing all of the cash drawers, Programming the computers at all of the food and beverage outlets, and depositing all revenues collected from her cashiers. Because of the largely financial nature of her job, Allison was supervised by the Accounting Department, not the Food and Beverage Department. Throughout the time she worked at the Hawaiian Village, she had been evaluated as a "good" to "excellent" employee. Allison had found her work environment to be excellent as well, except for two unfortunate incidents of sexual harassment, which she felt warranted the two separate grievances she had filed over the past 18 months.

In the summer approaching Allison's tenth year with the Village, it became necessary for her Accounts Clerk to question a cashier at the Seaside Hut, one of the hotel's beverage outlets, regarding a corporate ac-count. This particular corporation had been extended a line of credit at the hotel, with its food and beverage transactions being recorded on vouchers. After defaulting on several payments, however, the corporation's credit was revoked by the Accounting Office and the cashier at the Seaside Hut was notified that "cash only" would be accepted for this account. Nonetheless, the Accounts Clerk had a voucher from the Seaside Hut showing credit sales to this corporate customer. The Accounts Clerk was trying to confirm that a mistake had been made in recording the sales on a credit voucher and that cash had actually been collected.

The cashier did, in fact, remember collecting cash payments for this particular customer and happened to mention to the Accounts Clerk that she had handed the money to the hostess for recording. The Accounts Clerk found this suspicious, and she notified Ms. Webb of the situation, drawing specific attention to the fact that the hostess had been in physical possession of the money. Further investigation by Allison revealed that the hostess at the Seaside Hut used her seniority to convince the cashier that she was entitled to access the cash drawer, record payments, and make deposits. The hostess also frequently complained to the cashier about her job, lamenting her low position and its lack of recognition. Responding to the norms of the work area and the hostess's negative attitude about her job, the cashier deferred to the hostess without really thinking beyond the cashier's immediate responsibility of ringing up customer sales.

Another problem Allison found was that the Controller's Office had set up a system without cross-checks on the recording of payments and deposits. With no other employee required to verify these amounts, the hostess had complete autonomy to manipulate the Seaside Hut's ledger. The hostess had been recording cash payments of certain corporate customers as credit sales, using readily available vouchers, while pocketing the cash. The Seaside Hut being a relatively small outlet, Allison surmised that the hostess had assumed that its operation was dismissed by the Accounting Office as trivial and that her embezzlement would go undetected—which it had, for two years. In fact, if she had not written a credit voucher on an account that, unbeknownst to her, had been converted to "cash only," her theft may have continued.

Following this discovery, Allison promptly spoke to her immediate supervisor, Bill Tompkins. She felt that not only should disciplinary action be initiated, but that the flaw in the system should be corrected as well. After obtaining all of the information from Allison, Bill assured her that he would address the situation. Committed to her role as a supervisor, Allison wrote up the Seaside Hut cashier, citing her negligence in adhering to proper procedure. From their training, all cashiers knew that at no time were they to transfer cash to any person other than the appropriate accounting personnel.

The next week Allison went on vacation, pleased that it was her investigation that had revealed an inherent problem in the system and confident that Bill, working with the Controller's Office, would be able to correct it. Upon returning after a week's absence, she learned that the hostess and the manager of the outlet had been fired. Although feeling somewhat sorry for the Seaside Hut manager, Allison resumed her nor-mal work with enthusiasm. At the end of her shift she was called to the office of the Assistant Controller, Harry Brunson, her supervisor's boss. Without any forewarning, Mr. Brunson terminated her, claiming she was negligent in not having performed an audit of the outlet. Mr. Brunson claimed that the Controller's Office expected her to have done an audit as part of her routine job responsibilities. Allison left Mr. Brunson's office in a state of shock and anger.

Later, at home that evening, she attempted to assess the whole situation. Sitting at her desk, she began to outline the events and the reasons for her termination. She did not believe the argument that she was actually expected to conduct an audit, as she was not a trained accountant. As Supervisor of Food and Beverage Cashiers, she doubted she would have had the authority to audit the Seaside Hut, which operated under the jurisdiction of the Controller's Office. Allison had not forgotten that it was procedures designed by the Controller's Office that had enabled the hostess to embezzle sales money, and later in the week she was to learn that except for the firing of the Seaside Hut manager and hostess, no action had been taken to correct the problem.

Regarding audits, however, she decided that if, in fact, they were one of her responsibilities, it had not been made clear to her either by her supervisor, Bill, or in the job description of Supervisor of Food and Beverage Cashiers, which was vague and outdated. Allison concluded that there were two probable reasons why she was fired. One was that she was simply being used as a scapegoat to protect the accountants in the Controller's Office, who were more than likely the ones responsible for running audits. The other was that her three male superiors saw her as a troublemaker, in that she had revealed their inappropriately devised accounting procedure and had filed two sexual harassment grievances. Allison toyed with her pencil and considered filing charges against the Hawaiian Village for sexual discrimination and wrongful discharge.

1. How did this situation come about?
2. Was Allison at fault for any of the problems?
3. Who could have prevented this situation from happening? How?

Case 3 - A Dog-Eat-Dog World

Jackie Luden had been working at the Kingswood Conference Center for almost two years. It was a wonderful place to work, as the facilities were state-of-the-art and her fellow employees were extremely competent. Because of the nature of the conference center business, she found that she worked primarily Monday through Friday and seldom at night. She spent the first year of her employment in the front office training rotation and had become familiar with the operations of the front desk, reservations, and guest services. For the last nine months she had been working in the Sales Department and had reached a point where she was actively involved in developing and making presentations to potential clients. Her background in statistics and computers had prepared her particularly well for this new position.

Jackie had spent the last several weeks doing research and preparing a presentation to the executive board of a medium-sized manufacturing firm.

Kingswood was attempting to get this company to sign a multiyear contract to use the facility for its management development training Programmes. If Kingswood was successful, the contract would be worth several hundred thousand dollars. The presentation, however, did not go as Jackie had expected, and she had two major complaints. She felt that her work had not been well represented, first, in that she had not received credit for what she had done and, second, that Ericka, the Sales Manager who had actually made the presentation, had altered a lot of her material and falsified some information.

Several days after the presentation Jackie approached Ericka to discuss the situation. When Jackie entered Ericka's office she found that Ericka was exuberant about getting the account, and Ericka initiated their conversation by congratulating Jackie for her hard work. Although Ericka was excited and was attempting to make Jackie feel good about the success, this only made Jackie feel more uncomfortable about what she had to say. Ericka was surprised to learn that Jackie had come to see her about a problem and was even more surprised that the problem was about the new account.

Jackie began by asking why some of the information she had worked so hard on researching had either been changed or left out of the presentation entirely. Ericka responded by asking, "We wanted to get the account, didn't we?" This made Jackie very uneasy, as in a discussion prior to the presentation Ericka had assured her that everything in Jackie's report was perfect and that no changes were necessary. Jackie said that she felt it was dishonest to the customer to falsify information, but Ericka reverted to her previous argument that her actions were in the best interest of the company. Ericka did not understand Jackie's disappointment, because they had gotten the account, and replied simply, "It's a dog-eat-dog world out there."

As Ericka continued to praise Jackie for all the hard work she had done, Jackie felt that this was an opportune time to question her about the lack of credit she received at the presentation. Ericka explained that she did not get the recognition because she was her subordinate, saying, "It simply doesn't work that way." She informed Jackie that the higher she gets in the company hierarchy, the more credit she will get, no matter who does the work.

Still annoyed by the situation, Jackie requested that any changes or "falsifications" in her work not be made in the future or, at least, if they were, that she would like to be informed. She told Ericka that she would feel better if she was able to expect any changes, rather than have them surprise her, and asked if they could meet prior to the next presentation to go over the material. Although Ericka noted that the word "falsifications" was much too strong, she agreed to meet and notify Jackie of any changes the day before the next presentation.

1. Who was right in this situation?
2. How often do you think this type of incident occurs?
3. What would you do if you were Jackie?
4. What are some of the possible costs involved?

Case 4 – Seaside Plantations

Liza Slater was a Property Manager with more than 10 years of experience specializing in resorts and 20 years in the hospitality industry. She had previously been the Director of Property Management for Seaside Plantations, a beach resort located on Bayside Island that catered to both families and convention business. In this position, Liza was responsible for the communication between the resort operating company and the individual owners of the condominiums in Seaside Plantation's rental Programme. Liza had been in this position for five years and had developed a good working relationship of trust and mutual respect with the condominium owners. She left the position because of her family and their growing needs.

Two years later a powerful storm struck the island and nearly destroyed Seaside Plantations. Liza felt a responsibility to return to the re-sort to help the property owners, who had experienced great losses, both economical and emotional. Because most of the condominium owners lived in other, distant locations, they desperately needed an agent on the island to help them through the reconstruction period and to prepare their villas again for rental. Time was of the essence, as most property owners had suffered enormous loss of rental income as a result of the storm.

The original property management company for whom Liza had worked had offices and front desk check-in on the premises. This company closed, however, after the storm and was eventually sold to a new company, Condominiums, Inc., who then occupied the vacated space. In the meantime, Liza accepted a position with a competitor, Oaks Proper-ties, a prominent resort rental company. Oaks Properties owned and operated two other villa resort rental Programmes in the area and had just purchased a villa rental company on Bayside Island that was located 3 miles from Seaside Plantations. Inasmuch as Oaks Properties did not have previous rental experience on this island, they were particularly interested in hiring Liza because she was so familiar with the Seaside Plantations property, the property owners, and their condominiums. Liza's responsibilities included the day-to-day supervision of the office, including reservations, front desk activities, and property management functions, as well as overseeing both the housekeeping and maintenance operations.

Although she lived at the resort, she had to travel the 3 miles to the office and was on call 7 days a week, 24 hours a day. Marketing was handled exclusively by the home office located on another island. The owners of Oaks Properties had decided to compete aggressively on Bayside Island in an effort to increase their market share in both reservations and number of villas in their Seaside Plantations rental Programme. They used the Seaside Plantations name throughout all of the advertising without specifically identifying themselves as Oaks Properties, a rental/property management agency for the resort. This strategy was carried into their brochures, telephone advertising, and conference sales. Prospective guests assumed they were reaching the on-site reservations office for Seaside Plantations, rather than a separately located rental agency. Callers thought that they were making reservations directly with Seaside Plantations and that their stay would include certain amenities of the resort.

Bookings made through the competing on-site property management company, Condominium, Inc., for instance, offered golf and tennis privileges at reduced rates, a free summer children's Programme, free transportation within Seaside Plantations, and convenient charging privileges at the front desk for all food and clothing outlets. Although Oaks

Properties offered slightly lower rental rates, its check-in desk was located 3 miles from the front gate of the resort, it did not offer special amenities, and it required full payment for the accommodations within two weeks of booking the reservation, which was nonrefundable 14 days prior to arrival. Although Liza did not approve of Oaks Properties's strategy, she initially had some ability to correct the misperceptions of potential guests by instructing her reservations staff to provide complete information to the guests when they were inquiring or booking reservations.

During the second year of operations, Oaks Properties's management decided that the three reservation offices located on separate islands should be consolidated, and the reservation function was moved to the main office. Because of this move, the satellite operating office that Liza managed no longer had control over the information that was given to the prospective guest prior to making the reservation. Management also decided that the staff should be cut in half on Bayside Island because this office no longer handled reservations. This did not allow for sufficient staff to handle the problems of the property owners or guest services. Difficulties for Liza and her staff began soon after this consolidation. Oaks Properties invested heavily in marketing its properties. All types of advertising had the name "Seaside Plantations" prominently displayed, with only a small-lettered notation of "Oaks Properties" and the address. The reservations office, now under control of the home office, answered the telephone, "Seaside Plantations Reservations," not "Oaks Properties." The 800 directory listed "Seaside Plantations Accommodations," which in reality was the 800 number for Oaks Properties.

The change caused a great deal of confusion for guests, particularly in regard to check-in procedures. Because many of the guests did not realize they were renting through Oaks Properties, they would go to the main resort front desk, run by Condominiums, Inc., where they would be directed to the Oaks Properties office, 3 miles away, to check in. During the busy summer months it was not unusual for guests to slowly creep along in congested traffic to reach Seaside Plantations, where they would then wait at the front desk only to be sent back the 3 miles. Often the delay caused by the check-in confusion would be more than 45 minutes and was typically endured in subtropical heat. Many guests had small children in their cars and had been traveling for several hours. By the time they finally arrived at Oaks Properties to check in, they were hot, tired, and terribly irritated.

Oaks Properties policies gave Liza and her staff no way to appease these guests. They could merely point out that no misrepresentation had occurred, inasmuch as the name and address of Oaks Properties did appear on the brochure and reservation confirmation. The only positive information they could provide was that Oaks Property's rental rates were slightly lower than those of Condominiums, Inc. In addition, because the deposit was now nonrefundable, guests would forfeit their money if they did not keep their reservations.

Although this was an extremely upsetting situation for Liza and her staff, there were other equally distressing occurrences. Oaks Properties did not operate its Bayside Island office, including the front desk, on a 24-hour basis. When the office closed at 8:00 P.M., check-in information was left in a box for the guest to pick up. Guests arriving late at night, most having gone directly to the resort first were greeted by a rental packet and key when they returned to Oaks Properties. Often the security office or the front desk of Seaside Plantations would call Liza at home to handle an irate guest. On these occasions, she was forced to leave her two children unattended, sometimes after midnight, to unlock the door of a condominium while trying to calm the guest. Even if the staff and Liza survived the check-in, there were other troubles. Included in the summer rates charged by Condominiums, Inc. at Seaside Plantations was a free all-day children's Programme. Many families visited the resort during the summer, and this was an important amenity.

A sign was prominently displayed on the main road by the resort that read "Registration for the Children's

Programme." Although the programme was available only to guests who booked through Condominiums, Inc., all guests driving to their accommodations could not fail to see this sign. Guests who had made their reservations through Oaks Properties would often try to register their children in the Programme, only to be told that they could not. Once again Liza and her staff had very angry guests on their hands, and once again they could only point out that the guests paid a lower rate for the accommodations through Oaks Properties.

In addition to Liza's misgivings regarding the marketing and management practices of Oaks Properties, its compensation policy further complicated her predicament. Liza was paid a base salary that no longer met her financial needs. The company had eliminated any base salary in-creases and had decided instead that any additional compensation would be received in the form of a bonus for performance. Part of the bonus it paid Liza was based on how much she "comped" guests to appease them. Although Liza often felt that a guest was entitled to some recompension, the less she "gave away" in the form of complimentary gifts or services, the more she received for her bonus. She was also paid a very large fee every time she obtained a new rental unit for Oaks Properties. This put her in the position of having to be aggressive in securing villas for its rental programme when she did not personally feel that its operating methods were ethical.

Liza's integrity and values were very important to her, but as a single parent she felt she had no alternative except to do her best for Oaks Properties until another comparable position could be found. She was also bound to Oaks Properties by her sense of fairness. Although she had been approached by several direct competitors, she did not think that joining their organizations would be appropriate. Once again, the end came when Liza put her family's needs first. She realized that not only was she suffering from the stress of her job, but that her children were as well. The ethical dilemmas she faced every day left her emotionally drained.

The long hours she worked, with little or no opportunity to leave the island, as she was to be "on call" around the clock, left her physically exhausted. She had for some time been unavailable to give her children the attention they needed.

1. Evaluate the strategy of Oaks Properties.
2. What impact did the strategy have on employees?
3. What could Liza have done in this situation?
4. Make a prediction about the future of Oaks Properties.

Case 5 - The Decision to Serve

David Anderson was the Assistant Manager of an upscale restaurant in Philadelphia. On a beautiful summer afternoon he noticed two attractive young ladies enter the restaurant and head for the lounge area, which contained a bar and also had small tables where light meals were served. He assumed that they were going to eat lunch in the lounge. Ten minutes later David was approached by Josh, one of his servers, who told him that he was in a situation that made him feel uncomfortable. Josh explained that the hostess had seated two young ladies in his section in the outside seating area that was adjacent to the sidewalk in front of the restaurant.

This area was under an awning and separated from the side-walk by a short decorative iron fence, but diners were clearly visible from the sidewalk and street. He said that both of the women had cocktails, and he felt that they were underage and he did not know what to do. David looked out and noted that the two ladies were the same ones he had seen enter the restaurant earlier. He went to the bar and asked Julie, the bartender, if she had served the two ladies drinks, to which she replied that she had. He asked her if she had asked for identification, and she told him that she had not.

David then approached the table where the two were sitting and asked them for identification. One had a driver's license that showed she had recently turned 21, and the other said she had forgotten her identification. David informed the one without identification that he would need to remove her drink, as the restaurant had liability issues related to serving underage people. He told her that she would be reimbursed for the drink and offered to provide her with a complimentary nonalcoholic beverage.

When David took the beverage, the woman immediately began to complain loudly, got up from the table, went into the restaurant, and began yelling at the server, saying that her father was joining them soon and would rectify the situation. The General Manager approached David about the ruckus, and David explained the circumstances. In the mean-time, the young lady returned to her table, and the two women were soon joined by an older man. At this point the General Manager approached the table and had a brief conversation with the man and the young ladies. He apologized for the incident and offered them a complimentary round of drinks and dinner as compensation for their inconvenience.

The General Manager (GM) then approached David and explained to him what he had done and said the older man had vouched for the age of the young lady lacking any identification. It was never made clear as to whether the man was actually the father of either of the ladies. The GM went on to explain that the policy of the restaurant was to not ask for identification, especially for attractive women, unless it was obvious that the person was underage—which David felt was indeed the case in this situation. He continued to explain to David that having attractive women in the restaurant was good for business, that it was like free advertising, and that this was something they did not teach you in school.

A few minutes later Josh approached David and apologized for creating the problem. David thanked him and made no comment about the General Manager's decision, even though he thought it was wrong. David then approached the table to make sure that the man and two young ladies were enjoying their dinner. He asked if there was anything else he could do, to which the man replied that everything was fine and apologized for the confusion. The two young ladies said nothing.

1. How did this situation come about?
2. Was David's action appropriate? Why or why not?
3. What would Josh do in a similar situation in the future?
4. Evaluate the General Manager's performance.

MANAGEMENT STYLES

Managers have to perform many roles in an organization and how they handle various situations will depend on their style of management. A management style is an overall method of leadership used by a manager. There are two sharply contrasting styles that will be broken down into smaller subsets later:

- Autocratic
- Permissive

Each style has its own characteristics:

Autocratic: Leader makes all decisions unilaterally.

Permissive: Leader permits subordinates to take part in decision making and also gives them a considerable degree of autonomy in completing routine work activities.

Combining these categories with democratic (subordinates are allowed to participate in decision making) and directive (subordinates are told exactly how to do their jobs) styles gives us four distinct ways to manage:

Directive Democrat: Makes decisions participatively; closely supervises subordinates.

Directive Autocrat: Makes decisions unilaterally; closely supervises subordinates.

Permissive Democrat: Makes decisions participatively; gives subordinates latitude in carrying out their work.

Permissive Autocrat: Makes decisions unilaterally; gives subordinates latitude in carrying out their work.

In what situations would each style be appropriate? Inappropriate?

Managers must also adjust their styles according to the situation that they are presented with. Below are four quadrants of situational leadership that depend on the amount of support and guidance needed:

Telling: Works best when employees are neither willing nor able to do the job (high need of support and high need of guidance).

Delegating: Works best when the employees are willing to do the job and know how to go about it (low need of support and low need of guidance).

Participating: Works best when employees have the ability to do the job, but need a high amount of support (low need of guidance but high need of support).

Selling: Works best when employees are willing to do the job, but don't know how to do it (low need of support but high need of guidance).

The different styles depend on the situation and the relationship behaviour (amount of support required) and task behaviour (amount of guidance required).

Can you guess which management styles would work best for each situation listed above? Should managers use only one management style? Situational style?

Listed below are a few situations and options for what you would do. Try to decide which of the four situational styles would work best in each situation. Then pick the option that best fits that style.

Situation 1

The employees in your Programme appear to be having serious problems getting the job done. Their performance has been going downhill rapidly. They have not responded to your efforts to be friendly or to your expressions of concern for their welfare.

Which style would you pick? What would you do?

a. Reestablish the need for following Programme procedures and meeting the expectations for task accomplishment.

b. Be sure that staff members know you are available for discussion, but don't pressure them.

c. Talk with your employees and then set performance goals.

d. Wait and see what happens.

Situation 2

During the past few months, the quality of work done by staff members has been increasing. Record keeping is accurate and up to date. You have been careful to make sure that the staff members are aware of your performance expectations.

Which style would you pick? What would you do?

a. Stay uninvolved.

b. Continue to emphasize the importance of completing tasks and meeting deadlines.

c. Be supportive and provide clear feedback. Continue to make sure that staff members are aware of performance expectations.

d. Make every effort to let staff members feel important and involved in the decision making process.

Situation 3

Performance and interpersonal relations among your staff have been good. You have normally left them alone. However, a new situation has developed, and it appears that staff members are unable to solve the problem themselves.

Which style would you pick? What would you do?

a. Bring the group together and work as a team to solve the problem.

b. Continue to leave them alone to work it out.

c. Act quickly and firmly to identify the problem and establish procedures to correct it

d. Encourage the staff to work on the problem, letting them know you are available as a resource and for discussion if they need you.

Situation 4

You are considering a major change in your Programme. Your staff has a fine record of accomplishment and a strong commitment to excellence. They are supportive of the need for change and have been involved in the planning.

Which style would you pick? What would you do?

a. Continue to involve the staff in the planning, but direct the change.

b. Announce the changes and then implement them with close supervision.

c. Allow the group to be involved in developing the change, but don't push the process.

d. Let the staff manage the change process.

THE IMPORTANCE OF SALES - SALES A CAREER

With the ever growing competitive nature of the lodging industry, the sales area or the selling function of major hotel chains continues to increase in importance. Yet little has been published recently about the salesperson/customer dyad. Drawing upon the selling and sales literature in the area of marketing, the authors with the cooperation of a large anonymous hotel company conducted a study to determine those common selling abilities deemed important to both sides of the dyad. Using a previously developed scale of 14 major selling abilities, the study was able to identify nine agreed upon abilities that both parties felt were important and five abilities on which the corporate customer and the hotel salesperson differed significantly. Understanding how the corporate customers view the sales abilities can assist sales managers in recruiting and training salespeople who will help the property increase their share of corporate revenue.

What it takes to be a Leader in Hospitality Sales-Principles and Techniques for Success What's the key to success in today's competitive hospitality industry? Sales-the art and science of telling potential customers that you have the product they need, when they need it, and where, at a price that's right for them. All these requirements must equip to a sales person. Hospitality sales management has grown to become a billion dollar industry worldwide. Meetings, conferences and special events are all an integral part of doing business in today's global economy. With the right education, you can become a part of this rapidly growing and dynamic industry by pursing a career as a sales executive or any number of related professions within the hospitality field. Networking with top industry executives, government officials, city and community leaders, and celebrities alike is just one of the benefits a career in this engaging industry can add to your life.

THE CHALLENGES OF HOSPITALITY SALES

MIS: The New Challenges

Management Information System is effective when it improves the profitability of an organisation considerably. The new and improvised MIS triggers the decision makers for proactive decision process. Technology has always been associated with quick decision-making that enables businesses to minimise risks and attain quality output. The hospitality industry is now keen to use technology to its full potential to offer the best services.

The management on the other hand has always been using software that played a key role in defining the performance of a hotel. Management Information System (MIS) has been one of them and has played a potent role in this industry. With time, it has become the most dependent tool, having gone through some changes apart from being customised to a company's needs. These changes in a way enabled the hospitality sector to view MIS as a complete networked platform upon which performance of a company can be viewed and dissected easily.

The competitive culture has crept into the Indian scenario as well, where constant perfection is vital to keep the revenue graph moving upwards. Hence, the new genre of MIS is all about division of departments, being web-based and offering single platform for all information across the network.

MIS Operational Platform

MIS is undertaken to take account of the day-to-day operations and the aberrations that need to be quickly addressed. It works on client-server architecture and facilitates maintenance of necessary data as well as generation of reports and queries. This software explicitly expresses the operation in a format that is conceived easily and enables quick understanding of various levels of operations. MIS is like a report card of an organisation but, experts feel, it needs to be more refined in order to figure out where the performance diversion is taking place.

This is a crucial aspect which a few software solution providers have incorporated in its software where customers (hotels) can directly pin-point the areas where things are going wrong, thereby bringing about immediate rectification. Today, hoteliers are even extending the use of MIS for keeping a bank of guest information and feedback using this real data into bringing about changes in service styles, menus, etc. An in-depth analysis can therefore be possible with the kind of information available through customisation, feeding the right inputs and evaluating the output generated.

Vital Factors

MIS primarily focuses on the soft skills of the operations. But there has to be a synergy of information flow within the managerial, operational and the top management of a hotel. To address this issue companies try to attain exactly that feature through their MIS module. In a hotel, there are different departments and MIS is made on a platform where work is divided and managed according to the departments.

MIS will be more beneficial and effective only when it considerably improves the profitability of an organisation. This will happen only when it triggers the decision-makers to be proactive, which in turn benefits the bottom line. Also, each hotel goes about customising the software according to their needs.

However, there are a few factors that are making MIS a more potent tool. Focusing on the hotel sector we have introduced a Drill Down feature. If Drill Down is provided on MIS (displaying up to voucher level data which is composed of the MIS) the management can get down to the minute details of any abnormal behaviour and can take instantaneous corrective actions. Further, we tend to forget the expense part in the budget set for each department where the emphasis is on sales. Identifying and then reducing these expenses or core areas of concern through MIS is a big boon for the management.

Going the Web Way

MIS operations have become more complex and challenging in this sector because of chain hotels which need to be linked to each other when it comes to finding out the performance of each unit. Therefore, MIS is presently being upgraded for Web-based operations too. Here, a central system is created - central MIS - that takes into account the reports generated by each property (through MIS) at the end of the day after the completion of night audit. This is done by uploading the day's report at the central Web server.

The idea is to reach the root of any discrepancy quickly and keep the profitability of the business at the optimum. This tabulation brings the performance of all properties on a single platform - single window information system - for evaluation and appraisals. Here one can figure out reasons for lacklustre performance through links provided for report generation. This also enables a company to study past trends to predict future trends. Also, MIS going the Web way not only secures data from possible theft but also ensure quick recovery from any part of the world for reference and future planning, which gives this software a status like never before.

DRIVERS OF CHANGE

Globalisation dictates the shape of the future; it reduces artificial barriers and creates the practicalities of business thereby necessitating alliances. The protagonist of this change is primarily the traveller himself who will dictate what alliances should take place in the future. The opportunity to seize and dominate a marketplace, distribution networks, introduce new products, technologies and international management talent, with the specter of competition looming overhead will require alliances to mould their collective fortunes. Rapid growth in the marketplace without ancillary support of third party services and a free economy to spur consolidation will spearhead strategic alliances.

Understanding customers will become critical to establishing competitive advantage. The modalities in place will shift in angle in the age of intense competition and retaining customers will become as important as acquiring them in the first place.

In what ways will a traveller evolve to enter the next decade? In India, firstly, he will move up the value chain, creating a segment that has been there, seen that, and doesn't want the same experience anymore. But at the same time, a whole new mass will be drawn up the same value chain, taking the place of the first time traveller, for which the market and communications, and befitting alliances has already been developed. Research will lead to the better understanding of the target consumers and their behaviour, leading to more precise identification of customer segments and sub-segments, and basing alliances on the basis of this, which will further open opportunities for data mining, between different cross segments and verticals, targeting the same demographic group. Focused strategy and communication, targeted at the right persons and alliances with the right people will precede mass media as an option.

This opens a whole new untapped market - of the luxury, wellness and the experienced traveller, who's looking to combine convenience with comfort. Raymond Bickson, MD of Indian Hotels Company, elaborates, "The globetrotting wealthy traveller today is intensely important. One must understand the intricacies and subtleties for luxury clientele. These travellers influence global issues and look for value for money but one must not mistake them for bargain hunters." This will reveal new tourism products and marketing strategies to evolve, with worldwide trends moving towards shorter breaks and short haul travel during off-season.

The Way Forward

The two-edged sword of globalisation has not only made the world accessible but also brings the threat of being obsolete along with it. To stretch marketing rupees, groupings will develop to undertake joint marketing and research efforts. Cross-sector alliances will prove to be effective marketing formats, with access to database and direct marketing tools, with verticals looking at other segments to associate with. This will increase the retail, arts, cultures and others on a bigger framework and canvas than it is today.

Global opportunities will create more openings for health and wellness tourism and medical tourism - a market that the Indian government has already realised as a growing one. Its worldwide medical tourism campaign is proof enough. And not without reason; according to market statistics, the medical tourism market in India is touching US $300 million (with an estimated 1.5 lakh foreign patients visiting India every year) and growing into a US $2 billion business by 2012. The Leela Palaces & Resorts, according to its president, Peter J Leitgeb, is the first five-star hotel group in the world to offer special packages to travellers from the UK at its Kerala property after having tied-up with Globe Health Tours.

Meanwhile, hotels will try to differentiate their products even more, and expand through the management cum franchise route by integrating marketing synergies. Standalone properties are bound to integrate under the umbrella of a known brand. Alliances to differentiate the product, both with consumer brands and retail in addition to marketing alliances worldwide, will become a compulsion for Indian brands to compete against the giant franchises and managed brands.

While evolving into the next decade, it would be the visibility of a brand and its penetration into the marketplace that will be the first step to forge an alliance. Accordingly, a hotel will select the right fit for furthering its growth through the right associations, since one-size no longer fits all. And it would be the right partnership. This, in some cases, might lead to inorganic growth but nonetheless will be a win-win situation for all.

Chapter 2

The Marketing Plant

THE STEPS OF A MARKETING PLAN

The homogeneous mass market, which has dictated the offerings of U. S. producers since the dawn of the industrial revolution, is confronting its demise. At least, that's the word from advertising and marketing experts as we stand at the threshold of the new millennium. If you don't believe it, look no further than assembly-line hamburger maker, Burger King, which was a forerunner in realizing that customers want it "their way" and their way is not necessarily everyone else's.

As touted in its advertising, Burger King offered "customized" burgers based on a patron's preferences - down to the ketchup - a far cry from the typical one-way-suits-all quarter-pounder. Because the mass market is splintering into fragments, now is an opportune time to figure out which fragments are yours. Writes prophetess of trends Faith Popcorn in her latest version of The Popcorn Report, "Markets are becoming niches and niches are growing smaller. As this market miniaturization occurs, customers gain more stature - and they know it." Reaching those customers requires a new strategy. The scattershot advertising approach, which wasn't necessarily all that effective in the past, will be even less so in the 21st century. The most obvious alternative, shifting to narrower and more specialized markets, is already being tried by many small firms with substantial success.

Find a Niche

Atlantic Publication Group in Charleston, South Carolina, spent four years offering broad-based, general interest magazines to a market already saturated with competition. Then in 1989, company president Marvin Jenkins decided it was time to change direction and develop products for specific niches. Now APG produces 28 publications for many different kinds of organizations. It has grown from four to 11 employees and revenues have tripled. Every APG product is developed in response to a particular need. "Specifically, we search for groups that have a database of readers and are looking for ways to communicate with them," Jenkins explains.

APG enters into multi-year contracts to produce publications for groups such as trade associations, economic development entities, municipalities, regulators, architects and others. When a resort needed a services directory for its 40,000 guests, for example, APG produced it. Clients grant APG exclusive rights to publish the information and sell advertising to defray production charges. The cost to the clients varies with each situation. Sometimes there is no cost at all. For instance, the state of South Carolina annually publishes a book of hunting and fishing regulations, which also carries advertising. The publication used to cost $40,000; now the price tag is zero, thanks to the advertising APG sells. "Niche marketing is really refinement of product," Jenkins asserts. "The trick is to be open-minded. Look honestly at what you're doing and whether it is working. If not, small companies have the flexibility to change direction."

Tapping specific niches can also help small firms stand out from the crowd. "A business must differentiate itself in ways that are important to the customer," notes Philip Kotler, professor of international marketing at Northwestern University. "Small firms are uniquely positioned for niche marketing. If a small enterprise sits down and follows the principles of targeting, segmenting and differentiating, it doesn't have to collapse to larger companies. "A business can actually be more profitable by going for the niche rather than the volume," he elaborates, "and new technology presents many opportunities for new niches."

Riding the Superhighway

Advances in communications technology really do add a valuable new arrow to the small firm's marketing quiver. An increasingly wired population is turning for information to computer online services, cable TV and the information superhighway. Consumers will have a choice not only in the diversions they choose, but also in the method of delivery. The highly touted and publicized information superhighway, or Internet, may at first glance seem beyond reach to most small companies. But it is probably one of their most effective targeting mediums, and the cost of traveling it may be cheaper than you expect. One pioneering small business, Schoolkids Records in Ann Arbor, Michigan, recently decided to chance the superhighway's uncharted advertising territory. Founded in 1976, Schoolkids operated a main store and two smaller, separate stores devoted to classical music and alternative rock. In November 1994, the record purveyor opened a fourth store, this time on the Internet.

Customers can now read an electronic advertisement that lists the newest releases accompanied by brief reviews. The ad also includes the store's toll-free 800 number and even a map showing how to get there. Customers can order compact discs on line and, if their computers are properly equipped, even listen to samples of the music being offered for sale. "In the first few months alone, we've been receiving 400 to 500 calls a day, and the bottom-line results are very positive," notes founder and owner Steve Bergman. "We're also getting a lot of e-mail messages from Internet users who say they love the visual appearance of our ads. "When you're a small company as we are, you have to be creative," Bergman asserts. "And by being on the Internet, we have an opportunity to impress people the way we impress them in our store. We are convinced this advertising avenue will pay off, and are in it for the long term."

Owners of a tiny Texas company, Id, share Bergman's pioneering spirit. As creators of a computer software game called Doom, they faced a problem typical of software firms, especially small ones: how to advertise and sell Doom to the largest audience at the lowest cost. Id decided to try a technique that is gaining favor with software firms of all sizes. It posted a basic version of Doom on the Internet and let people download it at no charge. The strategy was to get players so hooked on Doom that they would send in $40 for a full version of the game. The plan worked beautifully. Since it was posted on the Internet in December 1993, millions of people have downloaded free versions of Doom and more than 100,000 have paid for a full copy.

"The kind of public recognition we've gotten with Doom - including movie offers and product endorsements - is unheard of," marvels Jay Wilbur, Id's chief executive officer and business manager. "'Shareware' endears us to the public, especially when we tell people who download Doom to play the game even if they don't want to buy it."

Market Research

The Internet is also an effective tool for finding out what your customers want. "More and more companies are using the Internet to communicate with their customers," reports Jane Torbica of CompuServe. (CompuServe, Prodigy and America Online are currently the three leading online services for small businesses.) "You can go on line to ask customers for product or service ideas or any other input you are seeking." The Internet also serves as a kind of online Yellow Pages. Firms listed on the Internet are categorized just like the printed version of the Yellow Pages, so it's easy for customers to search for the type of company and product they need.

Log on Carefully

While widely acknowledged as the wave of the future, the Internet still poses some challenges for advertisers. Because millions of people can tap into Internet transmissions, for example, it's risky for customers to e-mail their credit card numbers when making a purchase. Therefore, many companies are waiting for a secure way to exchange financial data and presently use the Internet to advertise while actually selling by phone, mail or in person. Even if online selling is secure, it's not expected to be all that popular in the near future. According to the San Francisco research firm Odyssey, only six percent of U.S. households currently has any online computer connection. Still, that works out to approximately 5.7 million families nationwide - a market well worth targeting. And the number of subscribers is forecasted to grow steadily.

The Personal Touch

A seemingly contradictory trend will also shape marketing efforts in the next century: that of personal customer service. Claims Faith Popcorn, "'New' will no longer be a compelling selling point, which is an amazing idea in the American marketplace. We've had 'new' all our lives. Now `new' is old. "`New improved' won't do much for consumers, either," she continues, "except make them say out loud what they've always wondered: 'Why didn't you make it good enough in the first place?' "What will make us buy one product over another is a feeling of partnership with the seller," concludes Popcorn. "Anonymous, impersonal selling is over. We want to buy from a person, a person whom we trust.

Trust will be implicit in every purchase." Nancy Ozawa, researcher at the Institute for the Future in Palo Alto, California, agrees. "To succeed in the future, companies will need to focus on their customers and reorganize around their needs. Once this is accomplished, it's time to get closer to your customers. One way of doing that," she suggests, "is to follow up with customers after transactions to find out if they are satisfied. "And by follow up I don't mean surveys." declares Ozawa. "Pizza Hut, for example, has a toll-free 800 number for complaints and a manager returns a customer's call within 24 hours. The managers are trained to carefully listen to people's voices in order to understand their level of frustration. As a result, customers feel comfortable that their problem is being resolved. Because nine out of 10 people who have problems don't tell you," she emphasizes, "it's important to use that one person who does to uncover the problems of the nine others and fix them."

A More Educated Consumer

In their book Future Tense, Ozawa's peers at the Institute for the Future, Ian Morrison and Greg Schmid, advise that "anyone connected with the business world must focus time and attention on understanding the driving forces changing today's business environment." Two of those forces are the widening and more proficient use of advanced technology and consumer expectations of more personal service. These two forces also define the 21st century consumer. "Businesses in the next millennium will serve consumers who are more sophisticated and educated," Ozawa predicts. "Well over 50 percent will have a high school diploma by the year 2000. "Tomorrow's consumers will also be more demanding and vocal, and will expect companies to meet their needs," she adds. "And they will use their wallets to vote for the winners."

STRATEGIES IN THE MARKETPLACE

The three primary strategies followed in the Indian hospitality industry are franchise agreements, marketing alliances, and representations.

Franchise Agreements

The primary motive of a brand franchise agreement is retaining ownership, while receiving a chain advantage. The areas where a company can gain through a franchise agreement is the accessibility of financing, easier start up, existing operating system, business assistance, established customer base, use of nationally recognised name, national marketing, access to discounted vendor relationships, benefit of loyalty programmes worldwide, etc.

Alliances in India are with highly experienced and renowned companies who bring with them management expertise and in-depth knowledge of the industry. They help in operating internally as one integrated hotel company while enhancing the distinct characteristics of each brand in the market. This model can be applied across all verticals with a few alterations. Some of the players dominating the market are Cendant Corporation, Choice Hotels India, Carlson Hospitality India, Sarovar Park Hotels & Resorts. Another version of this is the management franchise agreement that is increasingly becoming popular today.

Marketing Alliances

These reciprocal relationships are primarily for cross-promotional purposes. It includes joint marketing activities that include joint participation in trade shows, sales events, culinary promotions and niche marketing programmes and sales leads, mutual benefits for loyalty members (for instance the alliances between Taj Hotels and Shilla Hotels & Resorts, Korea and Taj Hotels-Raffles Hotels & Resorts).

Explaining the rational behind this is Ajoy Misra, senior vice president, (sales and marketing) of Indian Hotels Company, who says, "With continuous support from either sides, alliances can help us make forays into markets that would otherwise be uneconomical for us to move into, at least in the next five years. Singapore features as one of the top 10 source markets for us while India witnessed about 24,000 arrivals from South Korea in 2005 - an increase by 24 per cent over last year. All these indicators reflect that our alliance is a way forward in getting more business from these markets." He sees global alliances developing in the future with alliance partners having to move towards providing seamless travel and accommodation solution to their customers. "Merging of loyalty programmes and a wider airline route on which the customers can collect loyalty points is the way forward," he concludes.

Representations

Another visible strategy adopted by hotels is an alliance with a company to represent and market the brand internationally, a strategy followed by the Park Hotels with the Design Hotels, and Taj Hotels with the Leading Hotels of the World. V V Giri, associate vice president & general manager of The Park, Chennai cites, "This affiliation takes our company vision and expands it to the world gateways, giving us a place to market the brand internationally. Our brand mission is to lead by differentiation and Design Hotels fulfills that platform; it helps us reach like-minded travellers who believe in this brand philosophy."

MARKETING PLAN

There are two major components to your marketing strategy:

- How your enterprise will address the competitive marketplace
- How you will implement and support your day to day operations.

In today's very competitive marketplace a strategy that insures a consistent approach to offering your product or service in a way that will outsell the competition is critical. However, in concert with defining the marketing strategy you must also have a well defined methodology for the day to day process of implementing it. It is of little value to have a strategy if you lack either the resources or the expertise to implement it.

In the process of creating a marketing strategy you must consider many factors. Of those many factors, some are more important than others. Because each strategy must address some unique considerations, it is not reasonable to identify 'every' important factor at a generic level. However, many are common to all marketing strategies. Some of the more critical are described below.

You begin the creation of your strategy by deciding what the overall objective of your enterprise should be. In general this falls into one of four categories:

- If the market is very attractive and your enterprise is one of the strongest in the industry you will want to invest your best resources in support of your offering.

- If the market is very attractive but your enterprise is one of the weaker ones in the industry you must concentrate on strengthening the enterprise, using your offering as a stepping stone toward this objective.
- If the market is not especially attractive, but your enterprise is one of the strongest in the industry then an effective marketing and sales effort for your offering will be good for generating near term profits.
- If the market is not especially attractive and your enterprise is one of the weaker ones in the industry you should promote this offering only if it supports a more profitable part of your business (for instance, if this segment completes a product line range) or if it absorbs some of the overhead costs of a more profitable segment. Otherwise, you should determine the most cost effective way to divest your enterprise of this offering.

Having selected the direction most beneficial for the overall interests of the enterprise, the next step is to choose a strategy for the offering that will be most effective in the market. This means choosing one of the following 'generic' strategies.

- A Cost Leadership Strategy is based on the concept that you can produce and market a good quality product or service at a lower cost than your competitors. These low costs should translate to profit margins that are higher than the industry average. Some of the conditions that should exist to support a cost leadership strategy include an on-going availability of operating capital, good process engineering skills, close management of labour, products designed for ease of manufacturing and low cost distribution.
- A Differentiation strategy is one of creating a product or service that is perceived as being unique "throughout the industry". The emphasis can be on brand image, proprietary technology, special features,

superior service, a strong distributor network or other aspects that might be specific to your industry. This uniqueness should also translate to profit margins that are higher than the industry average. In addition, some of the conditions that should exist to support a differentiation strategy include strong marketing abilities, effective product engineering, creative personnel, the ability to perform basic research and a good reputation.

- A Focus Strategy may be the most sophisticated of the generic strategies, in that it is a more 'intense' form of either the cost leadership or differentiation strategy. It is designed to address a "focused" segment of the marketplace, product form or cost management process and is usually employed when it isn't appropriate to attempt an 'across the board' application of cost leadership or differentiation. It is based on the concept of serving a particular target in such an exceptional manner, that others cannot compete. Usually this means addressing a substantially smaller market segment than others in the industry, but because of minimal competition, profit margins can be very high.

Pricing

Having defined the overall offering objective and selecting the generic strategy you must then decide on a variety of closely related operational strategies. One of these is how you will price the offering. A pricing strategy is mostly influenced by your requirement for net income and your objectives for long term market control. There are three basic strategies you can consider.

A Skimming Strategy: If your offering has enough differentiation to justify a high price and you desire quick cash and have minimal desires for significant market penetration and control, then you set your prices very high.

A Market Penetration Strategy: If near term income is not so critical and rapid market penetration for eventual market control is desired, then you set your prices very low.

A Comparable Pricing Strategy: If you are not the market leader in your industry then the leaders will most likely have created a 'price expectation' in the minds of the marketplace. In this case you can price your offering comparably to those of your competitors.

Promotion

To sell an offering you must effectively promote and advertise it. There are two basic promotion strategies, PUSH and PULL.

- The Push Strategy maximizes the use of all available channels of distribution to "push" the offering into the marketplace. This usually requires generous discounts to achieve the objective of giving the channels incentive to promote the offering, thus minimizing your need for advertising.
- The Pull Strategy requires direct interface with the end user of the offering. Use of channels of distribution is minimized during the first stages of promotion and a major commitment to advertising is required. The objective is to "pull" the prospects into the various channel outlets creating a demand the channels cannot ignore.

There are many strategies for advertising an offering. Some of these include:

Product Comparison advertising: In a market where your offering is one of several providing similar capabilities, if your offering stacks up well when comparing features then a product comparison ad can be beneficial.

Product Benefits advertising: When you want to promote your offering without comparison to competitors, the product benefits ad is the correct approach. This is especially beneficial when you have introduced a new approach to solving a user need and comparison to the old approaches is inappropriate.

Product Family advertising: If your offering is part of a group or family of offerings that can be of benefit to the customer as a set, then the product family ad can be of benefit.

Corporate advertising: When you have a variety of offerings and your audience is fairly broad, it is often beneficial to promote your enterprise identity rather than a specific offering.

Distribution

You must also select the distribution method(s) you will use to get the offering into the hands of the customer. These include:

- On-premise Sales involves the sale of your offering using a field sales organization that visits the prospect's facilities to make the sale.
- Direct Sales involves the sale of your offering using a direct, in-house sales organization that does all selling through the Internet, telephone or mail order contact.
- Wholesale Sales involves the sale of your offering using intermediaries or "middle-men" to distribute your product or service to the retailers.
- Self-service Retail Sales involves the sale of your offering using self service retail methods of distribution.
- Full-service Retail Sales involves the sale of your offering through a full service retail distribution channel.

Of course, making a decision about pricing, promotion and distribution is heavily influenced by some key factors in the industry and marketplace. These factors should be analyzed initially to create the strategy and then regularly monitored for changes. If any of them change substantially the strategy should be reevaluated.

The Environment

Environmental factors positively or negatively impact the industry and the market growth potential of your product/ service. Factors to consider include:

- Government actions - Government actions (current or under consideration) can support or detract from your strategy. Consider subsidies, safety, efficacy and operational regulations, licensing requirements, materials access restrictions and price controls.

- Demographic changes - Anticipated demographic changes may support or negatively impact the growth potential of your industry and market. This includes factors such as education, age, income and geographic location.
- Emerging technology - Technological changes that are occurring may or may not favor the actions of your enterprise.
- Cultural trends - Cultural changes such as fashion trends and life style trends may or may not support your offering's penetration of the market

The Prospect

It is essential to understand the market segment(s) as defined by the prospect characteristics you have selected as the target for your offering. Factors to consider include:

- The potential for market penetration involves whether you are selling to past customers or a new prospect, how aware the prospects are of what you are offering, competition, growth rate of the industry and demographics.
- The prospect's willingness to pay higher price because your offering provides a better solution to their problem.
- The amount of time it will take the prospect to make a purchase decision is affected by the prospects confidence in your offering, the number and quality of competitive offerings, the number of people involved in the decision, the urgency of the need for your offering and the risk involved in making the purchase decision.
- The prospect's willingness to pay for product value is determined by their knowledge of competitive

pricing, their ability to pay and their need for characteristics such as quality, durability, reliability, ease of use, uniformity and dependability.

- Likelihood of adoption by the prospect is based on the criticality of the prospect's need, their attitude about change, the significance of the benefits, barriers that exist to incorporating the offering into daily usage and the credibility of the offering.

The Product/Service

You should be thoroughly familiar with the factors that establish products/services as strong contenders in the marketplace. Factors to consider include:

- Whether some or all of the technology for the offering is proprietary to the enterprise.
- The benefits the prospect will derive from use of the offering.
- The extent to which the offering is differentiated from the competition.
- The extent to which common introduction problems can be avoided such as lack of adherence to industry standards, unavailability of materials, poor quality control, regulatory problems and the inability to explain the benefits of the offering to the prospect.
- The potential for product obsolescence as affected by the enterprise's commitment to product development, the product's proximity to physical limits, the ongoing potential for product improvements, the ability of the enterprise to react to technological change and the likelihood of substitute solutions to the prospect's needs.
- Impact on customer's business as measured by costs of trying out your offering, how quickly the customer can realize a return from their investment in your offering, how disruptive the introduction of your offering is to the customer's operations and the costs to switch to your offering.

- The complexity of your offering as measured by the existence of standard interfaces, difficulty of installation, number of options, requirement for support devices, training and technical support and the requirement for complementary product interface.

The Competition

It is essential to know who the competition is and to understand their strengths and weaknesses. Factors to consider include:

- Each of your competitor's experience, staying power, market position, strength, predictability and freedom to abandon the market must be evaluated.

Your Enterprise

An honest appraisal of the strength of your enterprise is a critical factor in the development of your strategy. Factors to consider include:

- Enterprise capacity to be leader in low-cost production considering cost control infrastructure, cost of materials, economies of scale, management skills, availability of personnel and compatibility of manufacturing resources with offering requirements.
- The enterprise's ability to construct entry barriers to competition such as the creation of high switching costs, gaining substantial benefit from economies of scale, exclusive access to or clogging of distribution channels and the ability to clearly differentiate your offering from the competition.
- The enterprise's ability to sustain its market position is determined by the potential for competitive imitation, resistance to inflation, ability to maintain high prices, the potential for product obsolescence and the 'learning curve' faced by the prospect.
- The prominence of the enterprise.
- The competence of the management team.

- The adequacy of the enterprise's infrastructure in terms of organization, recruiting capabilities, employee benefit programs, customer support facilities and logistical capabilities.
- The freedom of the enterprise to make critical business decisions without undue influence from distributors, suppliers, unions, creditors, investors and other outside influences.
- Freedom from having to deal with legal problems.

Development

A review of the strength and viability of the product/ service development Programme will heavily influence the direction of your strategy. Factors to consider include:

- The strength of the development manager including experience with personnel management, current and new technologies, complex projects and the equipment and tools used by the development personnel.
- Personnel who understand the relevant technologies and are able to perform the tasks necessary to meet the development objectives.
- Adequacy and appropriateness of the development tools and equipment.
- The necessary funding to achieve the development objectives.
- Design specifications that are manageable.

Production

You should review your enterprise's production organization with respect to their ability to cost effectively produce products/services. The following factors are considered:

- The strength of production manager including experience with personnel management, current and new technologies, complex projects and the equipment and tools used by the manufacturing personnel.

- Economies of scale allowing the sharing of operations, sharing of production and the potential for vertical integration.
- Technology and production experience
- The necessary production personnel skill level and/or the enterprise's ability to hire or train qualified personnel.
- The ability of the enterprise to limit suppliers bargaining power.
- The ability of the enterprise to control the quality of raw materials and production.
- Adequate access to raw materials and sub-assembly production.

Marketing/Sales

The marketing and sales organization is analyzed for its strengths and current activities. Factors to consider include:

- Experience of Marketing/Sales manager including contacts in the industry (prospects, distribution channels, media), familiarity with advertising and promotion, personal selling capabilities, general management skills and a history of profit and loss responsibilities.
- The ability to generate good publicity as measured by past successes, contacts in the press, quality of promotional literature and market education capabilities.
- Sales promotion techniques such as trade allowances, special pricing and contests.
- The effectiveness of your distribution channels as measured by history of relations, the extent of channel utilization, financial stability, reputation, access to prospects and familiarity with your offering.
- Advertising capabilities including media relationships, advertising budget, past experience, how easily the

offering can be advertised and commitment to advertising.

- Sales capabilities including availability of personnel, quality of personnel, location of sales outlets, ability to generate sales leads, relationship with distributors, ability to demonstrate the benefits of the offering and necessary sales support capabilities.
- The appropriateness of the pricing of your offering as it relates to competition, price sensitivity of the prospect, prospect's familiarity with the offering and the current market life cycle stage.

Customer Services

The strength of the customer service function has a strong influence on long term market success. Factors to consider include:

- Experience of the Customer Service manager in the areas of similar offerings and customers, quality control, technical support, product documentation, sales and marketing.
- The availability of technical support to service your offering after it is purchased.
- One or more factors that causes your customer support to stand out as unique in the eyes of the customer.
- Accessibility of service outlets for the customer.
- The reputation of the enterprise for customer service.

After defining your strategy you must use the information you have gathered to determine whether this strategy will achieve the objective of making your enterprise competitive in the marketplace. Two of the most important assessments are described below.

Cost To Enter Market

This is an analysis of the factors that will influence your costs to achieve significant market penetration. Factors to consider include.

- Your marketing strength.
- Access to low cost materials and effective production.
- The experience of your enterprise.
- The complexity of introduction problems such as lack of adherence to industry standards, unavailability of materials, poor quality control, regulatory problems and the inability to explain the benefits of the offering to the prospect.
- The effectiveness of the enterprise infrastructure in terms of organization, recruiting capabilities, employee benefit Programmes, customer support facilities and logistical capabilities.
- Distribution effectiveness as measured by history of relations, the extent of channel utilization, financial stability, reputation, access to prospects and familiarity with your offering.
- Technological efforts likely to be successful as measured by the strength of the development organization.
- The availability of adequate operating capital.

Profit Potential

This is an analysis of the factors that could influence the potential for generating and maintaining profits over an extended period. Factors to consider include:

- Potential for competitive retaliation is based on the competitors resources, commitment to the industry, cash position and predictability as well as the status of the market.
- The enterprise's ability to construct entry barriers to competition such as the creation of high switching costs, gaining substantial benefit from economies of scale, exclusive access to or clogging of distribution channels and the ability to clearly differentiate your offering from the competition.

- The intensity of competitive rivalry as measured by the size and number of competitors, limitations on exiting the market, differentiation between offerings and the rapidity of market growth.
- The ability of the enterprise to limit suppliers bargaining power.
- The enterprise's ability to sustain its market position is determined by the potential for competitive imitation, resistance to inflation, ability to maintain high prices, the potential for product obsolescence and the 'learning curve' faced by the prospect.
- The availability of substitute solutions to the prospect's need.
- The prospect's bargaining power as measured by the ease of switching to an alternative, the cost to look at alternatives, the cost of the offering, the differentiation between your offering and the competition and the degree of the prospect's need.
- Market potential for new products considering market growth, prospect's need for your offering, the benefits of the offering, the number of barriers to immediate use, the credibility of the offering and the impact on the customer's daily operations.
- The freedom of the enterprise to make critical business decisions without undue influence from distributors, suppliers, unions, investors and other outside influences.

PARTNERS

Fluidly interlocking into the fabric of business, alliances are indispensable drivers of growth in the hospitality industry. "The forces of a powerful ally can be useful and good to those who have recourse to them...but are perilous to those who become dependent on them." Niccolo Machiavelli, political genius and commentator, penned the aforementioned somewhat sinister version of alliances in his epochal 'The Prince'. While Machiavellianism alludes to alliances amongst unequals, the end justifying the means, in the realms of commerce it refers to a symbiotic relationship for mutual benefit between likeminded partners, equals in their own stead.

Historically, alliances resulted from spontaneous cooperation between people. The resultant synergies and innate power of a massive, yet heterogeneous body, with a unified objective furthered the interest of its constituent members. This flagged off its initial popularity in tourism, in a fragmented marketplace (multiple players, unique separately governed destinations), where resources were limited (state controlled budgets, limited resources to reach a global marketplace), and the industry - heavily regulated (traditionally and till date - aviation).

The composite benefits of these associations weren't always visible to the end consumer and government. Having been perceived as a threat to a free economy as cartels, they resulted in taking recourse to anti-trust immunity in extreme cases, an attempt to prove them as pro-consumer and pro-competition. The scenario here is now replicating global patterns. India, since independence, followed the socialist ideal with state control on resources, both natural and manmade. Most tourism policies were grounded in socio-political leanings and macro economic connotations with development restricted by the license-permit Raj. A tourism policy came into the picture as late as 1982 and a national Action Plan for Tourism, just 10 years later.

An isolationist approach followed by the democratic government, a crippling paucity of funds to fuel growth, and an absence of infrastructure kept demand to the minimal. This somewhat bleak and regulated landscape drove strategic alliances to the forefront, with partners leveraging benefits of access to additional resources and a strong brand to increase network. This was primarily outward, be it airlines through code-sharing or hotels through marketing and franchise agreements, and much later in the day, through tactical alliances.

The opening of the economy stimulated tourism, which was growing till then in spurts and gasps. Today, the world's eyes are focused on India, and rightly so. The World Travel & Tourism Council's (WTTC) projection of travel and tourism growth for 2006-2015 in India is a staggering annualised rate of 8.6 per cent. Logically, the scenario impels one to capitalise on and leverage the strength of a partner, before the dust settles.

The Fundamentals of Alliances

Alliances fall in the category of either strategic alliances at one end of the spectrum (such as a co-branded product and code-sharing which is demanding on resources) or a time-bound tactical promotion at the other end. Each segment has a valid reason for an alliance, objectives being clearly etched out by the partners, benefiting consumers and bringing economic benefits to the parties.

A critical aspect of an alliance is the partner. Most organisations have a diktat to affiliate with the right partner, a brand which is the right fit with their own growth as well as the time frame to meet mutual objectives, taking cognisance of investments. For a successful alliance, you look for a like-minded business for a partner along with a value proposition to the customer, and the speed and readiness for rolling out to retain competitive edge, so that both sides gain, with measurability of the campaign's outcome.

Alliance partners within tourism share a symbiotic relationship with each key player working in tandem with the other, either within the same vertical or outside. No single supplier (airlines, hotels, tour operators/travel agents, cruise liners, distribution channels) can be a claimant of success without an alliance, strategic or otherwise due to co-dependency. But were alliances the mainstay of all promotional activities and growth strategies? Not necessarily. They came into the picture only when the perceived success rate and profitability of the venture were compelling factors to cement their position.

Hotels traditionally looked at alliances to leverage a brand name. The examples of this were Holiday Inn franchisees or marketing franchise agreements in India, Taj Hotels and Shilla Hotels based in Korea - one of the oldest alliances being the marketing franchise between ITC-Welcome group with the Sheraton Corporation that lasted 30 years.

Each homegrown player strengthened its reach across borders, primed to capture a slice of the high spend market - primarily through the franchise route. This has been effectively employed by brands choosing to enter India, without taking recourse to sizeable investments. This strategy is not only popular with hotels but with other segments as well.

Choice Hotels India franchises its Quality Inn and Comfort Inn brands across India with the benefits of a chain affiliation accruing to partners, leveraging the brand's international reservations and optimising their yields. Vilas Pawar, CEO, Choice Hotels India, says, "Today it is difficult to create a brand. Establishing an identity needs a gestation period of about 50-60 years."

In such a scenario, a strategic brand partnership has found its roots within the segment, a popular recourse followed by many realtors foraying into the segment. But for the established brands, strategic marketing alliances with the additional bait of loyalty programmes are the preferred approach. For instance, Bharat Hotel's marketing alliances with the Intercontinental Hotel Group, such as Priority Club Rewards and the Ambassador Programme has ensured an increase in occupancy F&B revenues.

But it stretches to consumer goods too. Hyatt International has developed a strategic marketing partnership with Porsche that encompasses a range of joint marketing activities, in addition to one with Bang & Olufsen to specially design products and provide expertise to Hyatt, reveals Ratnesh Verma. Such alliances create an inspirational value to customers, and invariably, a brand connect and loyalty.

TYPES OF ALLIANCES

There are different objectives for forging an alliance with another partner, but they could be broadly categorised into the following:

Strategic alliances are long-term associations with a higher commitment of resources. It is essentially forged to build a long-term competitive advantage in the current business environment that is more global than regional, has more discerning and demanding consumers and is more dynamic than ever. Examples of this could be to launch a co-branded product, have a common loyalty programme or have a long-term joint marketing programme due to consonance between two brands in terms of customer demographics and image.

Tactical alliances are short-term associations, addressing short term needs. Examples could include sales promotion to boost sales in a lean period, acquire more customers into a loyalty programme or partner an event. It is also pertinent to mention that advances in technology and the evolution of the Internet have opened up new dimensions in this area (eg the Smart card, Web-based solutions, online distribution, etc).

Benefits of an Alliance

- Leverage of each other's brands through positive brand association
- Reach to a larger slice of their target audience through partner's database
- Gain competitive advantage by offering their customers more choices
- Stretch the marketing rupees (through joint advertising/ promotions, etc)
- Increased market share, revenues and incremental revenue earned
- Enhanced image and perception of the alliance partner

Increased share of mind space with end customers

INDIAN HOSPITALITY

In 2004-05, Visakhapatnam was the market leader in terms of occupancy, registering occupancy of 80.6 per cent. Bangalore achieved the second-highest occupancy at 79.8 per cent. It also had the highest (ARR), across all categories among the 30 cities, with an ARR of Rs 6,762. New Delhi was the second highest, registering an ARR of Rs 5,498. All India average occupancy was 63.6 per cent, an increase of 3.9 per cent occupancy points above the previous year's level, or 6.5 per cent in real terms. All India ARR increased by 26.9 per cent over the previous year.

Star category-wise occupancies ranged between 46.3 per cent to 72.1 per cent. Average rates showed a much greater spread, from Rs 5,499 for five-star deluxe hotels to Rs 643 for one-star hotels, an increase of Rs 1,052 and Rs 140, respectively, from the previous year. The All India average revenue per available room (RevPAR) increased substantially, from Rs 1,605 in 2003-04 to Rs 2,170 in 2004-05, reflecting an increase of 35.2 per cent. In the eight years of the survey, this has been the second-highest RevPAR growth (the highest was 46.2 per cent in 2003-04).

Rooms revenue, generally considered being the most important source of a hotel's overall profitability, was 57.7 per cent of total revenue for five-star deluxe hotels, 60.1 per cent of total revenue for five-star hotels and 56.6 per cent for four-star hotels. Overall (across all hotels) it represented 57.3 per cent of total revenue (an increase of 5.7 per cent from 2003-04). Food & Beverage revenue represented 28.3 per cent of total revenue across all hotels, a decrease of 4.6 per cent from last year. (This reflects the increased share of rooms revenue in the total of 100). The all India average of Rooms department expense as a percentage of Rooms revenue declined further from 17.8 per cent in 2003-04 to 14.7 per cent in 2004-05.

Similarly, the all India average Food & Beverage department expense as a percentage of Food & Beverage revenue declined from 55.9 per cent in 2003-04 to 53.9 per cent in 2004-05. Minor Operated department expense as a percentage of Minor Operated department revenue registered an increase from 53.7 per cent in 2003-04 to 58.8 per cent in 2004-05. Telephone and other department expense, at 64.3 per cent of total revenue, was the highest departmental expense. Total departmental expense as a percentage of total departmental revenue reflected a further decline, from 37.4 per cent in 2002-03 and 33.7 per cent in 2003-04 to 30.9 per cent in 2004-05. This is partly owing to higher ARRs.

Percentage of foreign guests increased to 28.3 per cent in 2004-05, compared to 25.0 per cent in 2003-04, primarily as the percentage of foreign business travellers grew. Of the foreign guests, the UK provided the largest demand, at 16.2 per cent, followed by USA, at 12.8 per cent, and France at 7.2 per cent. Domestic guests continue to be the most important segment for the Indian hotel industry, accounting for 71.7 per cent of all guests in 2004-05, though this has decreased marginally from 75 per cent in 2003-04 and 76.9 per cent in 2002-03.

All India average stay of a business traveller has increased from two days to 2.4 days.There is an increase in foreign business travellers utilising five-star deluxe, five-star, four-star hotels and heritage hotels from 27 per cent, 18.6 per cent, 11.4 per cent and 11.7 per cent, respectively, in 2003-04 to 28.1 per cent, 21.4 per cent,13.7 per cent and 14.1 per cent, respectively, in 2004-05. Owing to all India increased occupancy, property operations and maintenance expenses per available room (PAR) has increased from Rs 69,735 in 2003-04 to Rs 91,981 in 2004-05. Average monthly occupancy was highest in December (at 71.7 per cent), followed by November (at 67.8 per cent) and January, February (at 65.8 per cent).

Direct enquiry and advance reservations by travel agents and tour operators cumulatively comprise 75.9 per cent of reservation source for the Indian hotel industry. Five-star deluxe hotels are making the best use of GDS as 8.1 per cent of the total reservations for five-star deluxe hotels come from GDS, against the all India average of 1.7 per cent. GDS reservations generally provide higher room rates compared to the other channels.

Print advertising is the most popular medium used by the Indian hotel industry with the all India average at 92.2 per cent of hotels using it, followed by 82.5 per cent using direct mails. Radio advertising features as the least utilised marketing media at 8.4 per cent, followed by merchandising at 24.5 per cent, by the Indian hotel industry in 2004-05. All five-star deluxe hotels (sample size 32) used the hotel website at 100 per cent as a marketing medium in 2004-05.

Credit cards as a mode of transaction increased from 27.7 per cent and 30.4 per cent in 2002-03 and 2003-04, respectively to 32.5 per cent in 2004-05. Credit cards remained the most popular method of payment at five-star deluxe hotels at 47.4 per cent. Visa (41.8 per cent) was the most widely used credit card by hotel guests in 2004-05, followed by Mastercard (37 per cent). American Express charged the highest credit card commission at 2.9 per cent against 1.7 per cent by Visa and Mastercard.

Comparison with the results of the survey in 2004-05 with the previous year, shows that nearly all categories (except one-star hotels) saw an increase in occupancy and a significant increase in average rate (except heritage hotels). This resulted in a major increase in RevPAR across all categories with the highest RevPAR growth in four-star hotels at 41.9 per cent and an all India RevPAR growth at 35.2 per cent. The demand for rooms has been positive and owing to lack of adequate new supply, hotels in nearly all categories have managed to simultaneously increase the occupancy and average rates.

Among environmental issues, electricity consumption is the most monitored attribute, followed by water consumption. Five-star deluxe and five-star hotels continue to monitor environmental issues most closely. Energy expenses accounted for 8.9 per cent of total revenue in 2004-05 against 10.5 per cent of total revenue in 2003-04 and 12.3 per cent in 2002-03. This may be partly attributed to rising revenues and partly to the increase in efforts made to conserve energy by the industry in India.

Other Significant Trends

All India average revenue per hotel has grown significantly, from Rs 9.15 crore during 2003-04 to Rs 11.49 crore during 2004-05, and is expected to see further improvement in the next few years owing to an increase in occupancy and average rate. House Profit (Gross Operating Profit after deducting franchise and management fees) as a percentage of revenue increased from 34.8 per cent in 2003-04 to 40.7 per cent in 2004-05. The all India average net income (income before depreciation, interest payments and taxes) per hotel also increased, from Rs 2.80 crore (34.8 per cent) in 2003-04 to Rs 4.08 crore (40.7 per cent) in 2004-05, reflecting the overall health of the industry.

July has the lowest monthly occupancy in the year. However, occupancy for all months was higher in 2004-05 compared to the last five years. The year 2004-05 saw a continuation of the growth momentum experience by the hotel industry in 2003-04. Most cities saw occupancy levels improve over the previous year and, consecutively for two years, both occupancy and average room rates have improved.

City Trends

The following paragraphs detail the expectations of new supply and performance for 19 important hotel markets, based on research undertaken and forecasts made by HVS International.

New Delhi

Occupancy witnessed a growth of 10.82 per cent in 2004-05. Average rates registered an increase of 29.43 per cent. The National Capital Region is expected to see an estimated 27 new hotels, serviced apartments and mixed-use developments with approximately 4,900 rooms in various categories over the next three to four years, with nearly 20 new hotels to be in Gurgaon alone. The new supply will start entering the market in 2007-08. This growth will be supported by significantly improved road and transport infrastructure (a six-lane section of National Highway 8 connecting Delhi and Gurgaon will open in late

2006), privatisation of the Delhi airport and demand induced by the Commonwealth Games, to be held in Delhi in 2010.

There will be further increase in hotel activity, especially in the mid-market and budget segment, after the much-awaited auction of sites by the Delhi Development Authority (DDA).

Mumbai

Citywide occupancy in Mumbai increased by 13.0 per cent and average rate witnessed an increase of 40.6 per cent in 2004-05. Mumbai (including Navi-Mumbai) is expected to see 19 new hotels, serviced apartments and mixed-use developments with approximately 4,950 rooms in various categories over the next three to four years. The bulk of the new supply will enter the Mumbai market by 2008-09. Most companies setting up operations in Mumbai now prefer to locate to new commercial districts in the suburbs like Andheri, Bandra-Kurla and Malad, and other periphery areas like Navi-Mumbai and Mulund; and, hotel development has shifted to these areas. Now, with availability of commercial space in the mills area, places like Parel, Lower Parel, Worli and Mahalaxmi will see increased hotel development activity. This is more so with the proposed development of Bandra-Worli Sea Link, which will significantly reduce the travel time between Bandra and central Mumbai.

Kolkata

Kolkata is expected to see 12 new hotels, serviced apartments and mixed-use developments with approximately 2,000 rooms entering the market in various categories over the next few years. The city is becoming a preferred location for conferences and seminars due to the relatively easy availability of space and at a lower cost as compared to other metros. It is also the commercial capital of the northeast region, with most companies basing their headquarters in the city.

Pune

Pune is expected to see 11 new hotels, serviced apartments and mixed-use developments with approximately 1,600 rooms in various categories over the next three to four years. The addition to supply, although quite high, is likely to be successfully absorbed, taking into account Pune's low room base of approximately 800 rooms and a continuous growth in the city's IT, ITeS, BPO and manufacturing industries.

Chennai

Chennai witnessed an occupancy increase of 15.7 per cent, following a decline for two consecutive years. The city saw a simultaneous increase in average rate by approximately 15.6 per cent. Chennai is expected to see 14 new hotels, serviced apartments and mixed-use developments with approximately 2,900 rooms in various categories over the next few years. The Old Mahabalipuram Road (OMR) connecting Chennai with Mahabalipuram is being developed as an IT corridor to house various IT and ITeS companies. As existing tech parks are full to capacity, software companies are also looking at sick industrial unit areas such as Guindy, Taramani, Ambattur and Padi, which are being converted into software technology parks (STPs). We see Chennai as a stable market and expect it to continue to show improvements in occupancy and average rate in the next few years.

Bengaluru

Bangalore's hotel market grew marginally in terms of occupancy and by approximately 64.5 per cent in terms of the average room rate. This is on the back of very high demand and lack of new supply. Approximately 7.0 million square feet of commercial space is likely to be absorbed this fiscal year (2005-06). Bangalore is expected to see, at last count, 27 new hotels, serviced apartments and mixed-use developments with approximately 6,100 rooms in various categories over the next few years. With work on the international airport having commenced the northern areas of the city will see pronounced commercial and hotel development activity. The first phase of the airport is estimated to open by October 2008. Road infrastructure, however, remains the biggest challenge for the city.

Goa

Goa is expected to see development of eight new hotels with approximately 1,200 rooms in various categories over the next 2-3 years. Goa is an extremely promising market with the highest average length (amongst the key cities) of stay by both foreign and domestic guests. The proposed Mopa airport is anticipated to witness much higher traffic flow than the airport at Dabolim. Accompanying the airport project will be a new ground transportation system, which will benefit the whole of Goa.

Agra

Agra has seen an increase in occupancy of 22.9 per cent. Average rates have decreased marginally by 1.4 per cent. This may be partly attributed to a higher base surveyed in 2003-04 and an increase in smaller hotels participating in the survey. Tourists typically make a day trip to Agra from Delhi; the increase in occupancy is owing to the meetings & conference segment, which has seen a significant growth for two consecutive years.

Ahmedabad

The survey indicates an occupancy decline of 7.7 per cent and a decrease in average rate by 8.9 per cent. This may again be due to change in composition of hotels participating in the survey. However, HVS's independent research indicates an estimated 15.0 per cent increase in both occupancy and average rate. Hotel activity will increase in the city owing to expected commercial growth on CG Road, Ashram Road, Satellite Road and SG Highway-particularly from the pharma, financial sector, telecom, retail, textiles, BPO and IT services.

Kochi

The survey indicates a decrease in occupancy of 4.2 per cent and a decrease in average rate by 22.3 per cent. This may be partly attributed to a variation in the hotels participating in the survey and does not reflect the true market condition. The city's hotel demand generators are mainly tourism related, with commercial demand borne out of shipping, Kochi Port, Cochin Shipyard, oil refineries and marine and agro export industries based in the city. Banking, financial services, insurance and the telecom sectors have seen growth over the past two years.

Hyderabad

In Hyderabad, overall occupancy increased by 3.3 per cent. Average rates registered an increase of 13.4 per cent over the previous year. HITEC City, HITEX, Genome Valley and ICICI Knowledge Park demonstrate the state's commitment to create world class infrastructure. The convention centre opening in 2006, with approximately 75,000 square feet of conferencing facility and 55 break-out rooms, is the first of its kind in South Asia. The convention centre will induce substantial demand for rooms in the city. The Hyderabad market will continue to witness a strong increase in occupancy and average rate in the next few years.

Jaipur

Occupancy levels increased by 14.2 per cent in 2004-05 and average rates increased by 10.0 per cent over the previous year. Besides being a preferred tourist and wedding destination, the city of Jaipur is gaining prominence as a commercial destination as well. This is owing to increased travel by buyers for gems, jewellery and textiles. With the proposal for a Jaipur special economic zone (SEZ), an international airport and an ethnic village, the city will see development of new hotel projects (approximately 1,200 rooms). There is a chance of Jaipur facing an oversupply of rooms in 3-4 years.

Lucknow

Occupancy levels increased marginally by 0.6 per cent in 2004-05 and average rates increased by 10.0 per cent over the previous year. Lucknow has been a very stable market and is witnessing a rise in average rate for the last two years. Lately, Lucknow has also seen increased retail activity.

Nagpur

Nagpur witnessed a decline in occupancy by 10.1 per cent and a decrease in average rates by 5.5 per cent from the previous year. The Nagpur market has now declined for two years consecutively.

Thiruvananthapuram

The city witnessed a decrease in occupancy of 7.0 per cent, and a growth in average room rate of 38.6 per cent. Being the state capital, the city is a hub of political activity. Moreover, Thiruvananthapuram, with its famous beaches, is among the top tourist destinations in India. The city has grown as a tourist and commercial centre, with the international airport being one of the gateways into Kerala.

Udagamandalam (Ooty)

Ooty city has seen a decline in occupancy by 9.0 per cent and an increase in average rate by 15.6 per cent. Mainly a tourist destination, Ooty is known for its picturesque locales. The city is unlikely to see any major hotel activity in the next 2-3 years.

Udaipur

Citywide occupancy increased by 19.25 per cent in 2004-05. Average rate showed a steep increase of 53.65 per cent. The increase in the average rate may be partly attributed to the inclusion of luxury/heritage hotels in the survey. Udaipur has lately seen an increase in international events and is attracting many domestic off-site meetings, conferences and weddings as well.

Vadodara

Citywide occupancy increased marginally from 62.5 per cent in 2003-04 to 62.6 per cent in 2004-05. Similarly, the average rate increased from Rs 458 in 2003-04 to Rs467 in 2004-05. The Gujarat government has also been promoting the state as a commercial destination and is giving incentives to various companies.

Visakhapatnam

Visakhapatnam witnessed a steep increase in occupancy by 15.0 per cent in 2004-05 and an increase in average rates by 18.4 per cent. In the past, the city experienced rapid industrialization with the onset of major industries: an oil refinery, a large fertilizer factory, the Hindustan Zinc smelter and the Visakhapatnam steel plant.

INDIA LACKS INFRASTRUCTURE

Even as the city of Bangalore witnesses domestic and international visitors in equal measure, much like any other international metropolitan, it is still lacking in the most basic of amenities - infrastructure. We have vehicles that ply the city with registrations from across the country and the city's inhabitants speak more than four or five regional languages. We have the best specialty restaurants. Despite this, the existing facilities don't even meet national standards, forget international proportions.

While she admits that there have been new hoteliers in the city most of whom are foreign brands, Marshall feels that all of this is sometimes a huge myth. "I believe in construction!" She adds, "Sometimes, projects remain on paper, barring a few projects. I do hear from industry sources and read in print that a certain player is in a management tie-up with someone and certain realtors are venturing into the project. But there has not been one stone turned in the name of construction."

While the international business travellers and domestic tourists who visit the city come looking for five-star properties, they all need to maneuver through potholes on bumpy roads. Marshall believes that unless basic infrastructure is not taken care of with immediate effect, things might worsen. She says, "Infrastructure is mandatory. However, it is amazing to see how the city is still thriving with business travellers despite everything. Sadly the supply of quality hospitality services still continues to be in short supply. But hopefully things will improve in future both for the city and the travellers."

Right in the Eleventh Try

Hosting five million visitors from abroad has been the tourism industry's dream for well over a decade and a half. In the quest for this magic number a dream paper (officially called a 'strategy paper') was drawn up in the early 1990s by the then cabinet secretary - an unusual level of initiative.

That paper had envisaged an investment of Rs 36,000 crore from both the public and private sectors and a whole list of actions were listed to build the infrastructure to service that many tourists. The move caused a lot of excitement among trade associations, a few ripples in the national media and received accolades from travel journals. As is the case with such grandiose ideas, industry leaders stopped talking about it. But the dream of five million arrivals somehow sustained itself as a reference point in any discussion on infrastructural requirements.

Then came a new tourism secretary. He revived the 'strategy paper' in his own name with a few changes in the previous draft, and it received the same interest from national and trade media as well as trade conventions as before. The next step of implementation was neither demanded nor taken. But the dream of five million tourists persisted. Then there was a change of government. Tourism success stories from our neighborhood had already made some dent on the socialism-stung leadership and the spirit of economic reforms wafted over the tourism sector as well. The prime minister's reference to the importance of tourism from the ramparts of the Red Fort on Independence Day confirmed that the sector was now on the national agenda. The Planning Commission made a five-fold increase in the allocation for tourism in the Tenth Plan. Aviation stepped out from darkness into brilliant sunshine. The rest is history.

This trip down memory lane was caused by the latest arrival statistics circulated by the tourism ministry. In the first nine months of this year, 3.06 million visitors came to India - an increase of 13.1 per cent over the same period in 2005. On the basis of this growth rate (actually many more people travel during the winter months) we should close the year with a count of 4.40 million, just 6,00,000 short of the coveted five million. And so 2006 will be remembered as the year in which we crossed the four-million mark. But wait; with a sustained growth of some 13 per cent in 2005 and 2006 so far, India can be sure of welcoming the five millionth visitor before 2007.

Interestingly, one entity to which the dream coming true will be no surprise is the Planning Commission. In its Tenth Plan projections, it had set a target of raising India's share of the world market from 0.39 per cent to 0.62 which many had thought was ambitious. Translated into numbers, the Commission's target (based on the then growth of world movements) would come to 5.6 million. Arrivals now projected would come pretty close to the Commission's calculations for which it deserves the industry's applause.

The Million Time-line

The country's march toward the five-million mark is also interesting. The first million was achieved in 1980. The second, fifteen years later, in 1995. It took another decade to reach three million in 2004 and only two years to get to four million in 2006. Hopefully, it will just take a year for its fifth million.

Tourism ministry mandarins would like us to believe that it is all thanks to the Incredible India campaign. Some analysts would give a fair share of the credit to economic reforms and the burgeoning corporate traffic from abroad. Industry doyens would hasten to remind you that this is all fine. Indian tourism is definitely on the upswing but in the global context it has miles to go. Look at China's 37 million arrivals and well over 10 million counts of smaller countries like Malaysia and Thailand.

Tourism ministry mandarins would like us to believe that it is all thanks to the Incredible India campaign. Some analysts would give a fair share of the credit to economic reforms and the burgeoning corporate traffic from abroad. We are in the final year of the Tenth Plan and the approach to the Eleventh Plan scheduled to begin in April 2007 is now under discussion.

Here is what the draft approach paper says on tourism: 'The contribution of tourism services in the GDP for 2002-03 is estimated at 5.83 per cent including direct and indirect effects. Tourism, as the third largest net earner of foreign exchange, earned some US $6 billion in 2005. Total employment, direct and indirect, generated by the sector is estimated at 38.6 million for 2002-03 constituting 8.27 per cent of the total employment in the country.

During the Eleventh Plan period, there is potential to generate 27 million additional jobs due to tourism. To fully benefit from natural, cultural, business, leisure, spiritual, religious, ecological, adventure and medical tourism, the Eleventh Plan should focus on creation of adequate tourism infrastructure like modernisation and expansion of airports, increase in accommodation facilities under star and budget category and improved road connectivity to tourist destinations.' Industry's lobbying for tourism's needs, it would seem, has reached the right address.

A robust economy, growing businesses, greater purchasing power, and surge in business & leisure travel has resulted in a flourishing and booming hospitality industry. But with the opportunity comes difficult challenges. Mounting competition and rising guest expectations are compelling the industry to take a fresh look at their businesses. The emerging technologies, capabilities and supporting infrastructure are 'must have' tools to overcome these challenges and ensure a better tomorrow. Integration of the latest technologies in hospitality are fast becoming the cornerstone of delivery for profitability, guest satisfaction, and most importantly, a differentiating factor.

Chapter 3

Marketing Strategies for the Growing Business

THE MARKETING AND SALES DIVISION

Marketing continues to be a mystery to those who create it and to those who sponsor it. Often, the ad that generates record-breaking volume for a retail store one month is repeated the following month and bombs. A campaign designed by the best Madison Avenue ad agency may elicit a mediocre response. The same item sells like hotcakes after a 30-word classified ad, with abominable grammar, appears on page 35 of an all-advertising shopper tossed on the front stoops of homes during a rainstorm! The mystery eludes solution but demands attention.

Putting the customer first is probably the most popular phrase used by firms ranging from giant conglomerates to the corner barber shop, but the sloganizing is often just lip service. The business continues to operate under the classic approach – "Come buy this great product we have created or this fantastic service we are offering." The giveaway, of course, is the word we. In other words, most business activities, including advertising, are dedicated to solving the firm's problems. Success, however, is more likely if you dedicate your activities exclusively to solving your customer's problems.

Any marketing Programme has a better chance of being productive if it is timed, designed and written to solve a problem for potential customers and is carried out in a way that the customer understands and trusts. The pages that follow will present the marketing concept of putting the customer first. Marketing is a very complex subject; it deals with all the steps between determining customer needs and supplying them at a profit. In addition to some introductory material on marketing, this publication includes practical material on the marketing approaches to budgeting, layout design, headline writing, copywriting and media analysis. You have to spend money on marketing; the purpose of this publication is to help you get the most for your money, or the most bang for the about the word marketing. Many people, including top executives, use it as a sophisticated term for selling. Marketing representative is commonly used in ads to recruit salespeople. Actually, marketing is a way of managing a business so that each critical business decision is made with full knowledge of the impact it will have on the customer.

Here are some specific ways in which the marketing approach differs from the classic, or sales, approach to managing a business.

1. In the classic approach, engineers and designers create a product, which is then given to salespeople who are told to find customers and sell the product. In the marketing approach, the first step is to determine what the customer needs or wants. That information is given to designers who develop the product and finally to engineers who produce it. Thus, the sales approach only ends with the customer, while the marketing approach begins and ends with the customer.
2. The second major difference between the sales and marketing approaches is the focus of management. The sales approach almost always focuses on volume while the marketing approach focuses on profit.

In short, under the classic (sales) approach the customer exists for the business, while under the marketing approach the business exists for the customer.

The marketing concept is a management plan that views all marketing components as part of a total system that requires effective planning, organization, leadership and control. It is based on the importance of customers to a firm, and states that

- All company policies and activities should be aimed at satisfying customer needs.
- Profitable sales volume is a better company goal than maximum sales volume.

SELF-ASSESSMENT QUESTIONNAIRE

In order to conduct a successful marketing Programme you must be able to answer the following questions:

1. What type of business are you in (manufacturing, merchandising or service)?
2. What is the nature of your product(s) or service(s)?
3. What market segments do you intend to serve? (Describe the age, sex, income level and life-style characteristics of each market segment.)
4. What strategies will you use to attract and keep customers?
   - Product
   - Price
   - Place
   - Promotion
   - Persuasion (personal selling)
5. What is your unique selling proposition (USP)?
6. Who is your competition, and what will you do to control your share of the market?

MARKET RESEARCH

To use the marketing concept effectively in a growing business, you should

- Analyze your firm's competitive advantage. What do you do best?
- Identify specific markets you now serve.
- Determine the wants and needs of your present customers.

- Determine what you are now doing to satisfy those wants and needs.
- Prepare a marketing plan that allows you to reach out to new customers or to sell more to your present customers.
- Test the results to see if your new strategies are yielding the desired results.

Market research must be used in each of these six steps to help define your business for your customer's interests, not your own. It is the process of learning what customers want or need and determining how to satisfy those wants or needs. It is also used to confirm whether the customer reacted to a marketing Programme as expected. The benefits of market research include:

- Learning who your customers are and what they want.
- Learning how to reach your customers and how frequently you should try to communicate with them.
- Learning which advertising appeals are most effective and which ones get no response.
- Learning the relative success of different marketing strategies, thus improving return on investment.
- Learning how not to repeat your mistakes.

The dilemma for the small business owner is that, properly done, market research is quite expensive, takes time and requires professional expertise. Acquiring all the necessary data to reduce the risk to your venture may cost so much and take so long that you may go out of business. The answer is to find a quick and inexpensive way of getting enough data to help you make the right decision most of the time.

Some obvious pitfalls are:

- Using a sample that does not represent the total market.
- Asking the wrong questions.
- Not listening to the responses.

- Building in biases or predispositions that distort the reliability of information.
- Letting arrogance or hostility cut off communication at some point in the marketing process.

If you have a limited budget, develop the skills to hear what your customers and potential customers are telling you. Some techniques worthy of consideration are:

- Advisory board – Occasionally convene a group of local people, whose opinions you respect, to act as a sounding board for new ideas. Choose your group with extreme care; one or two negative thinkers can distort the thought process of the entire group.
- User group – Gather customers together to discuss new ideas. Their opinions can help you keep your business on track. Pick a neutral setting where the people will talk. Be sure to reward the participants and share the credit for good ideas.
- Informal survey – If you seek feedback from customers by simply asking, How was everything? You can be seriously misled. Most people, even those with legitimate complaints, are reluctant to speak out because they are afraid of appearing foolish. This tendency is probably more widespread in smaller communities, where friendships often stand in the way of critical review. Also, if your attitude is such that customers feel complaining will not do any good, you may be antagonizing customers without even knowing it. One solution is to take a few customers aside and ask them some sincere questions about how your business met their expectations and where it fell short. If the customer appears uneasy, do not press the issue – you will only force him or her to give you pat answers to escape the situation. If you get a good response, take notes. Follow-up letters thanking the customers and telling them what you plan to do with their suggestions will bring you friends for life.

- Suggestion box – A suggestion box is a simple idea that works, but only if you do the following:
  - Read the suggestions on a regular basis.
  - Do something about the suggestions you receive.
  - Reward those who give you good ideas by posting their names, writing letters to them or rewarding them with money or other things of value.

The principle at work is: If you reward good results, you will get more good results. If you do not reward them, you will end up with an empty suggestion box and the mistaken idea that everything is fine.

- Sample survey – Canvass the neighborhood to gather data. If you wish to remain anonymous, line up some marketing students to perform the survey or engage a local marketing agency. Be sure you establish a technique for getting a random sample as most people naturally attempt to attract respondents with whom they feel comfortable. Be sure to test your questionnaire to see that the questions are easily understood and are meaningful .
- Focus group interview – Get 10 to 15 people together in a relaxed setting and encourage them to talk about products or services they like or dislike. Use a moderator who can lead the group discussion without inhibiting the thought processes or limiting the expression of ideas and opinions. Tape record the session for later analysis.
- Brainstorming – This is a variation of the focus group, in which participants are encouraged to freewheel in their thinking to produce as many suggestions as possible without analyzing them. Again, a trained moderator will obtain the best results.
- Complaint analysis – Encourage your customers to contact you directly if they have complaints. Respond

to every complaint with a courteous letter assuring that you will correct the situation. A few disgruntled customers can be harmful. If your customers feel that they can work with you to solve their problems, you are sure to be successful.

- Comparison shopping – Arrange with someone in a similar business located out of town to come to your town to shop your business and several of your competitors. Then return the favour and compare notes. This will avoid the danger of your becoming complacent about your premises and overlooking things that may be annoying or confusing to your customers.
- Customer analysis – Tabulate information about customers regularly to determine such data as :
  - Age.
  - Size of buying group (family, household, etc.).
  - Sex of the decision maker in the group.
  - Geographic location – Sort checks and sales slips by ZIP code, or ask customers to mark their home on a map with a colored pencil. Tabulate visitors versus local residents.
  - Average amount of purchase.
  - Coupon usage.
  - Response to recent advertising.
  - Radio station listened to.
  - Newspapers read.
  - Response to mailings.
  - Full price buyers versus those who respond to sales or specials.
  - Special populations in your area, such as college students, military personnel, senior citizens, hospital visitors, convention attendees, sports spectators, fair attendees, farmers, seasonal workers, car pools, pet owners, home owners, boat or recreational vehicle owners and athletic

participants. The more you know about your customers the better you will be able to satisfy and even anticipate their needs.

- Customer want list – Keep a notebook at your cash register and write down every request you receive for items you do not carry or have in stock. Periodic review of the list will give valuable clues about sales you are losing or new products and services you should consider carrying. You may learn of fad items, products being heavily advertised or items and services your competitors have dropped. Your customers may be telling you they are dissatisfied with your competition and would prefer buying from you. You will be able to tell if other businesses in the area are in trouble, even before they know it themselves. You may also discover ways to make additional income by adding new departments or product lines or by developing a special-order business if your customers are willing to pay the added shipping costs and wait for delivery.
- Industry analysis – On business trips or vacations, visit businesses similar to yours. Take pictures of signs, storefronts and displays, and talk to the owners to compare notes on new products, services and marketing techniques. Subscribe to trade journals and attend trade shows to keep current on marketing developments in your industry.
- Sales representatives – Representatives who call on other similar businesses in your area can provide valuable information on business trends, new items and changes in the industry. Be sure the information is reliable.
- Advertising notebook – Each ad that you run represents an investment. To make sure you maximize your investment, cut out each ad and tape it to a page in a three-ring notebook. (For a radio or TV ad, write a short description.) Enter the date, medium and cost of the ad. Record the results of the ad in sales,

inquiries or coupons redeemed. Divide the cost by the results to get a cost-per-inquiry factor that you can use to compare your ads and the media in which they appeared.

- Exit interviews – When someone leaves your employ, be sure to spend sufficient time to find out exactly why he or she is leaving. Probe deep to learn what may be occurring in your business that causes hard feelings, employee conflict or customer dissatisfaction. It is important that your employees leave with a good feeling about you and your business, so they will not spread unfounded rumors. Also, you may wish to keep them as customers. Employee turnover and training can be expensive to a business, so try to find out what you must do to keep employees and then decide if they are worth the price.

EXPANDING YOUR MARKET

When expanding your business, explore all the strategic alternatives available to you. Select the one that makes the most sense and then prepare a marketing plan on how to implement that strategy. There are at least a dozen common strategies and a variety of strategic combinations or special situations to choose from.

Expansion of Present Location

Learn to spot telltale signs of saturation in your present facilities. Grocery stores, for example, keep track of abandoned carts. When a shopper fills a cart and then leaves because the checkout line is too long, the grocer should realize that there is a serious problem. If you are experiencing bottlenecks, think about adding to your facilities. Determine how many additional customers you could service by building up or out and compare the additional sales to the cost of construction and temporary inconvenience.

Relocation

If it appears unlikely that you can draw more customers to your present location (at a reasonable cost), consider moving closer to your customers. A location on Main Street, in a shopping mall or an industrial park may cost you more in rent, but if you gain exposure to new customers it may be a sound investment.

Additional Outlets

Reaching the most customers may require opening several outlets at convenient locations throughout your market area. In addition to the added costs of real estate and multiple inventories, carefully analyze the cost and availability of labour and training, and the cost of hiring a manager for each location and installing an efficient monitoring system. Your advertising dollars may become more efficient since your radio, TV and newspaper ads cover your entire market. The multiple locations will make it more convenient for customers to find you.

Downward Vertical Integration

If your profits depend on the prices you pay for raw materials, your most profitable growth strategy may be to buy a farm, mine or processing plant to produce your own materials. This strategy also may make sense if your product quality is based on a consistent supply of goods at an acceptable quality level.

Upward Vertical Integration

Most small manufacturing businesses that start are forced to conform to the existing marketing channels and sell through established manufacturers' representatives, jobbers or dealers who have access to the market. As you grow, however, it makes sense to analyze your distribution system to see when you can improve your situation by hiring your own sales team, contracting with distributors, buying a truck fleet, opening retail stores or factory outlet stores or doing anything else you need to do to get closer to your market. Remember, every time someone gets between you and your customer, it either reduces your revenue or increases your operating costs. Also, it impedes the provider-consumer communication that is essential to a good marketing programme.

Exporting Goods or Services

Literally, there is a world of markets available to you if you are willing to learn how to get started. The U.S. Department of Commerce's U.S. and Foreign Commercial Service and the U.S. Small Business Administration can help you explore potential foreign markets for your product or service.

Tourists' Business

When you are looking for new customers, don't ignore tourists who could be attracted to your area. Work with your local convention and visitors' bureau to determine the impact if you cooperate with local tourist attractions or hotels and restaurants to get more people to visit and spend money in your community.

Franchises

Franchising as a growth strategy offers advantages if you are short of expansion capital, yet have a concept that can be packaged and taught to people who wish to invest in a business. The legal problems can seem overwhelming, but with a good plan and competent advice, you can develop a franchise system that could prove extremely profitable.

License Agreements

If you have a technical process or service, you may be able to find people in other markets who would be willing to pay you a royalty for the rights to use your process. Perhaps you could sell raw materials, secret ingredients, special tooling or promotional materials to your license holders.

Direct Marketing

Selling directly to your customers is one of the oldest and most effective methods of marketing. Today, there are few door-to-door salespeople; most direct marketing is seen in party plan selling and through mail, TV and magazines. Direct selling requires good selection and training techniques and a commission plan plus liberal incentives.

Telemarketing

If you have a good list of prospective customers, telemarketing may be an effective method of informing them about your business, qualifying them for sales follow-up or selling your product or service to them. Professional firms can be used, or you can set up your own telephone room. Here again, recruiting and training are critical because only a few people can do telemarketing well.

Private Label

One method of reaching out to new markets is to sell your product under the name of your distributor or retailer. However, you cannot build customer or brand loyalty because the consumer does not know you are the producer. Another potential problem is that, should the owner of the label find a cheaper producer, you may be out of the business.

PROBLEM SOLVING PLAN

The marketing plan is a problem-solving document. Skilled problem solvers recognize that a big problem is usually the combination of several smaller problems. The best approach is to solve each of the smaller problems first, thereby dividing the big problem into manageable pieces. Your marketing plan should take the same approach. It should be a guide on which to base decisions and should ensure that everyone in your organization is working together to achieve the same goals. A good marketing plan can prevent your organization from reacting to problems in a piecemeal manner and even help in anticipating problems.

Before your marketing plan can be developed, research must give you the basic guidelines: for whom you are designing your product or service (market segmentation), and exactly what that product or service should mean to those in the marketplace (market positioning). Below are some guidelines to help you develop a marketing plan to support the strategy you have selected for your organization.

Market Segmentation

Your marketing plan should recognize the various segments of the market for your product or service and indicate how to adjust your product to reach those distinct markets. Instead of marketing a product in one way to everyone, you must recognize that some segments are not only different, but better than others for your product. This approach can be helpful in penetrating markets that would be too broad and undefined without segmentation. No matter what you are making or selling, take the total market and divide it up like a pie chart. The divisions can be based on various criteria such as those listed below.

Demographics

This is the study of the distribution, density and vital statistics of a population, and includes such characteristics as

- Sex
- Age
- Education
- Geographic location.
- Home ownership versus rental.
- Marital status.
- Size of family unit.
- Total income of family unit.
- Ethnic or religious background.
- Job classification – blue collar versus salaried or professional.

Psychographics

This is the study of how the human characteristics of consumers may have a bearing on their response to products, packaging, advertising and public relations efforts. Behaviour may be measured as it involves an interplay among these broad sets of variables:

- Predisposition – What is there about a person's past culture, heredity or upbringing that may influence his or her ability to consider purchasing one new product or service versus another?

- Influences – What are the roles of social forces such as education, peer pressure or group acceptance in dictating a person's consumption patterns?
- Product Attributes – What the product is or can be made to represent in the minds of consumers has a significant bearing on whether certain segments will accept the concept. These attributes may be suggested by the marketer or perceived by the customer. Some typical ways of describing a product include

– Price/value perception – Is the item worth the price being asked?

- – Taste: Does it have the right amount of sweetness or lightness?
- – Texture: Does it have the accepted consistency or feel?
- – Quality: What can be said about the quality of the ingredients or lack of artificial ingredients?
- – Benefits: How does the consumer feel after using the product?
- – Trust: Can the consumer rely on this particular brand? What about the reputation of the manufacturer in standing behind the product?

Life-Style

Statements consumers make about themselves through conspicuous consumption can be put to good use by research people who read the signals correctly. By studying behavioral variables, such as a person's use of time, services and products, researchers can identify some common factors that can predict future behaviour.

MARKET POSITIONING

You must realize that your product or service cannot be all things to all people. Very few items on the market today have universal appeal. Even when dealing in basic commodities like table salt or aspirin, marketing people have gone to all sorts of extremes to create brand awareness and product differentiation. If your product or service is properly positioned, prospective purchasers or users should immediately recognize its unique benefits or advantages and be better able to assess it in comparison to your competition's offering. Positioning is how you give your product or service brand identification.

Positioning involves analyzing each market segment as defined by your research activities and developing a distinct position for each segment. Ask yourself how you want to appear to that segment, or what you must do for that segment to ensure that it buys your product or service. This will dictate different media and advertising appeals for each segment. For example, you may sell the same product in a range of packages or sizes, or make cosmetic changes in the product, producing private labels or selecting separate distribution channels to reach the various segments. Beer, for example, is sold on tap and in seven-ounce bottles, twelve-ounce cans and bottles, six-packs, twelve-packs, cases, and quart bottles and kegs of several sizes. The beer is the same but each package size may appeal to a separate market segment and have to be sold with a totally different appeal and through different retail outlets.

Remember that your marketing position can, and should, change to meet the current conditions of the market for your product. The ability of your company to adjust will be enhanced greatly by an up-to-date knowledge of the marketplace gained through continual monitoring. By having good data about your customers, the segments they fit into and the buying motives of those segments, you can select the position that makes the most sense. While there are many possible marketing positions, most would fit into one of the following categories:

- Positioning on specific product features – A very common approach, especially for industrial products. If your product or service has some unique features that have obvious value this may be the way to go.
- Positioning on benefits – Strongly related to positioning on product features. Generally, this is

more effective because you can talk to your customers about what your product or service can do for them. The features may be nice, but unless customers can be made to understand why the product will benefit them, you may not get the sale.

- Positioning for a specific use – Related to benefit positioning. Consider Campbell's positioning of soups for cooking. An interesting extension is mood positioning: Have a Coke and a smile. This works best when you can teach your customers how to use your product or when you use a promotional medium that allows a demonstration.
- Positioning for user category – A few examples: You've Come a Long Way Baby, The Pepsi Generation and Breakfast of Champions. Be sure you show your product being used by models with whom your customers can identify.
- Positioning against another product or a competing business – A strategy that ranges from implicit to explicit comparison. Implicit comparisons can be quite pointed; for example, Avis never mentions Hertz, but the message is clear. Explicit comparisons can take two major forms. The first form makes a comparison with a direct competitor and is aimed at attracting customers from the compared brand, which is usually the category leader. The second type does not attempt to attract the customers of the compared product, but rather uses the comparison as a reference point. Consider, for example, the positioning of the Volkswagen Dasher, which picks up speed faster than a Mercedes and has a bigger trunk than a Rolls Royce. This usually works to the advantage of the smaller business if you can capitalize on the American tradition of cheering for the underdog. You can gain stature by comparing yourself to a larger competitor just as long as our customers remain convinced that you are trying harder.

- Product class disassociation -- A less common type of positioning. It is particularly effective when used to introduce a new product that differs from traditional products. Lead-free gasoline and tubeless tires were new product classes positioned against older products. Space-age technology may help you here. People have become accustomed to change and new products and are more willing to experiment than was true ten years ago. Even so, some people are more adventuresome and trusting than others and more apt to try a revolutionary product. The trick is to find out who are the potential brand switchers or experimenters and find out what it would take to get them to try your product. The obvious disadvantage of dealing with those who try new products is that they may move on to another brand just as easily. Brand loyalty is great as long as it is to your brand.
- Hybrid bases – Incorporates elements from several types of positioning. Given the variety of possible bases for positioning, small business owners should consider the possibility of a hybrid approach. This is particularly true in smaller towns where there aren't enough customers in any segment to justify the expense of separate marketing approaches.

THE MARKETING BUDGET

Resource allocation is a critical part of any marketing plan. To simplify budget preparation, it is recommended that investments in labour, material and services be broken down into the five Ps of marketing:

- Product – The item or service you have to sell.
- Price – The amount of money you ask your customer to pay for your product.
- Place – Where a product is now and how it is transported to your customer.
- Promotion – The advertising and publicity necessary to complete a transaction.
- Persuasion – Personal selling of your business.

Each of the five Ps represents an investment in dollars, materials and services. We can represent this as a system of pipes consisting of a tank of money, which represents the total marketing budget, a main pipe through which the dollars flow and five valves that control the flow of money to each of the five. The concepts of market planning, segmentation and positioning are shown as filters. Budgeting is the process of setting the valves to meet the needs of each marketing task for each segment and then monitoring the results over time to make sure you remain on target.

As your market segments change, you will have to reset the valves. The important thing is to have in place an effective marketing research system that gives you the confidence to move in the right direction for the right reason.

THE PRODUCT (OR SERVICE)

When consumers think about using a product or service, they consider its advantages and disadvantages. In other words, they ask, What's in it for me? Therefore, it is not enough to define your product and its features; other questions must be answered. Think first of your perception of your product or service and then find out how your customers see it. Ask yourself questions such as

- What is a description of our product or service?
- What image does it have in the market?
- What are its features and benefits?
- In the eyes of the consumer, is there a way for us to provide our product or service more effectively?
- Where does our product or service fit in a product life cycle?
  - Introduction (maximum investment in development)
  - Growth (investment in marketing)
  - Maturity (maximize profits)
  - Decline

- Marketing decision – At some point during this declining stage, you must decide whether to invest more money in the product (i.e., create a new and improved model requiring additional investment and generating a new life cycle) or to discontinue it.

Price

There are a number of pricing strategies you can use to achieve your growth goal. Each has the potential of producing a profit, and most are tied to the critical relationship of price-to-sales volume and stock turnover. Some strategies you may want to consider are listed below.

Price Skimming

This refers to the practice of charging high prices for the purpose of maximizing profit in the short run. It works best when

- The product is unique and people are willing to pay extra just to have it. There are trendsetters in society who always are looking for something new and are willing to pay the price. A larger number are followers, and they will buy your product if it is accepted by the leaders. The followers, however, will not pay the higher price.
- The cost of development is high and there is a chance of early obsolescence or imitation by competitors.
- You have a strong patent position, or your product would be difficult to copy.

The real disadvantage of skimming is that it attracts competition. Your competitors will soon figure out what you are up to, and the high profit potential will encourage them to copy you. They may produce cheaper versions of your product or style, referred to as knockoffs in the market. Once you have meaningful competition on price, your skimming days are over and you run the risk of ending up with a warehouse full of products that cannot be sold at any price.

Penetration Pricing

The opposite of skimming is to introduce your product at such a low price that you will quickly gain a large share of the market. The purpose is to discourage competition. However, eventually you will have to raise your prices to start making some profit and, when you do, you will learn much about customer loyalty.

Buying a Market Position

A variation of penetration pricing is to buy your way into the market with free samples or heavy coupons, for example, 50 cents off on a 69-cent purchase. This tactic is usually used by big companies because it takes considerable financial backing and it may be six months or more before it starts to pay off. Small marketers can use it to the degree they know what they are doing and can control the process. Frequent follow-up is important to ensure samples are not going to professional collectors but are reaching potentially strong customers.

Loss Leader

This refers to promoting a few items at a sizable reduction to attract customers. The idea is that the increased traffic will result in greater sales of your regular-priced merchandise. The reductions have to be on recognized brands and items purchased frequently enough so customers know the prices and can recognize the savings. You must keep switching leader items – people are not going to buy catsup four weeks in a row regardless of its price. The danger is that you may develop a following of cherry pickers who will breeze into your store, scoop up the specials and buy nothing else.

Multiple Unit Pricing

You can increase the size of your individual sales by offering a meaningful discount for larger purchases. A liquor store usually will offer a discount or throw in a free bottle of wine when you buy a case. The same idea applies to the baker's dozen, a discount on a set of tires or selling beer and soft drinks by the pitcher. This is a good technique for building customer goodwill, but you will not see your customers as often. The trade-off, of course, is that you save time and money on containers and packaging, save time by writing up fewer sales and, perhaps, can make your delivery service more efficient by selling by the truckload. Variations are two-fors, six-packs, cheaper by the carton and bulk price.

Suggested Retail Pricing

This is the practice of selling at prices set by your suppliers. It is convenient because many product lines are available prepackaged and prepriced. However, you lose flexibility and must live with a set percentage markup. (To combat this disadvantage, some suppliers offer two-for-three options using the retail price). Because suggested-retail or retail-price-maintenance plans are illegal in some states, the practice usually is a loser. Using a slightly different strategy, Panasonic published a minimum retail price list showing a higher average retail; some stores use such gimmicks as compare at or nationally advertised at to imply that the official price is at a certain point.

Discount Pricing

The discount store usually offers lower prices as a trade-off for spartan interiors, lack of sales help and the efficiency of central checkouts. These stores typically work on a 35 to 38 percent markup compared to 42.5 to 45 percent for a department store. Since discount stores depend on the efficiency of greater volume to cover operating costs, they must maintain, or at least promote, good prices.

Full-cost Pricing

This pricing is calculated by adding the costs of the product or service plus a flat fee or percentage as the margin of profit. During inflation, you must keep track of your costs to make sure that you are charging enough. In many business lines, owners have come to realize that when they replace their stock, the wholesale price has often risen above their retail price. If they do not raise prices rapidly enough, they are faced with diminishing inventories at a constant dollar investment or with having to invest more money to restock their shelves at the constant level.

Keystone Pricing

This refers to the practice of setting the retail price at double the cost figure, or a 100 percent markup. It is most common with jewelry items and in specialty shops, high-ticket fashion shops and department stores. Typically, the merchandise is subject to drastic clearance markdowns on items that are slow sellers or held past the season.

Price Lining

This is the technique used by most retail stores of stocking merchandise in several different price ranges. A hardware store, for example, may carry hammers in good, better, and best categories at $3.49, $6.49 and $9.98, respectively, and a professional model at $17.95. The theory is that people buy products with different uses in mind and with different expectations for quality and length of useful life. If you do not carry a range of prices, you may lose the customers who cannot find the product at the right price. Price lining simplifies buying and inventory control because you buy only for the price levels that you know your customers will accept and eliminate those goods that fall outside the levels you want to carry.

Competitive Advantage

Here is where you copy or follow the prices set by your competition. Based on your service image, you can set your prices equal to, above or below those of your competition. This strategy requires constant vigilance by reading the ads and shopping your competition. It is a more passive technique because you're always following your competitors. Chances are your more aggressive competitor can make better purchases than you. A variation of this is the we-won't-be-undersold routine, where you offer to meet or beat the prices of all your competitors.

Pre-season Pricing

Many manufacturers offer price discounts or dated billing as incentives to buy early. This is important to manufacturers because of production planning and the lead time necessary for ordering raw materials. For the retailer, the same principles apply; also, off-season specials may be a way to profit in business on a year-round basis. When you sell at a lower price to get the early sales, you may be borrowing from later full price sales. On the other hand, anyone who has tried to buy snow tires during the year's first snowstorm knows the extent of delivery problems. In this case, early sales at a lower price would have allowed the merchant to serve the customers better and to capture sales that may be lost due to limited service facilities.

Price Is No Object

This refers to certain marketing situations in which the quality of the product or service is far more important than the price. If you need a kidney transplant, for example, you are not going to shop around and haggle over price. And even if you do press the doctor, he probably will quote you a range with a $5,000 spread rather than giving a specific number. The same is often true with high-ticket fashions and jewelry. Using the same psychology, expensive automobiles and boats are not sold on price. They may use a starting at or base price to get people interested, but the prices of the options are usually in very small print. The extreme of this attitude is that if you have to ask the price you probably cannot afford the item anyway.

Place

Where the product is located when the potential customer is exposed to a buying opportunity can often mean the difference between success or failure. The distribution plan for a given product may be determined by several of the factors listed below.

Product Characteristics

- Perishability – Refrigeration or frozen storage requirements can severely restrict place options and raise operating expenses.
- Bulk – A product requiring large display space, or one that is heavy, may restrict transportation options as well as display opportunities.
- Displayability – Package design that prevents stacking on store shelves can severely restrict customer exposure. (Log Cabin syrup was originally packaged in slanted-roof metal containers. As supermarkets placed increased value on shelf space for customer selection, the inability to stack the log cabins forced a change in package design.)
- Buying requirements – If the item must be tried on to determine fit or if it must be demonstrated before the sale can be made, the place element is more restrictive than for a product that requires no package opening at the time of purchase.

Customer Characteristics

- Impulse versus planned purchase – Items displayed in a high-traffic area can increase unplanned purchases.
- Frequency of purchase – Items purchased once a week usually require more outlets than those purchased once a year. Grocery stores, for example, always outnumber retail furniture outlets.
- Distance – How far is the customer willing to travel to purchase your goods or services?

Use Characteristics

How the customer uses the product after purchase also can determine place characteristics.

- Do you need to train the customer to use your product or supply instructions or a repair parts list?
- Can you make more sales for service contracts, accessory items, consumable supplies, repair parts or companion items?

Location

For most small businesses, especially those involved in retail, finding the best location at the lowest price becomes an important consideration. You can draw customers to a poor location but the cost of advertising is often prohibitive. You should learn how much money you have to pay for the better location and see how that compares to the cost of drawing the same number of customers to the poorer location. Do not overlook parking, public transportation, quality of the neighborhood, sign restrictions, lighting, traffic flow and other factors that determine your store's convenience and safety.

Promotion

Perhaps the most versatile of the five marketing Ps is promotion. It covers all phases of communication between the seller and the potential customer. It is versatile because a change in budget, media or target audience can be made quickly. Promotions also can be effectively changed for specific market segment efforts. Major promotional concerns include the following.

Budget

Because promotional costs can originate from several sources, it is vital to establish a written budget and closely monitor actual costs. The budgeting procedure is simplified if separate budgets are prepared for advertising and promotional activities. Sales goals in dollars, units or both are usually the basis for promotional budgets.

Timing

Selling when the consumer wants to buy is a fundamental factor in the marketing concept. Promotional efforts, whether in-store or through mass media advertising, should be timed to coincide with maximum seasonal or cyclical demand.

Distribution of Promotional Efforts

- Advertising – The major portion of a firm's promotional budget is advertising. Some advertising media, such as the Yellow Pages, where a specific amount is charged each month, can be budgeted as fixed advertising expenditures. The mass media – newspapers, radio, TV, direct mail and magazines – should be individually budgeted to achieve sales goals, improve your image and expand your customer base.
- Promotion – Many firms classify promotion as a separate budget category. In this case, promotional efforts include in-store displays, sampling, specialty advertising, giveaways and other nontraditional media efforts.
- Publicity — This is the no-cost element, meaning there is no charge by the newspaper or other medium for carrying a news release or feature. There will be an internal cost, however, for the preparation of publicity releases and photography. Many businesses miss publicity opportunities because they do not have a written marketing plan. Every promotion or addition of personnel is an opportunity for free publicity, but only if the news release is prepared and sent to the media. Business expansion, remodeling, automation or changes in product name all deserve a publicity Programme.

Promotion Strategy

All advertising and other promotional activities should be in tune with the firm's stated position in the marketplace. This suggests that not only advertising themes but also media selection must be based on building and strengthening that position.

- Benefit approach – Regardless of your media, to make your marketing concept work in advertising messages you must analyze each product and service in relation to these two elements:
  - Product point – Those features built into the product or service. Product points are usually highly touted in advertising messages, but they are relatively ineffective unless they are integrated with the second ingredient.
  - Benefit – The advantage a customer receives after purchasing the product. Your advertising should promise benefits and make those promises believable by naming the product points that will produce the benefits. For example, "You'll feel better about your family's safety (benefit) when they are riding on the new steel-belted radials from Armstrong – thanks to the interwoven blankets of steel embedded deep in the tread (product point)."
- Media – Consider many types of media in your promotional campaigns.
  - Newspapers
  - Shoppers
  - Television
  - Radio
  - Billboards
  - Direct Mail
  - Magazines

A full discussion of these media is included under Media Available to Advertisers.

In summary, the importance of promotion in the overall marketing strategy suggests you devote time to its written plan and constantly monitor the plan's performance. Be creative but avoid cuteness. Stick to the benefit approach, and your customers will respond.

Persuasion

Your business's success will depend on your ability to persuade others to take actions that will help them while also helping you. This is referred to as a win-win situation. Both parties in the transaction must receive a benefit in value or in satisfaction. There are many buying motives that may bring a customer to your business:

Gain	Utility	Conformity
Time saved	Productivity	Saved effort
Health	Convenience	Money saved
Comfort	Happiness	Need
Protection	Pride (vanity	Want
Pleasure	Fear	Economy
Amusement	Love	Luxury
Security	Profit	Safety

The key to successful selling is to determine which motives brought the customer to you and then develop a sales presentation that will convince the customer that you and your product can meet those needs. This process can be broken down into a series of steps:

- Prospecting – This is the activity of identifying potential customers or running ads to entice people into your store.
- Pre-approach – This includes planning what you will say to customers and what evidence or displays you will need to enhance your presentation.
- Approach – This may include a greeting, statement of objective or series of questions to determine exactly what the customer wants. Learn as much as possible about the customer and his or her buying motive before you begin your presentation.
- Presentation – This is the opportunity to tell customers everything they need to know to make an intelligent buying decision.

- Dramatization – Show enthusiasm for your product or service.
- Proof – Words may not be enough. You may need to show facts and figures, endorsements, testimonials or other means of backing up your claims.
- Visualization – your customers visualize the satisfaction they will derive from buying now.
- Demonstration – If possible, let the customer experience the product. Many items are difficult to sell without a test drive.
- Trial close – This is a statement or question designed to let you know how close the customer is to making a buying decision.
- Uncover objections – Find out why the customer is not ready to buy.
- Meet objections – Go back over your presentation to clear up misunderstandings or doubts the customer may have.
- Final close – Ask a question that causes the customer to make a buying decision in your favor.
- Follow-up – This includes all the steps you take to write up the sale, arrange delivery, receive payment and ensure customer satisfaction.

The above process may be inefficient in many selling situations. The genius and creativity of advertising is its flexibility in preconditioning the customer and answering some objections. Certainly your reputation, attitude and the atmosphere of the selling situation can do much to alleviate fears or concerns in the mind of the customer. Your best prospect often is a satisfied customer or the friend or relative of a satisfied customer.

For many products or services, direct mail and telephone selling can be used to complete the sale or to qualify prospects for a personal follow-up.

Motivation is an essential ingredient in persuasion. You and your employees must maintain a positive mental attitude. You must learn to sell yourself, your company and your product. And your attitude must be one of serving the customer first, with the realization that your success depends completely on your ability to serve the customer.

THE ADVERTISING BUDGET

This section will concentrate on how to prepare a written, detailed advertising budget. This differs from a budget that details specific dollar amounts for anticipated receipts and expenditures, usually handled by a certified public accountant (CPA) or other financial advisor. These professionals seldom do more than allocate a specific amount for advertising and treat it the same as rent – i.e., as an annual expense item.

Returning once again to the marketing approach, a sound advertising budget should be based on consumer habits and preferences. Unfortunately, most retail advertising today appears as an attempt to solve a store's problems. Promotions reading We Are Overstocked, We Must Reduce Inventory and Our Loss Is Your Gain are commonplace and do very little to stimulate the reader to action. The first requirement of successful advertising for the retail store is to work toward solving the consumers' problems. This publication's approach to preparing an advertising budget will, therefore, be based on the following assumptions:

- Timing of advertising will be determined by consumers' preference for buying rather than when the store would like to sell.
- Items to be featured in advertising will be selected on a basis of probable popularity with customers rather than on a store's desire to reduce inventory.
- Headlines and copy for advertising will always be customer-benefit oriented.
- Any medium will be selected on its ability to reach the right prospects. Personal favorites and prejudices prevent objectivity in media selection.

The complete advertising budget must provide specific written answers to each of these questions:

- How much should I spend?
- When should I spend it?
- Where should I spend it?
- What media should I use?

How Much Should I Spend?

Since the cost of advertising must be paid from sales revenue, it should always be expressed as a function of expected sales dollars. The two most popular approaches are

1. The number of dollars considered necessary to successfully promote the sale of a given item at a given price. (Example: $10 of the $300 selling price for each refrigerator will go to advertising so that $3,000 in advertising should sell 300 units and produce $90,000 in sales.)

2. A flat percentage of every anticipated revenue dollar will go toward advertising. (Three percent of an estimated $100,000 annual sales volume will result in an advertising budget of $3,000.)

This section will concentrate on the second approach because it allocates advertising costs for all product lines. Although fewer than 50 percent of the items carried by most stores are never advertised, their sale is the direct result of customer traffic created by the advertised items and, therefore, all merchandise sold should contribute to the overall cost of advertising.

Setting Sales Goals

In both approaches, the first step in preparing an advertising budget must be setting sales goals. Just how many television sets do you expect to sell in a month, a season, a year? Or what will the retail sales volume for the entire store be in each time frame?

Setting sales goals can be a guessing game, but basic research into past sales performance, the quantity and quality of competition, the economic forecasts for your area and characteristics of the population in your market area can help make the guess an educated one. The U.S. Department of Commerce publishes statistical information about consumer expenditures, retail sales and expense statistics. An hour or two spent in the government publications section of your local public library can pay big dividends. Another source for statistical data is the business association that serves your industry.

Although the first sales goal you set will be an annual figure, monthly sales goals can never be determined by merely dividing the annual figure by 12 months. One of the certainties of marketing is that consumer habits change constantly. Yet those very changes make the consumer predictable since there is a predictable pattern of consumer desire for almost every known commodity. While this consumption pattern may vary from month to month, the annual pattern repeats itself with remarkable consistency. The chart shown in Appendix B will give you an idea of the variation in annual sales patterns for just a few stores. For example, while the average retail jewelry store can expect 23 percent of its annual sales volume in December, the lumber yard or building materials store can expect only 8 percent of its annual sales during the same month. The figures on the chart represent average figures from stores of all sizes and from all parts of the United States. They have been recorded and averaged for five consecutive years, so your store's actual percentages may vary slightly.

Your next step after setting an annual sales goal is to determine what percentage of that annual volume you should anticipate for each calendar month. You may elect to use the national figures for your industry, but using your actual sales figures will give much more reliable numbers. To determine what percentage of your annual sales were achieved in any given month, merely divide that month's dollar volume by the annual dollar value and multiply that amount by 100. Your monthly share of sales percentages will be even more accurate if you compute it for each of your last three or four years of sales and then average the percentages for each month.

MAKING ADVERTISING WORK FOR YOU

Appeal to Consumers' Needs

Human behaviour, according to psychologist Abraham Maslow, is always the result of one or more of five basic needs or motivating forces. Maslow classified these in a sequence he refers to as the hierarchy of human needs. His theory is that until a lower-ranking need is satisfied there is no desire to pursue a higher-ranking need. Below are the five human motivators, beginning with the basic or lowest-ranked need and continuing to the highest.

1. Physiological needs – Include hunger, thirst, reproduction, shelter, clothing, air and rest.
2. Safety-security – The need for security, stability, dependence, protection, structure, order, law, tenure, pension and insurance.
3. Love-belonging – The need for belonging, acceptance, love, affection, family and group acceptance and friendship.
4. Self-esteem – The need for recognition, respect, achievement, responsibility, prestige, independence, attention, importance and appreciation.
5. Self-actualization – The need for satisfaction, the desire to achieve fulfillment through reaching self-set individual goals or aspirations.

The advertising practitioner will do well to become familiar with the Maslow theory of human motivation because it stresses once again that motivation is always an individual act. The most your advertising message can hope to do is to present an appeal strong enough to stimulate action toward satisfying one of the basic human needs.

If there is one rule that will be most helpful in preparing effective advertising, it is this: The message must put the desire of the potential customer before the advertiser's desire. Please read that one more time! The rule may sound like a simple one to follow, but frequently advertising messages take the form of a plea to customers to respond and solve the advertiser's problem.

Visualize the felt tip pen you probably use every day. When it was manufactured the raw materials were converted into these product features: a plastic barrel, a plastic cap, a supply of ink, a felt tip and a metal pocket clip. These are the total product points in the felt tip pen. What's amazing is that none of those things have anything to do with why you will buy the pen! You buy any item only for how it will benefit you. The key, of course, is benefit. Effective advertising must promise the consumer some benefit he or she will receive after buying the goods or services advertised. Product features should be cited only to make the promised benefits believable. Here is an example of how you can advertise the felt tip pen by promising benefits and then using the product features to make promised benefits believable.

- You can drop this pen on concrete from 20 feet in the air and it will not break because it is made of a strong plastic.
- You can draw a jet black line for more than 100,000 yards, thanks to the large supply of quality ink.
- This pen will not leave an ink stain on your shirt or in your purse, thanks to the snug-fitting plastic cap.
- When you bend over this pen will not fall from your pocket because it features a strong spring steel clip.

Although this technique appears logical, many advertisements ramble on and on with all the product features while the potential customer asks, What will it do for me? Using the benefit approach can be simplified by preparing a worksheet on which each product you plan to advertise is dissected into (1) the benefits the buyer will enjoy by owning this product and (2) which product features will help convince the potential buyer that the promised benefits are likely to be true. Using the benefit approach is the best advertising technique for each advertising medium. It is also the selling technique used by all top salespeople.

Techniques in Presenting the Advertising Message

The buying decision is seldom a purely rational one – emotions influence your behaviour. As you explore various techniques for presenting your advertising message, do not ignore psychological and emotional appeals. For example, red, a strong colour suggesting excitement, increases reader interest when used in sales ads. While the principles discussed here relate most specifically to print ads, they can apply to all media.

Determining Layout Shape and Design

Behavioral scientists have determined that of all the rectangular shapes, the vertical rectangle of approximately three units wide by five units deep is the one the public is exposed to most and, therefore, the one people find most comfortable. The advertising world refers to this shape as the golden rectangle of layout. It is believed that an advertising message receives higher readership when presented in this size.

In Appendix H is a drawing of this three-unit by five-unit shape. Notice the dot on the vertical center line, one-third of the way from the top of the ad. This is called the focal point. It is the point to which the eye is attracted first, at which the eye enters the ad. Next, note the wavy line extending from the upper left-hand corner of the ad to the lower right-hand corner. This reverse s is the path that the eye follows, called the gaze motion path. Your objective should be to reinforce the ease with which the eye can follow this path. How you place elements of your ad can invite the reader's eye to follow this path or to leave your ad completely before getting your message. If your artwork, for example, is located near the curves in the gaze-motion pattern, it will invite your reader to leave the ad at that point and turn the page. The gaze motion also reinforces the principle that the best place for a headline is at the top of the ad where the reader starts the visual journey through the ad. The worst place for your logo is the lower left-hand corner; the eye prefers to leave the ad at the lower right-hand corner, so your logo will have greater impact there.

The dotted lines divide the ad into vertical and horizontal halves to stress balance in your layout. Formal or symmetrical balance occurs when the elements on the left side of the vertical center line are in the same position and of the same size or density as corresponding elements on the right side. This formal balance is not as interesting to the eye as informal or asymmetrical balance, obtained by balancing weights on one side of the center line with weights of varying densities at greater or lesser distances from the center line on the other side of the ad. Visualize ad balance as being similar to a see-saw where weight near the outer end of the board can be balanced by heavier weights nearer the fulcrum on the other end of the board. In designing your ad layout, place illustrations, copy blocks, headlines and other elements so they appear balanced without formality.

Communicating Desired Layout to Printer

In submitting any printed advertising message to the media, the only way to ensure that your ad looks the way you intended is to provide adequate instructions. Layout means blueprint to the typesetter or printer. Your layout should be a full-size replica of what you want the finished advertisement or brochure to look like. Here are some guidelines to use in preparing layouts.

1. A layout should accurately indicate where all parts of the completed message are to be located with respect to the borders. This must include the location and approximate, if not actual, dimensions of all artwork.

2. There are five parts to a comprehensive layout:

   Headline – Print all headlines right on the layout sheet, making the headline fill the width you want. Give the printer a close approximation of the desired type size by the size of your lettering. On each line, put the exact words you want to appear and use capital letters or upper and lower case letters the way you want the type set.

Illustrations – Use a copy machine, if possible, and paste a copy of any artwork or photograph on the layout sheet where you want it to appear. If you plan to reduce or enlarge the artwork, show the finished height, width and the location on the layout sheet.

Copy – Copy refers to the text in your advertisement. Do not letter in the copy on your layout sheet. Use two parallel lines to represent each line of copy and draw these lines in the exact position on the layout sheet. These parallel lines should show whether you want the copy set flush on both right and left margins or if you prefer a ragged edge on the right margin. Each block of copy should be positioned properly on the layout sheet and then should be keyed, i.e., assigned a circled letter of the alphabet that matches a separate block of copy supplied on copy sheets. Copy sheets should be typewritten, double-spaced and should include all words and prices to be typeset, including any headlines you have lettered on the layout. Leave a two-inch left margin on the copy sheet to give the mark-up person space to code for type style and size.

Price – It is generally a good idea to letter your prices right on the layout if they appear anywhere other than within regular copy lines. Show the price as it should appear, including the relative size of the cents to dollars portion of the price and any dollar or cent signs you want used.

Logo – The logo is your firm's name, whether you have a standard, exclusive design or you merely want your name set in type. Let the layout show the desired location and size. It also is helpful to letter in your address and phone number. If you have a logo design, do not paste the original art work on the layout. Make a copy and paste the copy in the desired position. Ask the printer to make a photo reproduction (PMT) of your logo and keep the original artwork for future use.

In addition to these key elements, your layout also should contain instructions, written outside the ad borders and circled. A line from an instruction circle may lead to the specific area within the ad if it helps clarify instructions. Instructions should include the dimensions of the ad stated in inches (width depth). For a newspaper ad, the width should be stated in columns and the depth in inches or lines, depending on the paper's policies. Other instructions can include the insertion date, reference to the enlargement or reduction of artwork, the names of typefaces desired and special typesetting requests. Remember, your layout will serve as the blueprint for your ad. The finished product can be only as effective as the original layout. The copysheet that accompanies your layout also should contain the size of the ad and the insertion date. Use a paper clip rather than stapling the copy sheet to the layout. This will prevent tearing when the two sheets are separated for production.

STRENGTHENING THE ELEMENTS OF ADVERTISEMENT

Headlines

Since the headline is the first contact your readers have with your message, it must reach out to them. Promise them a benefit. Tell them how they will be better off if they read the rest of the ad. Use action verbs. Save ten dollars is a stronger heading than Savings of ten dollars because of the verb. Headlines can be classified into the following five basic types; effective headlines frequently combine two or more of these kinds.

News Headlines

This form tells the reader something he or she did not know before. Using the word news does not make it a news headline. Now – a copy machine that copies in colour is an example of this type headline.

Advice and Promise Headline

Here you are promising something if the reader follows the advice in your ad. Switch to Amoco premium, no-lead gasoline, and your car will stop pinging.

Selective Headline

This headline limits the audience to a specific group. For example: To all gray-haired men over forty. Caution! Be absolutely sure you do not eliminate potential customers with this type of headline.

Curiosity Headline

The intent here is to arouse the reader's interest enough to make him or her read the ad. The danger is that this headline often appears cute or clever and fails in its mission. An example: Do you have trouble going to sleep at night?

Command or Demand Headline

Watch out for this one as most people resist pushiness, especially in advertising. Do it now! or Buy this today! This headline generally can be improved by changing to less obtrusive wording such as: Call for your key to success!

One common misconception about headlines is that they must be short and easy to understand. This is not always true. Here is a headline that was used extensively in print ads by Ogilvy and Mather for one of their clients: At 60 miles an hour, the loudest noise in this Rolls-Royce comes from the electric clock.

Illustrations

There are three primary reasons for using illustrations in an advertisement.

- To attract attention to the ad.
- To illustrate the item being featured.
- To create a mood in the mind of the reader.

Everyone has heard a picture is worth a thousand words; in advertising, the illustration frequently helps the reader visualize the benefits promised. You can almost feel the warmth of the tropical sun when you see the photos in January travel ads. Cost and practicality may dictate whether your ad uses photographs, artists' drawings or merely canned artwork. Any of these can make the ad more appealing to the reader's eye.

Copy

If you follow the three principles of good copy, your ads will be effective:

- Good copy should be clear.
- Good copy should be crisp.
- Good copy should be concise.

Clear, crisp and concise the three Cs of copywriting suggest that the words in your advertising message merely do a good job of communicating. Do not use big words when small words can make your meaning clear. Use colorful, descriptive terms. Use the number of words necessary to make your meaning clear and no more – but also no less! Selecting the right words is critical to the success of the ads. Recent research conducted at Yale University found that the following 12 words are the most personal and persuasive words in our language.

You	Discovery	Safety
Money	Proven	Results
Love	Guarantee	Save
New	Easy	Health

Price

Should you or shouldn't you put prices in your ad? Yes! Yes! Yes! Since price is the one factor that allows the consumer to determine whether an item represents an adequate valuc, an ad without price makes the buying decision difficult if not impossible for the reader. Can you imagine how uninteresting your daily newspaper would be if there were no prices on the food store ads or the department store offerings? Yes, price belongs, and it belongs whether you are advertising a home for $175,000 or a ballpoint pen for 49 cents.

Logo

Can you visualize the corporate logos for such firms as Chevrolet, Ford, Playboy, Borden or Levi Strauss? There is an identification advantage in developing a logo design exclusive to your firm. Using a logo also helps give your advertising continuity. Use the logo consistently on all printed pieces, including stationery. Use it in Yellow Page advertising, on the side of your truck or company car, on bags or boxes and anything else your customers or prospects may see.

Type

The typeface you use in advertising plays an important role in how the message comes across. Printers are very knowledgeable about typefaces and happy to help you make choices. A selection of typefaces is illustrated in Appendix I.

Media available to Advertisers

If you understand the concept that advertising is a multiplication of a selling conversation, then the basic ingredients of advertising media are easier to grasp. First, there must be an audience. A newspaper printed as a single copy could not function as an advertising medium unless the single copy were passed from person to person to create a worthwhile audience. (In that case, the advertiser probably could go from one individual to another and be more effective while reaching at least as many prospects in the same amount of time.) A potential advertiser will require evidence that an audience does exist, and will want to know the size and location of the audience, as well as other characteristics.

The second ingredient on which an advertising medium can be evaluated is its acceptance in the marketplace. Acceptance is related not only to the total number of customers in an audience, but also to the composition of that audience as compared to the target audience of the advertiser. Advertising over a closed circuit television Programme received only by occupants of nursing homes would not be very profitable for a real estate firm attempting to sell starter homes.

In addition to an audience's acceptance and size, the medium also must have a usable *frequency of exposure.* Most retailers and other local business establishments rely on their advertisements' reaching potential buyers regularly, some even several times daily. A medium with a once-a-year or even a once-a-month frequency might deserve nothing more than a very small part of a retailer's advertising budget. Remember, one way advertising functions is by repetition; a commercial message increases in audience awareness after more than one exposure.

Various advertising media will be examined from the standpoint of these three basic ingredients: the audience (coverage) each enjoys; the acceptance (impact) of the medium on the audience; and the ability to expand its initial impact by being available more than once or twice in a particular time frame (frequency).

Paid-circulation Newspapers

Almost every community has a newspaper. About 1,700 of the paid-circulation papers in America are daily papers and several thousand additional local papers are published weekly. Paid circulation means the audience reached pays to have the paper delivered to the home or pays a per copy price to pick it up at a newsstand or vending machine. Newspapers are the most popular advertising medium for most local businesses.

Today's newspaper no longer enjoys its former role as the almost exclusive source of news; that privilege applies only in those very few areas not served by radio or television. Newspapers remain, however, a strong factor in their sphere of influence. Below are some characteristics of paid-circulation newspapers that make them appealing to advertisers.

1. Most paid-circulation papers, both daily and weekly, reach the majority of homes in their primary city or town.

2. The size of the audience is easy to determine and verify.
3. The newspaper offers a predictable frequency of publication: once, twice or up to seven times a week.
4. Newspapers generally are bought by people representing all segments of the population. High- and low-income families, urban and suburban residents – all are subscribers to the local newspaper.
5. Newspapers offer several options to advertisers. Large or small ads, words alone or words with graphics, black and white or colour, news or specialized feature page positioning.
6. The printed advertising message has both permanence and desired obsolescence. A reader can refer back to or even clip and save your ad, yet tomorrow's edition is new and fresh and eagerly sought by the same reader.
7. The newspaper is the only medium in which the audience also advertise. The want ad or classified section of most newspapers serves as a local marketplace where individual buyers and sellers gather to trade their treasures and buy and sell each other's services.
8. Newspaper pasteup permits you to request special locations for ads that tie in with your market segments. Sports, business, society, food and news are the most common sections.

There are limitations to the newspaper as an advertising medium.

1. You could possibly miss potential customers who choose not to have the paper delivered.
2. Your advertising message must fight for the reader's attention. There may be hundreds of ads in one paper, as well as dozens of articles and features for the reader to spend time on. If the total time spent

with a newspaper is only 20 minutes or so, as some surveys have found, you can see the odds against your one ad reaching a really significant number of subscribers.

3. To some advertisers, another limitation of newspapers is the time required to get the message into the reader's hand. The advertising deadline for some sections of large metropolitan papers may be one week or more in advance of publication date.

Advertising in newspapers is always priced by units of space. Rates for classified advertising may be priced per word or per line while display ads (the bordered ads that frequently contain illustrations as well as words) are usually priced per column inch or agate line. A column inch is a space one column wide by one inch deep. The agate line is 1/14th of a column inch. The cost of newspaper advertising is determined by the size of the circulation, the degree of the paper's dominance in the marketplace, and by the increasing costs of newsprint, ink, labour and transportation. The paid-circulation paper is the oldest of the mass media and continues to be the largest, as measured by volume of advertising dollars. It is used by industry giants as well as the corner drugstore. As a retailer or other small business owner, some of your advertising budget will most likely end up in your local paid-circulation newspaper.

Free-distribution Newspapers

Although far from new (the first newspapers in our country were distributed free), today's free-distribution paper is different from paid-circulation newspapers. Although the shopper type papers contain mostly advertising and little feature material, they remain a highly productive advertising medium in hundreds of cities and towns. Many of the earlier shoppers have grown into full-fledged newspapers with news, comics and features, and a frequency of delivery that approaches seven days a week. They offer the advertiser most of the advantages of paid-circulation papers, including the permanence of print, the versatility of colour and graphics, and high readership of personal want ads. One advantage over paid-circulation papers is their ability to reach a very high percentage of the market area. Because they are free, they are delivered to every home. If readers like what they read, they soon come to depend on the paper. Studies show penetration and acceptance by more than 90 percent of the residents in the circulation area of free-distribution papers.

To verify the number of papers delivered, publishers of free-distribution papers may employ auditing firms to come into the delivery area and certify the number of copies printed, the number of carriers used and the number of households that regularly report receiving a paper. Many of these papers have audited proof of coverage approaching 100 percent of the homes in their markets.

The phenomenal growth of free-distribution papers in recent years is related to the increased sophistication of marketing and advertising technology. The computer made possible the measurement of sales in market share. Not only do today's merchandise movers target to sell more of their products each year, but also to sell them to ever larger shares of the total population in each area. Since daily and weekly paid newspapers often do not reach a substantial number of consumers, the total coverage concept of the free-distribution papers has proven they have outgrown their reputation as throwaways! Today, Sears, K-Mart, JC Penney and dozens of smaller department, discount, food and apparel chain organizations regularly use the free-distribution papers for total coverage of certain market areas.

Another growing function of the free-distribution papers is their ability to serve as the distribution vehicle for advertisers' own preprinted flyers, sections or merchandise catalogs. Many publishers will custom design for your special promotion a delivery system that will deliver the preprinted section to every home within a specified area, such as the 12 square blocks immediately surrounding your business.

If there is a free-distribution paper in your market area, it deserves an inquiry. Advertisements in it may prove to be the most effective dollar invested in your advertising budget.

Direct Mail

We would be remiss not to mention the U.S. Postal Service and its ability to deliver your advertising message. The direct mail advertising message can be highly personal and powerfully effective. You know how saturated your home mailbox is with nothing to buy contests giving you chances to win new houses, cars, world cruises and big checks for every month as long as you live. While there is no obligation for you to buy anything, there is always something available for sale – subscriptions, books, records, videos, personal products, real estate – usually at discounted prices. The giveaways are possible only because enough people are tempted by what is available, and what they buy can be traced to direct mail advertising. In almost every business there is an opportunity for increased business through intelligent use of direct mail advertising.

Because the per-piece cost of direct mail is much higher than most forms of print, it must be used carefully, selectively and efficiently. Mailing lists are difficult to prepare, expensive to buy and are partially obsolete the day after they have been completed. Because people die, move away or get mad at you at an alarming pace, keeping an accurate mailing list is not easy. Still, direct mail can be an efficient way to deliver a sales message to a specific target audience. If your audience is composed of doctors, lawyers, dentists or school teachers, for example, only direct mail offers you the chance to direct your ad to that target audience with no waste circulation. Direct mail also makes couponing and sampling practical. It can help isolate advertising response to one segment or another and compare returns in one area with those in another.

The most critical part of any direct mail Programme is the mailing list. Keep a list of all your customers, either by asking them to fill out a mailing list card or by taking their names off the checks you receive each day. Hold contests to get your customers to fill out an entry form. As your list grows, you may need to buy a computer or hire a mailing firm to keep the list current and to prepare mailing labels.

Magazines

Print media also include magazines. While most national magazines are not practical as an advertising medium for local businesses, some local magazines may be. City magazines are now published in hundreds of cities and towns. They may look as sophisticated as their national counterparts, and they are edited to local tastes. They use colour, photography and professional writing and editing to create high-interest stories about people, places and things. They frequently are distributed free to certain people on special lists restricted to higher income families. In this way they can reach relatively exclusive audiences, but the frequency of publication (usually monthly) restricts their use as a basic medium.

Many regional and national magazines include classified ad sections that may be useful for promoting the availability of a catalog or for selling individual products. The advantage of magazines is that they have highly defined readerships that allow you to focus on specific market niches. If, for example, you run an ad in a boating magazine, you can be fairly sure the people who subscribe either own a boat or are looking for one. The Standard Rate and Data Service (SRDS) publishes a complete listing of all the magazines that serve particular market interests; it is available in the business section of most libraries.

Brochures

For many small businesses, a printed brochure may be helpful to establish credibility and tell your story in more detail. Computer typesetting and laser printing have reduced the cost of producing a brochure. Free layout help is available at many copy centers. You can keep your costs down by using standard 8.5x11 inch paper and by using a triple-fold design that will fit into a standard business envelope.

Other Local Print Media

Don't overlook drop-point media such as booklets available for free pickup in high-traffic areas like convenience stores, banks and motels. These may include guides to local television Programmes, listings currently available from real estate firms, entertainment or sporting events. Evaluate each booklet on its ability to provide enough value to justify using it.

Radio

In America, 280 million people own more than 300 million radios! Only radio can take your advertising message to people while they ride bicycles, walk in the park, ride in cars or climb mountains. Radio brings a sense of urgency to its listeners that is second to none. Contrary to the predictions of doom during the advent of television, radio is alive and well today, and radio advertising is a major part of the plan for advertisers of every size and description.

In its pre-television days, radio was the national advertisers' most economical way to communicate with millions at a time. Syndicated Programmes of music, drama and news were a common part of the American life-style. With the advent of television, radio moved to the automobile and the beach. Along came the transistor and radio moved to the shirtpocket. Today radio is everywhere. Millions awake to the sound of clock radios, and for many the radio is the last sound they hear before going to sleep. How can a small business use this sound-only medium for effective advertising? Only by understanding it and capitalizing on its strengths.

Today's radio station is judged on its effectiveness not only by the number of its listeners, but also who those listeners are. Many of today's stations have positioned themselves to reach a selective audience instead of a total market. In one marketplace, one station may play only country-western music, another rock music, a third only religious music, while others feature 24-hour news broadcasts or talk shows. As an advertiser, format programming allows you to buy advertising on stations whose listener characteristics most closely coincide with the profile of your firm's customers. Buying time on a given station also can help you reach audience segments that you may want to target to help expand your firm's total market segment.

Radio advertising is sold on the basis of time. That time can vary from an entire Programme, which includes your commercial announcements, to spot announcements ranging from 10 to 60 seconds. Price ranges are higher during drive time (the hours in the morning and evening when the maximum number of people are in their cars going to or from work, school or other daytime activities) and lower during the time when more people are watching television. Most stations offer package rate plans with a specified number of commercials guaranteed within a particular time slot. Also, consider buying flights of commercials, i.e., an intense saturation of 30-second or 1-minute spots in a relatively short period of two or three weeks. Repeat this flight technique during key promotional times of the year.

The sounds you can employ on radio include not only the monologue of a man's or woman's voice, but dialogue and dramatic conversations, vocal and instrumental music, and sound effects of every imaginable nature, used individually or in combinations. The size of radio's audience, like the circulation of newspapers, is audited by independent organizations and available to advertisers through station sales representatives. Arbitron, one of the auditing firms, conducts its survey by having a sample number of households keep a written diary of the radio listening habits of each occupant during a predetermined period (usually one week). Arbitron then summarizes the various stations' listeners by time of day in 15-minute segments by sex and age of listener. An advertiser can use the Arbitron data to select the station or stations that best cover the desired target audience.

Radio advertising frequency is as high as you can afford. Many stations now broadcast 24 hours a day, seven days a week. The number of commercial minutes any station can air in each segment of programming is limited by the Federal Communications Commission (FCC), but there is still the opportunity to have a message repeated frequently in any given period. It is also possible to have the radio station come to your business for a remote broadcast with customer interviews, prize giveaways and other crowd-drawing techniques.

Television

Watching TV is the most common leisure activity in our country today; many surveys report average daily television viewing time as high as five or six hours. It is no wonder it has grown into a giant advertising medium. Television always has been a popular medium for large retailers, but its effective use by small- and medium-size businesses is becoming more popular because of lowered production costs and the ability of cable TV to reach smaller market areas.

The power of television is its ability to appeal not only to sight and hearing simultaneously, but also to strengthen that appeal by the dimensions of movement and the realism of full colour. If you have invented a new product, TV advertising can show and tell many people about it and actually show them the benefit of ownership. Since they saw how it works and the package it comes in, customers will recognize it when they are at the store and be psychologically reminded of how it works and how great it would be to have it. If the hammer had never been invented until you came along, just imagine the number of words in print advertising it would take to equal the effectiveness of a 60-second television spot during which a hammer pounded a nail to fasten one piece of wood to another!

Television advertising is sold by the time the message takes. There may be additional charges for writing, talent, props, on-location filming, music and editing. Audience loyalty is a disadvantage in TV advertising. The audience tunes to a given channel for entertainment they know they will find at a particular time. If a football game, popular movie or some other preferred form of entertainment appears on another channel, the viewer does not hesitate to change channels without leaving the couch. While viewers are loyal to the entertainment value of television, they show very little loyalty to the station itself, especially as cable can bring 40 to 50 viewing alternatives into the home. Viewers, however, do tend to have favorite news, weather and sports telecasting personalities, which can influence the size of your audience and its consistency during certain time periods.

Other developments that could affect television advertising are the availability of many different stations through cable companies, all-shopper channels, all-sports channels, all-news stations, the use of home television screens as monitors for in-home computer and game systems, and the popularity of video movie cassettes. All of these may reduce the size of the audience a television station can guarantee its advertisers.

Many rating services measure the size of television audiences. National Programmes are measured daily and a station's audience size can be estimated fairly well. Your local television representative can explain television's penetration within the station's area of dominant influence (ADI) and how that area may conform to your firm's trade area.

Outdoor Media

Despite restrictive legislation, billboards and other outdoor display signs still perform a strong advertising task in many areas. Instant communication is the key to successfully using billboards. Directed at drivers with only split seconds to divert their eyes and to passengers who can at best get a fleeting glance, wordy or complex messages are worthless. Photos or striking art combined with a firm name and a one- or two-word headline or slogan are common.

Audience totals are determined by how many sign locations you buy and the total traffic passing each sign. Outdoor advertising is usually sold on a basis of gross rating point (GRP) evaluation. The GRP of any medium is the number of persons exposed to a message compared to the total number of persons that make up the market. One shortcoming is that the same person may drive by the same billboard three or four times a day and be counted as four separate people. Your local outdoor sales representative can explain how many locations are necessary for you to achieve 50, 75 or 100 gross rating points, and what that exposure will cost you over varying time periods.

Other Media for Advertising

We could spend considerable time just trying to complete a list of all the other ways a business can advertise and probably still leave some out. Pencils and pens with your firm's name imprinted, skywriting, business cards and even sandwich boards all can perform an effective advertising role for some advertisers. You must evaluate each one on its ability to get your sales message to the maximum number of prospects in a believable manner and at a reasonable price. No textbook or consultant can do the job for you. After you have read and listened, go to your local media representatives and ask for their help. They have everything to gain and nothing to lose by putting your firm's best interest ahead of their desire to make a sale.

Refining your Advertising for Greater Results

Every item you advertise and every word and illustration you use becomes a part of your firm's image. Your ability to develop a USP depends on your knowing what you want your image to be and then doing those things and only those things that reinforce that image. A men's clothing store can become the store with fashions for the man who thinks young. A nursery can create the image of the home of the talked-to plants that will respond to you. A car dealer can develop a following and a reputation for his automatic three-year trade-in plan. Once you have arrived at a USP that you think will appeal to your customers, translate the idea into a selling slogan of three to ten words that can be used as the theme of your advertising campaign. Use it consistently until our customers learn to associate your business with the selling slogan.

But be careful. A few years ago Excedrin decided to position itself as the headache remedy for many different kinds of headaches, like headache No. 43 or No. 27. Their TV commercial showed the agony of each headache by the number. What happened? People went to their drugstores and said I think I've got headache No. 43. Give me a package of Anacin. They sold the concept of the headaches beautifully but not the exclusivity of Excedrin as the best relief.

If you want to position your business in the marketplace, select your target market. How old are they? What do they have in common? What are their goals and ambitions? When you have learned all you can about them, go back and learn more! Then start talking to them, and only to them, in your advertising. Talk to them about themselves and their desires. Then tell them how the goods or services you sell are perfectly suited to helping them achieve those desires.

Timing Each Ad for Impact

While your budget will tell you how much you have to spend each month, you must refine your plan to know how many ads will run each week and on which days. In planning your ad insert schedule, be aware that the best results are obtained by strengthening already strong sales days, not by trying to make bad days better. If large employers in your area have paydays on the first and fifteenth of the month, time your advertising to coincide. If you use more than one medium, attempt to coordinate your efforts by scheduling a radio blitz to coincide with a big print campaign or special store event.

Using Colour

Adding colour to a black-and-white advertisement not only increases readership, but can substantially increase the sales response. Retailers, however, frequently use too much colour in their ads. Remember, colour works because of its contrast with noncolour areas; use it in one or two strong clustered areas rather than scattering it throughout your ad. Keep in mind that colors also communicate psychologically. Here are a few popular colors and their common associations.

Red – Suggests excitement, heat, strength and is a good colour to use in a sale ad.

Yellow – Conveys brightness, airiness, refreshment. Warning: yellow gets lost on white paper, so always surround areas of yellow with a border of black or another dark tone.

Blue – As a cold colour, can convey formality and haughtiness in its darker shades and fragility, daintiness and youthfulness in the lighter tones.

Orange – A colour of warmth, action, power.

Green – Another cool colour, suggests cheapness and coldness in its darker tones while conveying freshness and crispness in its lighter shades.

Purple – A colour of royalty and stateliness.

Maroon – Suggests luxury, solidity, quietness.

Brown – Implies age, wholesomeness, utility.

White – Means purity, cleanliness, chastity.

Black – Conveys mystery, strength, heaviness.

Research on the productivity of colour in newspaper advertising invariably shows increased readership as well as increased sales from ads that use colour. Adding colour raises the cost of the ad, but the increased results are substantially greater than the increased costs.

Critiquing Your Ads

We can learn great lessons from the past. If your firm has been running ads, dig out a few from a year or so ago and see how many of these common no-no's you can find.

1. Does your ad contain words like our, I or other personal pronouns? They are poor communicators, try using you and yours.
2. Is the ad uninteresting to look at overall? It may be balanced too formally. Try using an odd rather than even number of illustrations to help achieve informal balance.

3. Does your firm have a logo? Develop one so the name of the firm is not just set in the same type as the rest of the ad.
4. Has your layout allowed the reader's eye to stray from the preferred gaze-motion path? If your invitation to the eye causes readers to leave your ad, you will not get them back.
5. Is your logo in the upper left corner or the lower right corner of the ad? Those are the two best spots for it.
6. Does your headline promise the reader a benefit?
7. Is your copy clear, crisp and concise? Be sure to use the product points that make the benefits you promised believable.
8. Have you used a headline in capital letters? Don't!
9. Have you told the reader what each item costs? It is very difficult to reach a buying decision until the question "How much is it?" is answered.
10. Does your ad contain any misleading statements? Any attempt to misinform or mislead the reader may lead to a sale, but in all certainty it will lead to lost customers and could lead to court. Honesty is still the best policy.

As you continue to expand your business in the months and years ahead, use the tips presented here. Prepare a budget and review it frequently. Select your items for advertising to help solve consumer problems and then present your advertising message as a form of planned communication. Ask your media representatives for help in understanding their product.

Chapter 4

Prospects Qualifying and Personality Traits

PROJECTING A PROFESSIONAL IMAGE

Projecting a professional image is important to those who value their careers. It is a major part of corporate image, and therefore important to the organization. Professional image can be enhanced by dressing and grooming appropriately, and by developing a positive self-image and strong group image. These activities will ultimately create a stronger organizational image, which is vital to its longevity. "If hospital 'A' presents a warm, friendly, and exquisitely polished image and hospital 'B' presents a frumpy, unkempt, and irritable image, and both are otherwise similar, which would you choose?" Given that professional image is self-controlled, can anyone afford not to build a more positive image?

Managing your personal and professional life is a lifelong balancing act due to situations that arise in the course of expected and unexpected normal life events. Identifying and dealing with these issues in your own life will likely make you a stronger leader in the eyes of your employees who often struggle with similar issues. Acknowledging these struggles among your employees can help create community in work teams, which ultimately translates into retention. Advocating for work life policies in your organization will transform personal compassion into organizational culture and, ultimately, into corporate policy. When we perceive others we do it through four of our five senses:

1. Sight
2. Sound
3. Smell
4. Touch

The fifth sense, "taste", we will set aside because it is irrelevant to this subject. But we will include an intangible quality, a "sixth sense", so to speak, which we will identify as "something extra". The vague notion we get about somebody which we are unable to quantify. It is an all-round subconscious combination of everything else that we perceive about the person. We have all felt it. We all project it. It's the thing we speak of when we say or think the words:

- "I feel as though I can trust this person" or
- "I think I feel safe in this person's presence" or
- "it seems as though I have known this person a long time" or
- "I just don't feel comfortable when he (or she) is around" or
- "this person makes my skin crawl."

Call it gut feeling, animal instinct, intuition or whatever you want. We all possess it and we all project it. Some are more receptive at what comes in and others can mask what goes out. But there are signals. So let's examine each of the above attributes briefly to see what sort of "persona" or image you are projecting for others to "read".

Sight

What do you see when you look in the mirror? What do you look like? Not everybody has movie star looks or a perfect athlete's body. However, we should all be making the most of what we have got. There is simply no excuse for an unkempt appearance. Are you a man who only shaves every second or third day? If so, why? Are you a woman who has unruly hair? It has been proven that people judge you mostly by what they see. If you make a poor initial visual presentation then you have to rely on everything else to work overtime to overcome it.

Consider this. Think about your lawyer, accountant, doctor or any other "professional" person. When you first met that person how did they present? Were they well groomed and in fine clothes? Almost certainly they were. Now, every time we see that person we judge them by that first presentation appearance. You may see your accountant one weekend down at the hardware store in his or her grubbiest work clothes - but you still have that image of them in their professional attire. Let's reverse that. Let's assume that you bump into that person in the hardware store, you strike up a conversation, during which, they reveal to you that they are an accountant. But you see them in their filthy weekend work gear. Is it convincing? You decide to visit them at their usual place of work at a later date. Hey presto! Out comes this person looking very professional. Is your mind in conflict?

The point is this - the first impression is the lasting impression. When you see somebody for the first time and they are professionally attired, that is the way you invariably categorise that person from that point on - even if a subsequent meeting shows them wearing lesser clothing. It just doesn't work in reverse. My point is - if you want to project a certain image - dress for that image. But that is not to say that you need to wear your best clothes all the time when you are away from your work. The above example was just to illustrate my point.

Sound

What words do you use? Do you speak appropriately and knowledgeably for your profession. Are you prone to "um" and "er" your way through conversations? Do you think before you speak? Is your verbal language sprinkled or even littered with profanities or expletives? Gutter language is a sure way to lose customers and clients. So are sarcasm, racial prejudism, sexual connotation, rudeness, ignorance, criticism and a host of other poor language traits.

Do you revise and edit your written language in letters or emails before you send them - particularly when you are in conflict with a person or corporation? Do you screen your writing for blatant errors or possible misunderstandings? Being pleasant but firm creates a much better environment for resolution than a harsh and angry tone. Do you wait before you send your mail and revisit your words before posting? Do you put yourself in the position of the receiver of the correspondence?

Smell

Do you smell? Many people have deficient nasal receptors. Their sense of smell is either diminished or non-existent. Often such people can reek of offensive body odour simply because they are unaware of it themselves. Some people have heightened nasal receptors. Their sense of smell can be so sensitive that all sorts of odours cause them discomfort. Therefore, if you are a man who drowns himself in after-shave you might save yourself a lot of money by being less liberal with it. Similarly, women who walk down a corridor and leave a trail of perfume in their wake might also like to follow this advice. A hint of after-shave or perfume can be refreshing. A miasma of it can be just the reverse.

Touch

In today's society you had better be aware that excessive touching and feeling is completely unacceptable. If in doubt, you should offer and accept your hand in a hand-shake only. Many people find it very offensive when personal contact is made. If you are in the habit of giving people a hug just make sure that the "hugee" is amenable to the hug from the "hugger". All of the above add up to what can be described as a "general personal aura". You can send and receive these auras. They form part of that unquantifiable quality that we know of as the "sixth sense." Be aware that many of the subjects that I have described above can be modified to suit specific locations, customs, beliefs and relationships. There is no universal law. Awareness and common sense are the key.

There are several books, which go into great detail on these matters. By being aware of the signals that we send out when we deal with other people we can improve the way we interact with them. These are skills which can be learned and they can greatly increase our results in personal and business relationships. These skills are important because the greatest element in personal contact with your clients and customers is communication. Poor interpersonal skills will eventually cause a breakdown in confidence which will manifest itself in declining sales.

Imagine for a moment that you have a genie in a bottle, or a secret potion or wand that, that gives you the power to zap into being more of what you wish for. The truth is, it doesn't take a genie in a bottle, a magic wand or a secret potion, although these are fun 'reminders' of the awesome power that we hold! We are Divine Beings! The Bible says we are made "in the image of God" and that "what we reap we sowed." This means we, like God, are creators! We must learn how to help ourselves by co-creating, along with God, that which we desire by developing faith and applying focused thought. The best way to pray then is affirmatively, to visualize what we desire as if it is already in our experience, and to give thanks in advance, knowing that what we need and desire is available to us.

Another way of saying this is to use creative visualization. Creative visualization is the technique of using our imagination to create more of what we want in life. Everything we experience in "reality" has its beginnings in the non-physical. Every thought we think is a seed and every time we think the same thought over again, we water that seed. When we think thoughts filled with emotion, we fertilize those thoughts. The more intense our desire, and the degree to which we believe it is possible, the more likely it is to come into our experience and the faster it will manifest. The law of the soil and the law of the mind are the same.

The most successful people in any business are always the communicators. If you are an employee and you want your salary to increase, work on your communication skills. If you are a business owner and you want your turnover to increase, work on your own communication skills first then show all your employees how to do the same. The image that you project in the marketplace will directly affect your "bottom line". Think about it. What image are you projecting?

THE SALES KIT

A good hotel Sales Kit or Meeting Planners Kit is a necessary tool for the successful marketing of destination oriented and or primarily meetings market properties. Good design, comprehensive tightly-edited copy and clearly understandable plot plans, diagrams and space capacity charts are a must to effectively convey your message to the engager. Sales personal must know the business and the "hot buttons" of the meeting planner in today's competitive market. *Many hotels have beautiful accommodations and service but the engager must have confidence in "The Box" to book their meeting group with you.* Sale personal represents the company's strengths, direction and philosophy. It is what they do exclusively with affiliated hospitality businesses and are experienced with the dynamics and competitive environment that affect it's ever-changing marketplace.

Everyone wants to know what to expect in business as well as in life. It's easy to promise, harder to deliver. Quite simply, this is what to expect from Hotel sales personal:

1. A professional representative who will respond promptly to all requests within one business day.
2. An estimate for a project that will be detailed and all-inclusive based on the scope of work requested.
3. A fair price with quality service that will exceed expectations.
4. Timely delivery as outlined in the estimate, provided all required information and materials for the project(s) have been presented to them on a timely basis.

5. Friendly reminders of project due dates and deadlines that often fall through the cracks while customers are trying to do what they do best.... Sell, Market and/or Manage clients property and inventory.
6. A complimentary referral to a professional who can help customer with a project that may not fit into the scope of work of the company. All work orders will be processed either on-line or over the phone with courtesy, accuracy and attention to detail. All projects will arrive on time as promised (unless subject to acts of God, terrorism and/or any other unforseen natural occurrence).

KNOW YOUR MARKET

A sound marketing plan is key to the success of your business. It should include your market your market research, your location, the customer group you have targeted, your competition, positioning, the product or service you are selling, pricing, advertising and promotion. "You're in business to serve a customer need," says Derek Hansen, founder of American Capital Access. "If you're not sensitive to customers, don't know who your customers are, how to reach them and, most of all, what will convince them to buy your product or service, get help." Before developing your plan, you must do your homework.

Effective marketing, planning and promotion begin with factual information about the marketplace. Visit your local library, talk to customers, and study the advertising of other businesses in your community (including that of your competition) and consult with any related industry associations. Once you have all the necessary information, it is time to put your plan down on paper. It should accomplish the following:

1. Define your business
   - Your product or service;
   - Your geographic marketing area—neighborhood, regional or national;

- Your competition;
- How you differ from the competition—what makes you special;
- Your price;
- The competition's promotion methods;
- Your promotion methods;
- Your distribution methods or business location.

2. Define your customers
   - Your current customer base: age, sex, income, neighborhood;
   - How your customers learn about your product or service—advertising, direct mail, word of mouth, Yellow Pages;
   - Patterns or habits your customers and potential customers share—where they shop, what they read, watch, listen to;
   - Qualities your customers value most about your product or service— selection, convenience, service, reliability, availability, affordability;
   - Qualities your customers like least about your product or service—can they be adjusted to serve your customers better?
   - Prospective customers like least about your product or service but whom you aren't currently reaching.
3. Define your plan and budget
   - Previous marketing methods you have used to communicate to your customers;
   - Methods that have been most effective;
   - Cost compared to sales;
   - Cost per customer;
   - Possible future marketing methods to attract new customers;
   - Percentage of profits you can allocate to your marketing campaign;
   - Marketing tools you can implement within your budget—newspaper, magazine or Yellow Pages

advertising; radio or television advertising; direct mail; tele-marketing; public relations activities such as community involvement, sponsorship or press releases;

- Methods of testing your marketing ideas;
- Methods for measuring results of your marketing campaign;
- The marketing tool you can implement immediately.

The final component in your marketing plan should be your overall promotional objectives: to communicate your message, create an awareness of your product or service, motivate customers to buy and increase sales. Objectives make it easier to design an effective campaign and help you keep that campaign on the right track. Plus, once you have defined your objectives, it is easier to choose the method that will be most effective.

The essential idea is targeted marketing—making sure your message reaches the people you want to persuade. Today's marketplace is too fragmented and diffused to reach everyone without the expenditure of vast sums of money. This makes the formulation of a specific customer profile all the more important. "Before, we always tried to get everybody and their brother to buy from us. Need-less to say, that approach didn't work. Then we started a marketing plan that targeted a specific geographic area." says one long-time business owner, "and it brought in all the business we hope for."

BEING A HOSPITALITY PROFESSIONAL

The hospitality industry can offer a promising future for IT professionals wanting to make an exciting career. In recent years, the scope of IT professionals in this industry has been on the upswing. International brands are coming to India bringing along state-of-the-art technologies, which other local brands will need to match up to. This has begun to open up new avenues for the IT professional to implement, learn and to develop.

The accelerated infusion of computerised systems and sub-system transactions sweeping the hospitality industry has spurred IT professionals to look at the industry as a potential workplace. The challenge to integrate computer interface and the need to accelerate upgradation of technology usage so as to lower costs has added allure to this industry.

Just six years ago, all the IT professionals wanted to do was set base within the IT industry. But today the non-IT companies, including hotels, are proving to be equally lucrative. Jobs that are being targeted are in the areas of database management and administration, security and technical support. In fact, the hospitality industry holds sway over other industries as well. It is one sector which cannot choose to outsource simply because of the security aspect and a dedicated in-house team is considered to be better equipped to solve problems.

The worth of IT professionals is well recognised by the industry and an IT job is as important in hotels as in any other industry. No hotel can run without IT support these days. Moreover, the hotel industry offers unique challenges that make it more attractive to the IT professionals.

EDP Domain

The basic responsibility of the EDP or IT department in a hotel is to maintain all the computer systems, cater to troubleshooting of all hotel management software such as Fidelio, Point of Sale (POS) management system, Materials Management System (MMS), BOSS, etc, over and above managing the hotel's website. From the guests' point of view, IT should solve any frustrating computer-related problems.

Information management plays a very important role in hotels on a daily basis for successful management requirements of internal and external customers. With automation coming to the fore, there are packages used to support the needs of a unit or a group. This package may either be customised or taken off the shelf. To oversee the smooth functioning of the software package being used, most hotels have an EDP department where the manager is required to enhance the usability of the package. But this can be a remote requirement since in most cases the package bought by the unit comes with an after-sales service option. Indeed, the management laps up any form of automation, which may support the hotel's cause to generate customer satisfaction and retention.

IT requires constant upgradation and bringing in new advancements which involves the finance department at every step. Moreover, IT being in the know-how of valuable and confidential information related to finance, it is the finance department in many hotels that oversees the IT department.

The Right Man

The industry considers certain qualities as necessary for becoming a successful head of the hotel industry. These include job knowledge in becoming a successful IT head, knowledge in setting up networks, experience with various software packages (Micros, Fidelio), familiarity with different types of servers, switches, routers, etc. One should be in a position to work under pressure and meet timelines. The IT professional must be up-to-date and aware of new technologies introduced in the market. Other than this, he must be an effective listener, a team player and a quick learner.

An IT professional can grow in the hotel industry starting as an executive and moving up to become head of the department. There are various growth positions, but it calls for total dedication and continual improvement. When selecting candidates, hotels generally look for persons with good personality traits - the ability to communicate, educational qualification to match the post and experience. Other than the candidates' qualifications and personality traits, we also look for resourcefulness, his ability to keep abreast with new developments with in-depth knowledge of the technicalities and the ability to solve problems not just over the phone but attend to the needs personally. The aspirant should have good management skills and be a team player.

Growth Potential

This is one industry that makes an effort to constantly utilise its funds for upgradation and introduction of new technologies. Every IT professional wants to be associated with and learn about new technologies. The hotel industry gives such IT professionals a chance to broaden their horizons thus making it an attractive option.

One's growth is determined by one's capability and willingness to work. The pay is very rewarding. One's remuneration does not stop at the monthly pay package - there are hosts of incentives given while on the job. Over and above this, performance-based benefits and schemes provided make working for the hospitality industry that much more rewarding.

MARKETING BASICS FOR THE SMALL HOTEL BUSINESS

The essence of marketing is to understand your customers' needs and develop a plan that surrounds those needs. Let's face it anyone that has a business has a desire to grow their business. The most effective way to grow and expand your business is by focusing on organic growth.

You can increase organic growth in four different ways. They include:

- Acquiring more customers
- Persuading each customer to buy more products
- Persuading each customer to buy more expensive products or up selling each customer
- Persuading each customer to buy more profitable products

All four of these increase your revenue and profit. Let me encourage you to focus on the first which is to acquire more customers. Why? Because by acquiring more customers you increase your customer base and your revenues then come from a larger base.

How can you use marketing to acquire more customers?

- Spend time researching and create a strategic marketing plan.
- Guide your product development to reach out to customers you aren't currently attracting.
- Price your products and services competitively.
- Develop your message and materials based on solution marketing.

The Importance of a Target Market

When it comes to your customers keep in mind the importance of target marketing. The reason this is important is that only a proportion of the population is likely to purchase any products or service. By taking time pitch your sales and marketing efforts to the correct niche market you will be more productive and not waste your efforts or time.

It's important to consider your virtual segmentation by selecting particular verticals to present your offerings to. Those verticals will have the particular likelihood of purchasing your products and services. Again, this saves you from wasting valuable time and money.

Marketing Differs between Small hotels and larger hotels

If you are like the majority of small hotel business owners your marketing budget is limited. The most effective way to market a small hotel business is to create a well rounded programme that combines sales activities with your marketing tactics. Your sales activities will not only decrease your out-of-pocket marketing expense but it also adds the value of interacting with your prospective customers and clients. This interaction will provide you with research that is priceless.

Small hotel businesses typically have a limited marketing budget if any at all. Does that mean you can't run with the big dogs? Absolutely not. It just means you have to think a little more creatively. How about launching your marketing campaign by doing one of the following:

- Call your vendors or associates and ask them to participate with you in co-op advertising.
- Take some time to send your existing customers' referrals and buying incentives.
- Have you thought about introducing yourself to the media? Free publicity has the potential to boost your business. By doing this you position yourself as an expert in your field.
- Invite people into your place of business by piggybacking onto an event. Is there a concert coming to town, are you willing to sell those tickets? It could mean free radio publicity. If that is not your cup of tea, how about a walkathon that is taking place in your area, why not be a public outreach and distribute their material?

When you do spend money on marketing, do not forget to create a way to track those marketing efforts. You can do this by coding your ads, using multiple toll-free telephone numbers, and asking prospects where they heard about you. This enables you to notice when a marketing tactic stops working. You can then quickly replace it with a better choice or method. By being diligent in your marketing and creating an easy strategy such as holding yourself accountable to contact ten customers or potential customers daily five days a week you will see your business grow at an exceptional rate. The great thing is it will not take a large marketing budget to make it happen.

PROSPECT

For people who think this is the industry for them, they really think about their personality and be sure they can thrive (and survive) in the atmosphere. It truly is different from anything else. It is critical that they work for a hotel while they are still in school, preferably in a few different hotels, and departments, so they can get a feel for it and know where they would be the happiest and most successful. The growth in the services sector of the worldwide economy has been phenomenal in the last 25 years. In the United States, services currently account for more than 75 percent of the gross domestic product (GDP), which is a popular measure of an economy's productivity. Similarly, on an international scale, services continue to account for an ever-increasing percentage of economic activity. Most new jobs are created in the service sector, and the growth in the hospitality and tourism industry is a major contributor. Until the mid-1980s, the emphasis within the marketing community was on products. Now services have surpassed products and have taken on a more important role in marketing. Services, such as those offered by providers in the hospitality and tourism industry, have developed marketing strategies and practices that are unique. It has been established that the strategies, tactics, and practices that have been used successfully for product marketers do not always work successfully for those who market services. With the distinct differences between products and services in mind, the field of services marketing has evolved.

Services Defined

Unlike products, which are tangible, services are usually intangible. A service is not a physical good; rather, it is the performance of an act or a deed. This performance often requires consumers to be present during the production or delivery of the service. Service industries, including hospitality and tourism, are actually selling consumers an experience. Services have been defined to "include all economic activities whose output is not a physical product or construction, is generally consumed at the time it is produced, and provides added value in forms (such as convenience, amusement, timeliness, comfort or health) that are essentially intangible concerns of its first purchaser."1 Service employees such as front desk agents, housekeepers, hostesses, wait staff, car rental agents, flight attendants, and travel agents are responsible for creating positive experiences for customers. These frontline employees are critical to the success of service firms and play boundary-spanning roles because of their direct contact with customers. These roles are important because customers' perceptions of service firms are formed as a result of their dealings with the boundary-spanning employees. Several reasons underlie the remarkable growth in services.

The numerous reasons for this growth:

Changing patterns of government regulation: The reduction in government regulation has spurred the growth of services. In recent years, there has been a very noticeable shift toward the government taking a much less active role in the regulation of business activities. The most noteworthy of these shifts have been in the airline, trucking, telecommunication, and electrical generation and distribution industries. All of these industries have seen significant changes, as the barriers to entry have been removed and regulations governing such marketing elements as price have also been relaxed or entirely removed.

Relaxation of professional association restrictions on marketing: A new element of competition has been introduced into professions such as law and medicine as more of the practitioners in these areas advertise their services. Bans or restrictions on promotion have been largely removed. Within the hospitality and tourism industry, standards have also changed. We have seen an increase in advertising focusing on direct comparisons, or attacks, on competitors' products and services. This type of advertising strategy creates, or sustains, the perception of superiority in the mind of the consumer in favor of the brand being advertised.

Privatization of some public and nonprofit services: The term privatization was first used in Great Britain when the government adopted the policy of returning national industries from government to private ownership. This transformation has resulted in a greater emphasis on cost containment and a clearer focus on customers' needs. Later, in Central and Eastern Europe, following the fall of communism, we witnessed a continuing transformation from planned or government-run economies to market-driven economies fueled by private companies. Many of these countries' governments have released the control of airlines and travel agencies to private firms.

Technological innovation: Technology continues to alter the way firms do business and interact with consumers. In all types of businesses, consumers take a more active role in the service delivery process. For example, airlines, in an effort to reduce labour costs and increase speed of service to customers, have aggressively promoted self-check-in, both at the ticket counter and through their Web sites prior to arrival at the airport. Customers print boarding passes, receipts, and other documents without intervention by an airline employee. Express checkout for hotel guests has been in place for many years, but hotel chains continue to experiment with ways to enhance the service, thereby reducing labour costs and/or increasing the customers' perceived value.

In other settings, touch-screen computers collect feedback from guests, in much the same manner that comment cards have been used previously. The ease with which a company can maintain and access a database has permitted the development of sophisticated reservation systems and has led to more sophisticated frequent traveler Programmes. The use of more sophisticated reservations and property management systems has allowed hospitality and tourism firms to improve the level of service provided to guests. Guest history data serve as another example of how a hospitality organization can use technology to gain a competitive advantage. If a hotel guest requests a specific type of pillow, staff can record this preference within the individual's guest history file. When this guest checks into another hotel operated by the chain, the items that were previously requested can be waiting, without the guest even having to request them.

Growth in service chains and franchise networks: Much of the growth in service firms, including the hospitality industry, has been the direct result of franchising efforts by some of the major companies. Franchising represents a contractual arrangement whereby one firm (the franchisor) licenses a number of other firms (the franchisees) to use the franchisor's name and business practices. Notable lodging organizations such as Choice Hotels International and Marriott International, as well as food service firms such as McDonald's, Burger King, Taco Bell, and Wendy's, have all used franchising as a major vehicle for growth. The continued growth of the hospitality industry by means of franchising has put additional stress on independent owners and operators. In fact, each year the percentage of hospitality and tourism operations that are independently operated decreases.

Internationalization and globalization: Increasing shareholder value often remains directly associated with increasing company sales and profits, and globalization is one means of achieving this. As more and more of the prime locations are developed domestically, companies look internationally for expansion opportunities. This has been particularly true for fast-food franchisors: a significant proportion of their expansion during the last few years has occurred outside of their traditional domestic markets.

Pressures to improve productivity: In many industries within the service economy, competition stays very intense. This factor, when combined with the pressure from investors for higher returns on capital, has resulted in pressure to increase productivity and reduce costs. In many cases, managers seek to reduce labour costs by running leaner operations or using technology to replace humans for some tasks An example of this was when Delta Airlines encouraged passengers to check in via the Internet, thereby reducing the number of passengers who wanted to check in at the airport. They offered an incentive of 1,000 extra frequent-flyer miles to any passenger who used this service. While increasing productivity and profits remains a highly desirable goal, it must not be done at the expense of longterm customer satisfaction. Without long-term satisfaction, future profitability may exist in jeopardy.

The service quality movement: With the advent of consumerism, the public's perception is that service quality has declined. In response, successful firms are using the customer's perception of quality to set performance standards, rather than relying solely on operationally defined standards for service quality. They often conduct extensive research to determine the key elements that impact the customer's perception of service quality. When Ritz-Carlton won the Malcolm Baldrige National Quality Award, this was tangible evidence that paying careful attention to customers' service expectations can have a dramatic impact on the firm.

Expansion of leasing and rental businesses: The expansion of businesses that lease equipment and personnel to firms has been a contributing factor in the growth of the service sector. More and more firms are looking to outsource some elements of their operation, and they often start with elements that are not part of the firm's core product or business. For example, most hotels that host meetings and conventions have outsourced the servicing of the audiovisual needs of groups to a company that specializes in that type of business. The company in turn leases the audiovisual equipment to groups that are holding meetings in the hotel. The company is able to provide more up-to-date and specialized equipment to groups than the hotel might if it provided the service itself. The hotel does not have to maintain an inventory of equipment, and therefore capital costs are reduced.

Manufacturers as service providers: Some of the firms that traditionally manufactured and distributed tangible products have found it profitable to provide services as well. For example, most automobile manufacturers have consumer credit agencies to facilitate the leasing and purchasing of automobiles. In the hospitality industry, PepsiCo decided to enter the restaurant industry and distribute its products through acquisitions such as Taco Bell and KFC, but the company later reconsidered this strategy and sold these brands to Yum! Brands, Inc. In the computer industry, firms such as IBM and Hewlett-Packard provide services in addition to hardware and software. In most cases, the profit margins on services are higher than on products, contributing significantly to the bottom line of the firm.

Pressures on public and nonprofit organizations to find new income sources: All organizations are under pressure to increase sales, which often becomes difficult within the traditional products that a firm sells. There are many reasons for this, but increasing competition and mature industries are often contributing factors. In an effort to find new sources of income, firms often seek new services that will generate new net sales, without cannibalizing sales of existing products. For example, a limousine company might expand its city tour business in addition to the other services offered.

Hiring and promotion of innovative managers: In the past, managers in the service industries often spent their entire careers within a single industry, or perhaps even with the same firm. This situation no longer reintroduction to services marketing mains the same, especially at the corporate level of management. Firms often hire individuals from other industries to provide a fresh perspective and fresh ideas. The results can become dramatic. One such individual is Steven Bollenback, president and CEO of Hilton Hotels. Prior to his very positive impact on Hilton Hotels, he had engineered innovative financing at both Marriott International and Trump Hotels and Resorts.

THE NATURE OF SERVICES

Along with the growth in services, an appreciation for the ways in which services are different from products has developed. The traditional ways of marketing tangible products are not equally effective in services marketing. In many industries, marketing involves tangible manufactured products, such as automobiles, washing machines, and clothing, whereas service industries focus on intangible products such as travel and foodservice. However, before we can explore how services get successfully marketed, we need to examine the ways services differ from products.

Nine key differences:

No Ownership by Customers

A customer does not take ownership when purchasing a service. There is no transfer of assets.

Service Products as Intangible Performers

The value of owning a highperformance car or the latest computer lies in the physical characteristics of the product and to some extent the brand image it conveys. The value of purchasing services lies in the nature of the performance. For example, if you decide to celebrate a birthday or anniversary by dining at an expensive restaurant, the value lies in the way in which the service actors perform. When servers come to the table and present all the entrees simultaneously, the choreographed presentation appears in the same manner as a choreographed play or performance.

Greater Involvement of Customers in the Production Process

Because consumers tend to be present when receiving service within a hospitality operation, they remain involved in the service production. In many instances, they are directly involved through the element of self-service. Examples of this can be seen in fast-food restaurants as well as in hotels that provide automated check-in and checkout by means of either a machine or a video connection through the television. Airlines have greatly expanded self-service within their operations as a means of reducing labour costs. In any case, the customer's level of satisfaction depends on the nature of the interaction with the service provider, the nature of the physical facilities in which the service gets provided, and the nature of the interaction with other guests present in the facility at the time the service is provided.

People as Part of the Product

People or firms that purchase services come in contact with other consumers as well as the service employees. For example, a hotel guest waits in line at the front desk or the concierge desk with other guests. In addition, the guests share facilities such as the pool, the restaurant, and the fitness center. Therefore, service firms must also manage consumer interactions to the best of their abilities to ensure customer satisfaction. For example, a hotel's sales office would not want to book group business with a nondrinking religious group at the same time as a reunion of military veterans. The two groups are significantly different in behaviour, and the expectation is that they would not mix well within the facilities at the same time. Similarly, restaurants separate smokers and nonsmokers, and they should try to separate other patrons that show some potential for conflict.

Greater Variability in Operational Inputs and Outputs

In a manufacturing setting, the operational production can be controlled very carefully. For example, staff carefully manage inventory and precisely calculate production times. Services, however, are delivered in real time, with many variables not being fully under the control of managers. For example, if a guest has been promised an early check-in but all of the guests from the preceding night are late in checking out, it becomes more difficult for the hotel to honor the arriving guest's request. A service setting remains a more difficult site in which to control quality and offer a consistent service experience. Service firms try to minimize the amount of variability between service encounters, but much of the final product stays situational. There are many uncontrollable aspects of the delivery process, such as weather, the number of consumers present, the attitudes of the consumers, and the attitudes of the employees. Therefore, it becomes impossible to consistently control the quality for services in the same manner as the quality of manufactured products.

Harder for Consumers to Evaluate

Consumers can receive considerable information regarding the purchase of products; however, they often do not obtain it for services. Prior to buying a product, a consumer can research the product attributes and performance and use this information when making a purchase decision, especially an important one.

No Inventories for Services

Due to the intangible nature of services, they cannot be inventoried for future use. Therefore, a lost sale can never be recaptured. When a seat remains empty on a flight, a hotel room stays vacant, or a table stays unoccupied in a restaurant, the potential revenue for these services at that point in time becomes lost forever. In other words, services are perishable, much like produce in a supermarket or items in a bakery. It remains critical for hospitality and tourism firms to manage supply and demand in an attempt to minimize unused capacity. For example, restaurants offer early-bird specials and airlines offer deeply discounted fares in an attempt to shift demand from peak periods to nonpeak periods, thereby increasing revenue and profits.

Importance of Time

Hospitality services are generally produced and consumed simultaneously, unlike tangible products, which are manufactured, inventoried, and then sold at a later date. Customers must be present to receive the service. There are real limits to the amount of time that customers are willing to wait to receive service. Service firms study the phenomenon of service queues, or the maximum amount of time a customer will wait for a service before it has a significant (negative) impact on his or her perception of service quality. Airline companies offer curbside check-in for the most time-conscious passengers, and restaurants have devised practices such as providing guests with pagers and expanding the bar area in order to reduce the negative effect that results from waiting for service.

Different Distribution Channels

The distribution channel for services is usually more direct than the traditional channel (i.e., manufacturer-wholesaler retailer- consumer) used by many product firms. The simultaneous production and consumption normally associated with service delivery limits the use of intermediaries. The service firm usually comprises both the manufacturer and the retailer, with no need for a wholesaler to inventory its products. Consumers are present to consume the meals prepared in a restaurant, to take advantage of the amenities in a hotel, and to travel between cities by plane.

MARKET PLANNING WORKSHEET

Many people who try to start businesses have difficulty getting the business off the ground. They go through all the motions of getting a business set up, put an ad in the newspaper and then sit back and wonder what went wrong when no customers come knocking on their door. Don't let that happen to you. You can improve your chance for a successful business launch by doing a little research before you start the business. Use the marketing worksheet below to help you determine who your customers will be and what it will take to reach them.

Chapter 5

Telephone Sales

TELEMARKETING

Marketing is too important to be left to the marketing department. In a truly great marketing organization, you cannot tell who's in the marketing department. Everyone in the organization has to make decisions based on the impact on the consumer. Marketing is the business function that identifies customer needs and wants, determines which target markets the organization can best serve, designs appropriate products, services, and Programmes to serve these markets, and calls upon everyone in the organization to "think and serve customers."

Advertising, personal selling, sales promotion, and store retailers are traditional means of communication between sellers and buyers. However, these methods have faced a lot of pressure in the past several years. Today, the style of the consumer market is different, because of the increase in the number working women, the difficulty in getting to stores, and so forth. For these reasons traditional marketing cannot fit into today's market environment very well. Further, the cost of traditional marketing is growing. That means marketing organizations have to find and use a new marketing method – "Telemarketing."

Telemarketing has many benefits to companies and consumers. Consumers appreciate the speed and convenience of placing orders, reserving tickets, and contributing donations through 800 numbers. They also have grown used to settling problems and making complaints by telephone, effectively putting and end to the complaint letter. Companies like Telemarketing because it is fast, efficient, and less expensive than other marketing approaches, including person-to-person sales calls and conversations. It also provides immediate results, saves time, helps make field salespeople more efficient, increases the profits of each sale, conserves energy, and helps reduce pollution. Telemarketing has many advantages. It is becoming a popular and important marketing method in USA presently. Accordingly, to do the research on Telemarketing is very attractive and useful.

The Research Objective

This research project discusses a lot of things about Telemarketing. It includes Telemarketing theory, the influence factors of Telemarketing, the strategies of Telemarketing, and a review of related literature. The purpose is let everybody better understand this kind of marketing method, especially the "what", "why", "when" and "how to" of Telemarketing. In addition, field interviews by telephone were conducted to determine some of the responses, opinions, reasons, and acceptance of Telemarketing by consumers. I hope everybody can get a lot of help and ideas from this research project.

The Research Method and Process

This project includes three main parts as follows:

1. The Literature Research : First of all, to identify the scope and content of research, the Telemarketing literature was reviewed. The literature resources came from reference books, magazines, newspapers.
2. Field Interviews by Telephone: Using a random sample of 150, 60 effective responses were obtained from "Ameritech PagesPlus: Near North Suburban White and Yellow Pages," Then an analysis of the data was undertaken in order to understand the responses and opinions of residents on Telemarketing.
3. Review of Related Literature: Telemarketing belongs to Direct Marketing, Direct Marketing belongs to Non-

Store Retailers. A full understanding of Telemarketing requires some knowledge of the more general subject of direct marketing. Some of the aspects of direct marketing are discussed.

TELEMARKETING THEORY

The Scope of Telemarketing

The direct marketing expert Bob Stone defined Telemarketing this way:

"Telemarketing utilizes sophisticated telecommunications and information systems combined with personal selling and servicing skills to help companies keep in close contact with present and potential customers, increase sales, and enhance business productivity."

It is a new marketing discipline that uses telecommunications technology as part of a well-planned, organized, and managed marketing Programme that prominently features the use of personal selling, using non-face-to-face contacts.

In other words, Telemarketing uses the telephone as a direct marketing medium through which a variety of sales and market research activities can be carried out. It can also be a key source of information on a company's prospective and current customer base, markets, inventory, distribution channels, advertising and promotional efforts. When combined with information and management systems, it can bring trained personnel into computerized contact with potential customers, and maintain that contact profitably.

Why Telemarketing

Modern advances in computers and electronic technology have been astonishing. The telephone, invented over a hundred years ago, still ranks as our number one technological sales tool. Why Telemarketing? The reasons are evident.

- *Saves Time:* In business-to-business marketing, Telemarketing can be used in an appointment-setting Programme that can increase the total field selling time available. It stands to reason that if field sales reps can be provided with specific daily appointments, especially at the beginning and end of the day, management can be reasonably assured that the field sales organization is likely to be out doing what it is supposed to be doing: making sales presentations to qualified prospects. When Telemarketing used this way, effectively extends the field selling day, increasing sales productivity and reducing sales costs.

- *Cost Efficiency:* Because Telemarketing is lower cost, it can be used effectively with marginal accounts that normally wouldn't rate a field sales call. Such customers can frequently be turned into profitable accounts with Telemarketing. It can also be used with almost equal efficiency no matter what the customer's geographical location might be. Thus, penetration of new markets and major shifts in market geography can be accomplished soon with Telemarketing. Finally, the telephone can be a more flexible device than the field salesperson. For example, to do customers surveys by phone, to set up appointments, to announce significant changes in price of products, to upgrade orders and to check details.
- *Instant Response:* Because the person at the other end of the line can react immediately. If customers don't understand something, they can ask questions at once. If they have objections, they can make them, and you have an opportunity to respond.
- *Improved Cash Flow:* Telemarketing Programmes can have more immediate results than field sales Programmes, and they can often begin to generate orders almost instantly. Such immediate results, can allow cash flow to cover marketing costs, as well as permitting much tighter inventory control.
- *Expanding Territory:* Telemarketing can readily target new customers, efficiently making initial qualification

contacts, and closing the sale, all essentially independent of geographical considerations. Where field sales calls are required the prequalification process makes it much more likely that expansion can be accomplished with the existing sales force.

- *Customer Relations:* First, a phone call takes much less of the customer's time than a face-to-face sales. Secondly, phone calls can be more regular and frequent than face-to-face sales. Thirdly, since Telemarketing can be either inbound or outbound, the customers familiar with a company's Telemarketing operation can get much quicker response to ongoing problems or questions.
- *Seasonality:* Telemarketing allows the marketer to get around the restrictions of seasonal selling periods. Because of mailing times and delays, Telemarketing allows the marketer actually to extend the buying period by speeding up receipt of the order.
- *Lower Personnel Costs:* A Telemarketing staff, despite all the training and experience required, is much less costly to maintain than high-priced field sales personnel. In addition, Telemarketing needs fewer people, and there no bodies to transport, shelter, feed, and entertain.
- *Versatility:* Once a functioning Telemarketing operation is in place, it can be easily adapted to a wide range of functions. The same equipment can be used among other things, to sell, to do surveys, to announce changes or special offers, to make appointments, to qualify leads, to cross-sell, and to check credit.
- *Ease of Start-Up:* Since the equipment used in Telemarketing is readily available, and since Telemarketing operations can often be set up using existing space and personnel, a Telemarketing operation is relatively easy to start up.

The Constructive Factors of Telemarketing

There are three main factors of Telemarketing construction. They are professional staff, telecommunication equipment, and database. Telemarketing combines these three factors through a systematic plan and process to run a business. It costs a lot of money to establish a whole Telemarketing system, but it can improve sales. Generally on average, Telemarketing can rise sales from 10 to 20 percent. A good system can even double sales.

The Growth of Telemarketing

Experts agree that Telemarketing is growing by at least 20 percent per year. The rate of growth will likely continue, only to be accelerated with the growth of international Telemarketing.

In 1992, thirteen billion calls were made to 800 numbers, yielding sales of $7.73 billion. By 1997, sales from 800 numbers are expected to be $11.4 billion, with most growth expected from small-to-medium-sized business.

As sales and revenue grow, more and more companies establish or expand their Telemarketing operations. Between 1980 and 1985, the number of companies involved in telephone sales grew from 1,500 to over 80,000. By 1993, there were 565,000 Telemarketing operations in the United States.

The rapid development of information technology has certainly played an important role in the growth of Telemarketing. It has made Telemarketing more efficient and created the capability to provide more personalized service. In addition, it also provides huge employment opportunities for those who have the skills to enhance customer relations. Computer assisted Telemarketing systems, predictive dialing, and enriched databases are just a few of new developments. The growth of professionalism and the success of Telemarketing are predicted to result in one of the faster growth employment opportunities in this decade.

The Customer's Sale Cycle

The scope of Telemarketing applications varies by types of companies. But in exploring the extent of its scope, it is a good idea to review the eight selling stages followed by most marketing organizations.

The eight stages can be shown as a hierarchy of effects model.

Not all companies sales cycles include each individual step. In some cases, a few may be combined into a single step. But the organization is engaged in selling to business or in selling to consumers, most if not all of these steps in the sales cycle are involved- individually or in combination, and are incorporated into the act of selling.

Different industries fulfill each of the steps in the sales cycle with different communication vehicles.

There are many ways that Telemarketing can be used to support or replace field selling. To learn where, let us take the eight steps in the sales cycle and identify each in terms of five levels of interest (account calls that are nonrevenue producers (service calls), call made with accounts that are only marginally profitable (revenue in relation to the cost of the sales call), and primary accounts that demand and deserve attention from field salespeople plus the levels of high cost and low-cost products.

Telemarketing can be a good communications medium for moving prospects through many of the steps in the sales cycle. In exploring the opportunities, consider where Telemarketing might be used to support or substitute for other media, particularly field salesperson.

The face-to-face visit can be targeted for priority assignments. On the other hand, a Telemarketing Center can be assigned all service calls and can be called upon to displace the field salesperson in handling marginal accounts. In addition, Telemarketing Centers can supplement field salespeople in serving primary accounts.

Table : Integrating Telemarketing into the Sales Cycle

	Awareness	Inquiry	Information	Sales Desire Response	Pro-posal	Close Sale Purchase	Fllow Up	Service
Service Calls	T	T	T	T	T	T	T	T
Marginal Accounts	T	T	T	T	T	T	T	T
Primary Accounts	S	TS	TS	S	S	S	TS	TS
High Ticket Products	TS	TS	TS	TS	S	S	TS	TS
Low Ticket Products	T	T	T	T	T	T	T	T

T = Telemarketing S = Salesperson

Although handling nonrevenue calls becomes an expense that the account may not have borne before, it is low in relation to the cost of in-person visits. It becomes profitable as it uncovers qualified leads, assists in supplementing the salesperson's visits, and opens an opportunity to sell once the customer's problem is resolved.

In the case of marginal accounts and low ticket products, a Telemarketing Center can receive inquires, provide information, receive customer response, offer a proposal, close the sale, follow up, and provide answers to product problems. In primary and high ticket products, Telemarketing specialists can supplement salespeople at many steps in the sales cycle. For example, customer inquires often can be satisfied over the telephone, and information can be provided orally that suits the customer's need. And, as a follow-up after the sale, the telephone is a natural. By viewing the sales cycle as a fit, it can work alone or in concert with a face-to-face sales force.

THE TYPES OF TELEMARKETING

There are two main types of Telemarketing, they are Inbound and Outbound. Inbound is when a customer calls a business firm for customer service, and the business firm accepts the customer's query, complaint, or order. Outbound is when business firms call customers for selling, such as for a promotion, or exhibition invitation.

Inbound Telemarketing

Inbound Telemarketing relies on calls from prospects already interested in a product or service (interested enough to place an order, ask questions that will help them make a purchase, or make an appointment with a sales representative. During the call, the TSR (Telephone Sales Rep) may simply capture the information about the order or may try to increase the size of the consumer's order by suggesting complementary merchandise.

The people who want to reach companies call a special 800 number. This possibility has grown up only since the introduction of toll-free 800 numbers by AT&T in 1967, which made it practical to have call centers receiving calls from the entire country. In brief, toll-free service led to centralized nationwide call facilities which led to increased call volumes at single locations, which increased the incentive to maximize revenue and cut costs. In fact, Americans dialed AT&T 800 numbers over six billion times during 1988 (more than sixteen million times a day! AT&T estimates the number of calls is increasing by a billion calls a year. One of the biggest inbound operations in the United States is operated by the Home Shopping Network, which handles 200,000 inbound calls daily for its 24 hours shopping channels (such as channel 60 in Chicago area) and other clients. Airlines, hotels, and virtually every catalog company rely on inbound Telemarketing to take reservations and merchandise orders.

Inbound calls can also focus on customer service or consumer information. For example, at the General Electric's GE Answer Center, a force of 250 answer 250,000 questions a month about how to get the most from GE products, they rely on a centralized consumer product database that allows them to call up information on just about anything that has to do with GE products. Many companies now have consumer information lines to serve customers. Successful inbound Telemarketing Programmes are created by paying careful attention to such factors as the type of telephone service chosen, the carrier picked to provide the service, the planning to meet fluctuating call volumes, and the design of the advertising that carries the phone number.

Outbound Telemarketing

The objective of most outbound Telemarketing calls is to sell a product or a service to a new or existing customer. It is through telephone calls that lure customers to buy products or query the condition of customers using a product in order to improve selling and hold customer's demand. This is usually a "cold call", a call placed to someone who has no prior relationship to the firm.

Cold calls can generate leads to sell products. A good example of a lead-generating call would be one placed by an insurance agent to a new community resident about home insurance. The agent is trying to get his or her foot in the door and will not try to sell a policy until a subsequent face-to-face meeting. By contrast, a TSR who calls a consumer to subscribe to a product will try to take an order before the call ends.

According to the Direct Marketing Association, large numbers of companies place outbound calls to sell products and services to their customers. They include: 31 percent of all consumer publications, 70 percent of all business publications, 5 percent of all consumer catalogs, 25 percent of all business catalogs, 25 percent of all consumer products and service companies, 71 percent of all business products and services companies, 39 percent of all clubs and continuity offers, 18 percent of all financial services organizations, and 50 percent of all computer hardware and Programme software organizations.

Outbound Telemarketing also can be used to notify existing customers of an unexpected delay in shipments or other problems in an order, or to qualify leads from prospective customers by determining their interest in a product before passing the name on to a field sales representative for a personal sales call.

ANI, ACD, ARM, and WATS

There are two important technologies used in modern Telemarketing: ANI (automatic number identification) and ACD (automatic call distribution). When too many phone calls reach a particular number, they can be placed on hold, and assigned to the next available representative through automatic call distribution. In off-peak periods, calls can be evenly distributed among stations. If callers have waited a long time, overflow service can automatically shift the calls from a high traffic ACD group to a less congested one. ACDs process incoming or outgoing calls very quickly and effectively. These computerized devices are most effective when you have 15 or more lines in use on a consistent basis. The points to check out in ACDs include record keeping of calls made from individual telephones, backup operation in the event of a power outage and internal switching capabilities. And, with 800 automatic number identification, integrated data/phone terminals show the Telemarketing operator not only what phone number the caller is dialing from, but also important facts from that database about the caller's information before the call is answered. If desired, certain proprietary software can be used to capture name, address, and demographic information on incoming calls, without having the operator key it in.

ARM (Automatic Recorded Message) can be extremely cost-effective when a specific telephone presentation is to be made, i.e., a political message or an insurance company name change being relayed to a group of policy owners.

WATS (Wide Area Telecommunication Service) is available for outgoing and certain incoming calls, WATS lines are rented by long-distance carries based on hours of usage, location of calls (known as zones or bands) and a variety of other factors. Discounts are given for volume calling. The main disadvantage is the high cost for additional lines.

FACTORS THAT INFLUENCE THE SUCCESS OF TELEMARKETING

There are many factors that can influence Telemarketing's success or failure. The main important factors are preparation, staff training, information system, and management.

In any labour-intensive organization, the employees can make or break the bottom line. This is especially true of Telemarketing. The key component in a successful Telemarketing operation is management's ability to run the department. Even if the strategic concept is on target, and the prospect list is highly qualified, Telemarketing is doomed to failure without a richly sophisticated and experienced management to guide the Telemarketing effort. To capitalize on the sales potential that Telemarketing offers, a company must have a professional Telemarketing staff with a comprehensive grasp of the complexities of this type of management.

Preparation

Preparation for the Telemarketing campaign will take telemarketers from the planning stage right up to the first day of the actual campaign. During this time, telemarketers will have to establish their evaluation/control criteria and write their script. There are several points for preparation, such as:

1. Space
2. Equipment
3. Materials
4. Setting up the facility (Confirmation of arrangement for facilities and preparation of facilities.
5. Recruitment of staff and hiring of callers.

Staff and Callers Training

A good staff and callers training is very important; it can let a company do successful Telemarketing directly. Training is an on-going process.

Not everyone is cut out to be a telephone communicator. Direct-sales people are often ill at ease in a Telemarketing environment: they often miss the face-to-face eye contact, and the body language of the prospect. On the other side of the scale, people with prior acting experience seem to do quite well.

Most experts agree that there are five traits necessary in order to be successful as a telephone communicator.

1. Good communication skills
2. Persistent and able to bounce back from rejection.
3. Good organizational skills.
4. Ability to project a telephone personality
5. Flexibility: can adapt to different types of clients and new situations.

The first trait: "good communication skills" is a must. And the best way to evaluate these skills is with an initial telephone interview. Through the telephone interview the professional trainer screens out unlikely candidates.

Information System

If database marketing was nonexistent at this time, someone would have to invent it. For without database marketing, direct marketing, of which Telemarketing is an integral part, would be a shambles. Without a database a telemarketer cannot have segmentation. Without segmentation a telemarketer cannot have targeting. So, database marketing is a given for success.

The information system is important, it may include customers lists, customers data, selling record, trace record, other relevant data. To establish a complete information system is very necessary to telemarketers. I will discuss it in chapter four in detail.

Management of Organization

If the Telemarketing manager is high up in the organization, then there is leverage for placing Telemarketing into a high priority position, with the resources and support needed to achieve its objectives. Further, if the Programme is successful, with heavy resources committed and representing a key element in the corporate strategy, then there is every possibility that the head of the operation will be high up on the organizational ladder.

Both the Telemarketing organization plan and the person to head it are critical decision areas. The person selected must have both the experience and the capability to manage the operation technically as well as the credibility and support of top management. The plan is equally important to chances of success. If cost-benefit analyses, careful preparation, presentation of similar success histories and some pre-selling is not done, the chances of management even approving a trial Programme are considerably lessened.

In small organizations the plan be even more critical than in larger ones. The approval is not the issue; success or failure of the enterprise could hang in the balance. A marketing plan based on Telemarketing, and gaining the commitment of limited key resources had better be prepared.

Becoming sold on telemarketing and rushing into it without preparation and with expectations that it will cure all is a danger which may be averted with proper staffing and management. The subject of Telemarketing expertise is important as it relates to where in the organization it resides. The telemarketers themselves can certainly use experience in selling on the telephone, but the expertise and experience must be possessed by the person directly responsible for Telemarketing operations. The best situation is to bring in an experienced manager who has run the type of operation being set up Second best is to convert an on-board manager, but appropriate training and a strong desire to succeed must accompany the latter choice.

The character and nature of Telemarketing management is critical to the success of a Telemarketing operation in its relationships with other internal organization units and top management. The managers not only must perform their normal management duties but must justify the existence of his operation continually in the face of the newness and poor reputation of Telemarketing as a marketing discipline. The manager can follow set patterns only to the extent that they continue to produce results. Results are the lifeblood of Telemarketing, and the managers must produce them by whatever means they can. The Telemarketing manager's job is a demanding one, and not meant for the average person. For those willing and able to meet the challenge the rewards are there, and no manager will be more deserving. To sum up, a good management in Telemarketing organization is essential. A complete management will result in successful Telemarketing.

The 80/20 Rule

"Eighty percent of our business comes from 20 percent of our customers" is a frequent statement at any sales convention. There's hardly a sales executive who is not aware of the 80/20 rule. It's very amazing, we see scores of marketers ignoring it when it comes to allocating advertising and sales dollars, spending the same on all accounts.

The Telemarketing approach to lead generation and customer activation takes full cognizance of the immutable law (all prospects and customers are not created equal. Remembering that approximately 80 percent of sales come from 20 percent of customers. Telemarketers must spend their resources where they have the most return. Identify the key customers and develop them to the fullest. Next, spend part of efforts in calling on prospects to develop them as customers.

THE STRATEGIES OF TELEMARKETING

Most Telemarketing professionals consider Telemarketing to be a marketing discipline that uses remote selling and services techniques to execute a marketing strategy. In brief, it is far more than an 800 number, or a bank of operators waiting to take your order. Used properly, Telemarketing becomes a driving force in a company's strategic planning.

Preparing for the Telephone Sales Call

In telephone selling, a haphazard approach usually leads to haphazard results. To maximize your telephone time, it is essential to prepare. Preparation calls for a disciplined system. Successful telephone salespeople start with a call list and develop a system for tracking where they are with each call.

The fundamentals of any effective telephone system include:

- For prospecting, a concentrated block of time that you dedicate to your calls, not just one call between other activities.
- An objective for number of calls you want to complete per day.
- Your client or prospect list for the day – in priority order.
- A well-organized desk and environment.
- An objective (what you want to see happen) for each call.
- A record of each call. (It should be the client information, details, next steps)
- A memo system to trigger actions and follow-up.

Getting Through to the Right Person

Getting through to the right person is essential, whether are selling over the telephone or face-to-face. Not only is a presentation to the wrong person a waste of time, but it can also endanger the sale. Several points follow:

1. Finding the Decision Maker: When dealing with a small business, it usually is not difficult to identify the individual with authority to make a decision; however, it is not so cut and dried when calling a large organization for the first time. Naturally, when a reliable source has recommended a specific individual as the decision maker, there is not any problem. But without the advantage of such

information, getting through to the right person may require some fairly fancy footwork.

2. Getting Through the Third Party, the Screener: A third party stands between the salesperson and the individual he is trying to reach. It may be a receptionist, an assistant, or a spouse. The most commonly encountered third party is probably the private secretary, and he is also the most skilled at screening calls.
3. Speaking with Authority: This is especially important in getting through the screener, whose job is to separate trivial calls from important ones. Getting through the screener will never be a problem for you if you remember that you are important.
4. Leaving a Message: Leaving a message that works is an integral part of selling on the telephone. Often, you will not be able to get through to an individual on the first call, so it will be necessary for you to call back or to leave a message.
5. Calling Back: When an individual is difficult to reach and does not return your call, do not hesitate to call again. All these techniques take practice, but developing them is an essential part of good telephone selling. In short, you must get through to the prospect before anything can be sold.

There will always be some instances when a caller will have to make a series of calls before finally getting to talk directly with the prospect. One must work on establishing rapport with the screener, while maintaining an image of authority. Whether he leaves a message after the first call or the fourth, leaving an effective message also requires authority and a quiet suggestion of urgency.

Developing and Maintaining a Database

Developing a basic customer database is very important. Creative enhancements to the database can improve sales efficiency dramatically, but the first question to be answered is "What data should be included in the basic database?" The database requirement varies by category of business and/or type of customer.

For telemarketers, a key source of data is the call report. The call report should capture the history of each account and give direction for future servicing. Basic data, which should go into the database, include the following:

- Key contact
- Title
- Telephone
- Best calling time
- Time zone
- Mailing and shipping address
- SIC # (standard industrial classification) if a business firm
- Source of original contact
- History of purchases
- Current buying pattern
- Special requirements
- Credit limit
- Personal notes
- Other products/services in the discussion stage
- Log of call by dates
- Follow-up call cycle

With these data safely stored in the computer, carrying on meaningful dialogues with a customer base becomes a piece of cake. The computer makes sure that each telephone salesperson is given a list of scheduled follow-up calls each day. Prior to each call the total picture of the account appears on the screen. Complete recall results. Even though a salesperson might have a block of four hundred accounts, he or she can be as knowledgeable in conversation with a given account as if the salesperson had none other to serve.

The Telephone Presentation

Before talking about the telephone presentation, a caller should analyze ten questions first.

1. Do I use short, simple, uncomplicated words?
2. Do I mention a benefit to the prospect?
3. Do I express my prime message so it would be understood?
4. Do I maintain a positive mental attitude?
5. Do I emphasize the benefits of doing business with me and my company?
6. Do I have a professional way of "qualifying"?
7. Do I stick to a logical order in my presentation?
8. Do I have all the facts about my offering so I can answer any questions?
9. Do I smile before I pick up the telephone?
10. Do I ask for the order?

If the answer is "NO" to any of the above questions, positive steps must be taken to correct it. There are some rules that telemarketers should consider in marketing a telephone presentation:

1. Study your product or service: Write a list of all important features and, more important, their functions and benefits. Consider their price, quality, availability, and how they have helped others.
2. Analyze your prospect list: Determine your present customers, what they have been buying, and whom they've been buying from lately. If former customers, why did they stop buying? What do you know about them? Have you done your homework to determine their possible needs and wants? Also, what might they know about you that would make it easier for them to understand your company? The more information you have, the easier it will be to select the proper opening remarks and the best sales approach to use.

3. Write out or use your computer to list the key ideas you want to cover: Make sure all vital points are included. By covering all the main points you want to review, you are essentially preparing a presentation.
4. Get attention and interest, which is the warm-up portion vital to success in any effort to sell by telephone: Always smile, then (a) greet the prospect by name. During your opening comments, refer to how you obtained his or her name and company; (b) introduce yourself by making a simple statement of your name and company; (c) make an attention-getting statement by appealing to the prospect's self-interest or curiosity. It should be brief and to the point. A statement such as this deserves a great deal of care and preparation.
5. Create a desire for the product or service: Your voice alone has to do the selling. You have to tell your prospects what you are offering, why they need it; what it will do for them; and how, when, and where they can get it. The price and service may be discussed. Be creative and add a little sparkle to your sales talk. By knowing your product, you should be in a good position to create this appealing statement in such a way that the prospects can visualize from your words exactly what you mean.
6. You must describe the product realistically: Speak in terms that your prospect will understand and relate to. Smile before you pick up the telephone.
7. Give all necessary facts: Don't assume or leave anything to the interpretation of the listener be specific.

In addition, the following are some techniques of selling that the caller should take into account.

- Be prepared to talk when your prospect answers your call: Know about your product, its applications, availability, pricing, and benefits. Don't call unless you can devote your entire attention to the call. Review all past relevant information about the prospect before you pick up the receiver to dial.

- Speak distinctly in an ordinary conversational tone: You are talking with prospects and you want to make them friends and customers. Avoid technical phrases or jargon they may not understand. Talk your story; don't read it. Help your prospect to buy use word pictures to specifically describe your product and what it will do. Be specific in size, colour, application, and so forth. Use sparkle in your presentation. Avoid generalities and vague comparisons. Give customers a choice when you ask for an order or set up an appointment.
- Be polite, don't argue: You may win an argument and lose the sale. Smile before you pick up the phone so the customer hears a smile in your voice.
- Follow through: Do what you agree to do, whether it was to put something in the mail, follow up at a later date, set up an appointment, or contact someone else. Don't be discouraged in the course of your selling effort. The cost of using the telephone is so low that you can afford many unsuccessful calls to develop one good prospect or make a sale. The more calls you make without a sale, the closer you are to getting one. You should understand how to improve after each call.

Table : Do's and Don'ts of Telemarketing

DO NOT	DO
1 Scowl	1 Smile
2 Mutter	2 Speak clearly and politely
3 Sound tired	3 Be enthusiastic
4 Speak in a monotonous tone	4 Lower the pitch of your voice for friendly conversation
5 Be negative	5 Talk in a positive mood
6 Be overconfident	6 Be prepared to answer objections

7 Talk down into transmitter	7 Talk directly into mouthpiece
8 Ramble	8 Come to the point (ask for the appointment or sale)
9 Do something to the customer	9 Do something for the customer
10 Argue	10 Discuss
11 Hang up abruptly if service is refused	11 Politely thank the customer for listening to you
12 Assume you are understood	12 Ask to find out
13 Be overwhelming	13 Use a cassette recorder to hear how you sound

When to Call

When the salesperson approaches a prospect at the wrong time, nothing the salesperson says will bring a favourable response. Timing is of the utmost importance. The telephone company has prepared statistical information showing when is the best time for calling various people based on other priorities they may have their time:

1. Lawyers: between 11:00 A.M. and 2:00 P.M. or after 5:00 P.M.
2. Housewives and families: between 6:00 and 8:00 P.M.
3. Contractions and builders: before 9:00 A.M. and after 5:00 P.M.
4. Chemists and engineers: between 4:00 and 5:00 P.M.
5. Executives and heads of business: after 10:30 A.M.
6. Public accountants: any time but avoid January 15th through April 15th

Sales professionals analyze the work and home habits of their prospects and call at the appropriate time. When they get to the appointment, they ask, "What time would you prefer I call you in the future?" If you have trouble getting by a secretarial screen, try calling before 8 A.M., noon to 1 P.M., or after 5 P.M. Business people have a tendency to answer their own telephone when their secretaries are out.

Using an 800 Number

In 1992, thirteen billion calls were made to 800 numbers, yielding sales of $7.73 billion. By 1997, sales from 800 numbers are expected to be $11.4 billion. Offering a toll-free number encourages the customers and prospects to call, and many telecommunications companies have cost-effective services for small businesses. In many parts of the country, an 800 number service can be obtained and the area for which toll-free calling is provided can be specified. In other words, calls can be limited to certain parts of a state, region, or city, and a toll-free number provided just for customers in those areas.

Today, 800 number services are available through local Bell companies and through national long-distance firms, so there is usually a choice of vendors. Often an 800 service can be obtained without having to change the firm's phone number. Here's an example of some of the options and services that may be available. They are provided for customers of Pacific Bell who use "Custom 800" service:

- You may take your number with you if you move. For example, real estate agents working for one firm and using their own 800 number can take it with them if they move to another firm. (Clients will still call the same 800 number they are used to and still get the same sales agent)
- The area served can be as small as the territory covered by one three-digit phone number prefix, or you may specify several different areas.
- Printed reports from Pacific Bell, sorted by phone number, will tell you the prefixes your calls come from. They will also identify the area codes and prefixes for people who tried to call you toll-free but could not because they were outside your specified 800-number area.
- You can have calls routed to different offices at different times of the day. For example, if you have two offices that are staffed at different hours, you could have all 800 calls routed to one office during normal business hours and calls after hours routed to another office.

Services and costs vary substantially, so it's in a company's interest to check with different companies in an area. Firms levy setup charges and will charge extra for written usage reports in addition to the charges for each call. One question to ask 800-number provider is how the toll charges are billed. Some firms charge a flat rate per call, which may be more expensive than doing business with a company that bases the toll fees on the distance each call travels.

800 numbers are most commonly used in conjunction with direct mail offers, but once a number is established, the firm should use it on all materials such as stationery, brochures, specialty items, and so forth, as a benefit to customers. An 800-number can enhance the marketing power of promotional materials. A "hot-line" for answering questions can also be established. There are different types of toll-free numbers. The local phone company can discuss costs and options. However, if a firm goes through the expense of establishing an 800 number, it should make sure it has a staff person ready to answer the calls.

Americans order millions of dollars in goods over the telephone every day, establishing a toll-free phone number is an effective way to greatly increase the response rate of promotional efforts.

Using a 900 Number

The use of an 800 number, the cost is paid by the marketer. But, the use of the 900 number, the cost is paid by the consumer. The marketer determines the price.

The marketing advantages of the 900 number are as follows:

- Recoup the cost of promotions.
- Generate detailed customer databases.
- Provide national of regional coverage.
- Provide an instant response mechanism for print, broadcast, and direct-mail campaigns.
- Produce qualified leads for sampling and couponing.

- Offer measurability within hours or even minutes of a promotion or campaign.
- Provide an interactive "one-on-one" selling opportunity.

Since audiotex is integral to the 900 number process, the marketer gets an invaluable printout of the names and addresses of all who call. The value of this mailing list can be further enhanced with a demographic overlay that profiles the characteristics of the respondents. Thus the marketer gets a clear picture of the marketplace and knows what other media mirror the established profile.

The 900-number is a new way of marketing a business and in some cases it is the business itself. A 900-number is a real advantage to businesses who offer referral information or services for which people are willing to pay. Basically a business pays an installation fee and then can charge a caller from anywhere.

THE CRITICAL SKILLS ON TELEMARKETING

In each of the elements in the telephone call framework (opening, client, positioning, objections, close, and follow-up), the following six critical selling skills are used over and over. They are the tools for selling.

- Presence
- Relating
- Questioning
- Listening
- Positioning
- Checking

The skill level determines selling strength and flexibility. These skills are used over and over throughout the sales process as the telemarketer, finds needs, matches up a product or idea with the client's needs, resolves objections, and closes, these skills are used continuously. These skills are interdependent, they will help a telemarketer become a valued consultant to clients, know more about the clients, and sell more to them.

Presence

Presence is the level of comfort and confidence that a telemarketer projects. Through presence an individual can engage the audience's attention. Voice presence can have an impact on telephone sales success. Voice presence is created by tone, pace, diction, inflection, level of enthusiasm, confidence, wit, and the ability to think on one's feet.

Although sales enthusiasm may come naturally in face-to-face calls, it requires special effort in telephone sales calls. Most salespeople would not appear bored when meeting with a client face to face, but in telephone selling sustaining interest and enthusiasm in one's voice can be challenging. The more one modulates his voice, usually the more interesting he sounds. He can emphasize words with his voice.

Keeping an interested and positive voice when selling over the telephone is even more of a challenge in highly routinized and comparatively unchallenging telephone selling situations. Some selling borders on order taking, when salespeople have to take information only to make a referral to a different division. Salespeople in these rote roles can drift into sounding bored. To avoid this, remember that the objective at all times is to create a positive image of the organization to the client as well as to sell or close profitable business.

Whether a telemarketer is taking information or a message for a colleague, he should remember the following:

In conjunction with the other critical skills, presence adds to sales strength and flexibility and helps create a flow between the client's needs and the telemarketer's products.

Relating

If you cannot relate to your clients, you won't sell to them. This is as much a rule of human nature as it is a rule of selling. Relating is even more of a challenge over the phone, since the phone can depersonalize the situation. Yet it is possible to establish rapport and build relationships over the telephone.

Successful salespeople do have strong relationships with their clients, but they also know where to draw the line between what is friendship and what is business. A good relationship forms the basis for good business. What is a business relationship but a series of transactions? In most businesses, important transactions don't occur without a relationship. Whether it is primarily a one-time sale or there is the potential for ongoing business, rapport helps form the foundation so that a transaction or many transactions can take place. Rapport goes beyond small talk. Rapport is consideration and thoughtfulness; it is trust and value added.

Questioning

Being able to establish rapport and knowing how to question are the heart of consultative selling. Salespeople who increase their questions increase their sales. Because of the generic product environment of the nineties and the fact that product alone cannot be counted on to be the differentiator, questioning is more important than ever. This is because questions enable a person to position (tell a story from the client's point of view). But it is easy to fall into the trap of "telling," especially over the telephone. Of course there are times to tell, but how a person tells will be determined by what is asked and what is heard. Questions will help keep a person on at least a parallel track and eventually get on the same track as the client. Questions will also help qualify clients.

A look at the range of questions that will need to be asked and then the questioning skills which should be employed to ask them follows:

A. Decision-Making Questions

- Who are the key contacts on the account decision makers and influencers?

  "How does your decision-making process work?"

  "Who will be involved?"

  "How long do you need to reach a decision?"

B. Relationship Questions
- "How are we doing?" (How the client sees the relationship with you, performance, and his or her relationship with competitors.)
- "Am I doing the right thing?" "What do you want me to do?" (Action steps) (How you as an individual salesperson are meeting the client's needs.)
- "How satisfied have you been with our service except for this? How do you feel we handled...?"
- "Is our billing detailed and timely enough for you?" (Logistics of the account.)
- "When is a good time to call?" "When shall I call back?"
- "May I ask who you do business with?" "Who is the best? What do you like about them? Who else do you work with?"
- "Who else have you spoken to? Have you gotten proposals? What do you think...?"

C. Operation Questions
- "How do you do it?" (How does the client's production or organization work?)
- "How many or how often...? What is their...?"
- "What budget have you set?" (Does this customer qualify?)

D. Problem Questions
- "What is going on? What would your ideal situation be?" "What gaps do you see? (Don't ask this question too early (the right to have it answered must be earned.)

E. Strategy Questions
- "What is your strategy/thinking in...?"
- "May I ask why you want to go from X to Y?" (For example, manual to computer (find out why the customer wants to change.)
- "How will affect autonomy of..." (Changing roles in client organization.)

- "Longer range, how are you...?" (Checking the 5-year plan.)

F. Interpersonal Questions
- "Where do you live?" "Where do you go on vacation?" (What are the client's interests, family, situations?)

G. Need Questions
- "Where are you looking to achieve?" "How is that working?"
- "To what extent have you bought...?" (Likes/ dislikes(what does the client buy/not buy?)

Questions are the tools used to help clients. They get beneath the surface of demands, and they expose needs. If a caller doesn't let clients talk, he may never get to know what their concerns are, and will probably miss getting their business. Questions are the best way to get them to talk; then he must listen well and leverage what is learned.

Listening

Being a good listener is one of the critical skills in selling, whether the selling is face to face or over the telephone, but listening is even more important in telephone selling.

Some tips for developing telephone listening skills are:

- Do not interrupt. Be conscious of this. Let yourself be interrupted; stop talking and listen.
- Make an effort to focus on what the client is saying. You are "on duty," so stay tuned in. Don't mentally abandon your post. Take notes as you listen and underline words your clients underscore with their voices so you can incorporate them in what you say.
- Listen for pivotal words, wide words, key ideas, words that are inflected, and concerns and jot them down. These can be neon words that light up the client's voice or wide or ambiguous words you will need to clear up.
- Listen for tone and pace and match both to become congruent with the clients, not to mimic them. For

example, if the client is speaking softly and slowly, you are bound to be out of sync if you are loud and fast. Slow it up and soften it a bit to create a congruency. Pick up the client's approach and language. For instance, when the client is upbeat and highly articulate, be upbeat, articulate; when the client is serious and straightforward, be serious, straightforward. Always be professional. Avoid being down.

- Be careful in how and when you use jargon. Jargon is good shorthand only if everybody understands it. Often in a face-to-face call you can read confusion or a question from the client's expression, but over the telephone this is not possible. So limit your use of jargon unless you are absolutely certain the client is familiar with it. When you do use a term that your client may or may not know, briefly define it, almost parenthetically. And as you cover each key point, remember to check if the client has any questions.

Positioning Product

Positioning is truly the super skill. By knowing the client's perceptions, preferences, and needs a telemarketer will be able to craft his product or idea accordingly. Positioning enables one to personalize, tailor, and get into a flow with the client.

To help position a product as it is sold over the telephone a telemarketer can follow these suggestions:

Play devil's advocate before you pick up the telephone and ask yourself "What is in it for the client?"

Come up with three compelling reasons why this client might be interested in your product. But remember to use the reasons one at a time and to check (question) before and after each one.

Do your homework on your clients and their organizations(begin to identify their business and nonbusiness needs.

Know your features and benefits so you know what you are talking about.

Ask "open" need and strategy questions so that you will understand the client.

Listen

Tailor your statements and questions to the client you are approaching. An engineer may want to know details on how things work, but a purchasing manager may want to focus more on price and warranties.

Personalize your messages as well. Ask questions to get specific information on each client's approach and style.

Use your total offer. (core and value-added features and benefits)

Know your objective. For example, if you are an institutional salesperson, ask yourself if this is a call to do a trade now or a call to build the relationship for a trade in the future?

Plan your action step (know what your follow-up plan is and initiate it.

Use your features and benefits one at a time (at most two at a time) and check for feedback.

Use benefits early or your client is likely to say, "Listen, I've got to go."

When you don't have an answer, say, "Let me look into that. What specifically...? When...?"

Be selective. You have limited time over the telephone, so select key features and benefits and present them with an eye toward what the client wants to do.

Link features with their benefits by using words such as which means and so that to bond features with benefits. ("feature" which means "benefit")

Listen to what your clients say and incorporate their ideas into your responses.

Take notes as you listen so that you can incorporate your client's words now and again later. But don't repeat inflammatory words such as "absurdly low trade-in figure" which may further reinforce a misperception.

Listen to the client's voice. Read between the lines and adjust.

Speak your client's language

Avoid jargon unless you are talking to another "Pro." Jargon is a great shorthand only if everyone understands it.

Match the client's level of sophistication (avoid talking down to clients or talking over their heads.

Be accurate in the information you provide, but don't wait until you have perfect information. Let your clients know when your information may be imperfect, but also let them know you care about giving timely information.

Choose your own words selectively. Avoid phrases such as "You wouldn't be interested in..." or "I'm just calling about..." Instead, use persuasive, confident words.

Avoid the term product. It is better to say, "We have a way to increase interest..." rather than, "We have a product called X."

Check (ask for feedback, keep the dialogue going, get a measure of how you are doing throughout the call, especially since you don't have the benefit of reading the clients' facial expressions to gauge their reactions. Keep checking. Keep asking, "How does that sound?" Get feedback.

Checking

Checking lets a person get feedback from a client on what is being discussed. Checking means asking questions to gauge the client's reactions and is an essential skill in telephone selling, since one cannot see the client's reactions. Checking helps avoid waiting until the end of the call, if even then, to find out where the client is.

Checking means asking the client questions throughout the call to get direct feedback on what was just said. Checking allows one to find out something far more important than what he thinks. It helps find out what the client thinks.

Checking is not designed to get the client to say yes. It is designed to get at what the client thinks (Yes or No. Checking is an essential skill for salespeople who want to know, really know, their clients' needs and how well they stack up to meet them. It's designed to get good or bad feedback so that the salesperson can position and close.

All six critical skills (presence, rapport, questioning, listening, positioning, and checking (work together. They are interrelated, they form a skill set. A weakness in any one of these six critical skills will lower overall performance. The six critical skills are sales muscles; they provide sales strength and flexibility for salespeople.

THE FUTURE OF TELEMARKETING

Telemarketing has grown very rapidly over the past fifteen years, as Telemarketing grows, many important new trends emerge that can shape and influence Telemarketing quickly in the future.

Global Multilingual Telemarketing

Global multilingual Telemarketing is expected to increase during 1990s. thanks to the opening of world markets, the spread of international 800-number service, and the fact that for multinational firms, foreign sales are growing by 15 percent, compared to a 4.5 percent domestic growth rate.

How Telemarketing has prospered in other countries depends upon how many phones a country has. It's a fairly common apparatus in countries like France and Great Britain, but practically nonexistent in Brazil, which has only one phone for every eleven residents. Telemarketing is growing in Japan, although high phone rates mean it is used primarily as a business tool. But the growth rate for Telemarketing activities is surging everywhere as telephones proliferate and rates decline.

Whether calls are domestic or international, multilingual marketing lets firms expand into new markets and improve customer service and customer loyalty by enabling them to speak in a language their customers understand.

"We will see global Telemarketing expand a hundredfold in the future," says Ken Knecht, an expert of Telemarketing. "As international telephone rates come down, it will be possible to take calls from anywhere in the world and place them, too."

Tighter Labour Market

Labour market experts predict a 39 percent increase in marketing and sales positions in coming years, making it one of the fastest-growing segments of the economy. As opportunities for Telemarketing grow, the supply of qualified help will slow. To attract and retain employees, employers will have to offer a whole host of benefits designed to meet the needs of a new generation of workers. Part-time, flexible, and stay-at-home jobs are expected to increase as employers make their workplaces more family friendly. More generous family-leave policies and child-care subsidies can also be expected, because they help lower turnover and improve productivity.

But Telemarketing is not a recession-proof business, and some Telemarketing operations will fold. One example is Sears, when Sears shut down its catalog in 1993, it also closed seven of its eleven "telecatalog" centers and shifted the surviving centers from order taking to handling customer service calls.

Increasing Focus on Sales and Service

Many people believe that Telemarketing is the perfect growth tool for an economy that is moving from a manufacturing to a service base. "The more people this industry trains, the greater the potential for the U.S. service industry," "Telemarketing is all about customer contact, dealing with the public. It gets us away from the old manufacturing mentality." says Henry Greene, an expert of Telemarketing. "Telemarketing is finally coming out of the closet, as it were," says Greene, "Companies are using it proudly. It's not stuck in the basement, it's on the first floor. Over time, improved technology will make it an even more personal marketing tool."

Privacy Legislation

One trend that will absolutely affect the Telemarketing industry is the increasing demand for privacy regulation. The privacy controversy arose around the use of automatic outbound dialers that can be programmed to ring every number in a given exchange. Privacy advocates argue that outbound Telemarketing invades the sanctity of an individual's home and should be limited. Others don't mind receiving telephone solicitations, but believe that their hours should be limited. The only question is exactly what changes legislation might require.

The first major piece of legislation to limit Telemarketing was the Telephone Consumer Protection Act, signed into law by George Bush. It requires consumer marketers to: 1. Limit outbound calling hours to 8:00 a.m. to 9:00 p.m. in the recipient's time zone. This is no problem for today's sophisticated software, which automatically halts calls to each time zone at the given deadline. 2. Maintain a permanent "do not call" file of people who have asked not to be contacted by the marketer. It's up to the marketer, not the service bureau, to maintain this list. While consumer awareness of this new option is rising, only about 1 percent of consumers contacted request "do not call" status. The act also banned prerecorded commercial messages to residences without the consent of the called party, although this rule was later struck down by a federal judge.

In the face of new privacy legislation, some marketers are returning to direct mail to prospect for new business, reserving Telemarketing for calls made to customers or prospects they have already contacted. But legislation is not the only obstacle to Telemarketing. The same technology that permits massive Telemarketing applications also enables consumers to keep out unwanted callers. Consumers can use Caller I.D. to avoid calls from unknown numbers.

Neither legislation nor technology will have much impact on the business-to-business segment of Telemarketing. Buying and selling products and services is the heart of business, and it will continue despite the controls placed on outbound consumer Telemarketing.

The Electronic Superhighway

Much is made of the new "electronic superhighway" that is projected to replace today's telecommunication system. Now being constructed through an alliance of cable, telephone, and software companies, the system is expected to permit interactive communications between homes and businesses. The superhighway will allow consumers to choose from a vast selection of entertainment Programmes, or shop at home by viewing merchandise from an extensive menu and placing orders through a remote keypad.

Without a doubt, telecommunications technology will be essential in making the electronic superhighway a reality. The new interactive media can replace the need for a live voice on the phone.

Marketing of Telemarketing

The concern for quality is in the marketing portion of Telemarketing. Over the past several decades of growth, much more sophistication in telephone techniques has developed and the ability to move beyond simple telephone sales has been enhanced. But truly to earn the right to use the term Telemarketing the industry must go further.

If problems can be overcome and the industry keeps moving forward, the size and complexity of Telemarketing Programmes will continue to grow. The level of marketing expertise of clients whether internal or external, will certainly continue to increase. The number and the subtlety of suitable Telemarketing applications can be expected to explode to remarkable new levels. The range of quality and complexity of products and services offered by phone can be expected to rise dramatically. Both the total dollar volume and the average size of a Telemarketing order will continue to grow. And the sheer volume of calls will be staggering.

If the industry is not only to keep pace, but also to stay a step ahead of the complexity of challenges and opportunities that the future will bring, there is a very significant need for improvement in the quality and sophistication of the industry's marketing capabilities and techniques. The ability to coordinate with and use state-of-the-art marketing research, direct mail, print advertising, and the electronic media must improve. And the systems, software, and hardware required to use effectively the innovative new methodologies that have been developed must be created.

With the improvement in the quality and sophistication of those areas must come the development of more effective methods of results projection and Programme analysis. There is a need to increase sales and research capability while improving the back-end results and order fulfillment techniques.

On account of the above considerations it can be anticipated that several driving forces that will continue the expansion of Telemarketing:

1. Continuing demand for convenience and speed in the transaction of business.
2. Continued improvement in the capabilities and the price performance of computer technologies and telecommunication.
3. The abundance of software support systems that facilitate the development of more extensive and more creative databases about customers and potential customers.
4. Continued increase in the cost for other forms of communicating with customers.
5. Increase in the knowledge of how to develop successfully and operate telemarketing Programmes.

FIELD INTERVIEWS BY TELEPHONE

The Design of the Form Used in the Field Interviews

The purpose of the field interviews is to survey the some of responses and opinions of households on Telemarketing, and then to compile statistics and analyze the results.

All of the field interviews are made by telephone. The interview form includes a brief introduction and nine questions.

Part one:

Hello,

I am a graduate student doing a research on "Telemarketing," I would like to know your opinions about this marketing method. Your response is very important to me. Please take few minutes to answer a few questions. This brief introduction and request began the interview.

Part two:

Question 1. Have you ever received a "Telemarketing" phone call?

This is the most essential question, if the answer is "No," skip to last question and end this field interview. It was anticipated that almost all respondents would have received at least one call.

Question 2. How many times have you received Telemarketing phone calls in the past six months?

This question was intended to give some insight into how many times householders in the area of the survey received Telemarketing phone call in the past six months. Statistics were then compiled.

Question 3. Have you ever purchased anything as the result of a Telemarketing phone call?

This question was designed to determine whether the person interviewed had ever accepted a Telemarketing appeal or not. If the answer was "No," the interviewer skipped to question 6 to determine the reason.

Question 4. If you accepted the Telemarketing, what was the most important factor?

This question was meant to determine what the attractive factor was if the buyer accepted the Telemarketing.

Question 5. Were you satisfied with your purchase?

This question was asked to determine whether the buyer was satisfied or not with the products purchased as a result Telemarketing.

Question 6. Why didn't you purchase? (This question is for question 3 whose answer is "No.")

If the person rejected the Telemarketing in question 3, this question was asked to determine the reason.

Question 7. If sellers from whom you regularly purchase keep in touch with you by Telemarketing, what is your feeling?

This question was meant to determine the buyer's feeling about the sellers who keep in touch with buyers by Telemarketing.

Question 8. In your opinion, who is better at Telemarketing?

This question was intended to give some insight into how the sex of telemarketer influenced the buyer.

Question 9. What would be your response if you received a Telemarketing phone call? (This question is for those whose answer to question 1 was "No.")

If the person had never received a Telemarketing phone call, this question would determine what is his or her response would be if he or she receives one.

The Choice Method of Field Interviews Samples

The research used a near random sample method to choose people to contact. First a ten column and ten row table of random numbers was selected. Then ten 3x5 index cards were numbered from one to ten. These were shuffled and turned face down. One was drawn to select the column. The cards were shuffled again and a second drawing was made to determine the row. The first three digit number in the column and row selected was used to determine a starting page. The following one digit number was used to select a column and the next two digit number was to select a name. If an obvious business number was drawn, the next residential number was substituted for it. There are 556 pages, four columns per page, and about 80 rows in each column in this telephone book. A sample of 150 items was chosen from it and it was hoped that 60 effective responses would be obtained. As there were 556 pages and a sample of 150 was desired, one name was taken from every third page. When there was no answer at the number called, two additional attempts were made to contact an adult at the selected station. Altogether there were 60 useful responses yielding a forty percent response rate.

The Results, Statistics, and Analysis of Field Interviews

From the sixty effective responses, statistics were compiled and an analysis made for each answer in every question. To present the results more clearly, a flow chart and some pie graphs are used to display the responses and explain them.

The following are percentage analysis of field interviews for every response:

Q1. Have you ever received a "Telemarketing" phone call?

According to this response from all interviewed people, most people have received Telemarketing phone calls. That indicates that Telemarketing is very popular with sellers.

Q2. How many times have you received Telemarketing phone calls in the past six months?

According to the people that have received Telemarketing phone calls, 69% of them have received 5 or more calls, and most had received at least three calls in the past six months. That suggests that sellers use Telemarketing very frequently.

Q3. Have you ever purchased anything as the result of a Telemarketing phone call?

According to the people that have received Telemarketing phone calls, more than half of them purchased the product. This implies that Telemarketing is an effective tool of marketing, because more than half of people can accept it.

Q4. If you accepted the Telemarketing, what was the most important factor?

From this answer, reasons were obtained as to why people accepted Telemarketing. The most important reason is a "sincere attitude," the second most important reason is "credit" and "well-known company," the third reason is "professional knowledge" and "time length." From this result, it is concluded that projection of a sincere attitude is extremely important and the development of one should be part of effective screening and training of Telemarketing callers. Telemarketers should enhance their sincere selling attitude to get the acceptances of customers.

Q5. Were you satisfied with your purchase?

According to this result, more than three-quarters of the people were satisfied with their purchases. It appears that sellers know how to sell good products to the customers, and the customers are satisfied with the products, and will buy again.

Q6. Why didn't you purchase?

From this response it can be inferred why customers rejected to the Telemarketing. The most important reason is that they had "no interest in the product," with 60% of people choosing this answer. The next most important reason is their "concern about fraud," then "intrusion of privacy." This result shows if the customers have no interest in the product, or think that product is unnecessary, they won't buy it. In addition, about one-third of the people expressed concern about fraud and intrusion of privacy.

Q7. If sellers from whom you regularly purchase keep in touch with you by Telemarketing, what is your feeling?

In this result, nearly half of the people said they don't care whether the sellers kept in touch with them by Telemarketing or not. And, the feeling of good or bad is exactly equal half-half.

Q8. In your opinion, who is better at Telemarketing?

This is an interesting response. Half of the people are indifferent to the sex of the telemarketer. But for those who had a preference, most people preferred female telemarketers. Perhaps, customers feel female telemarketers are much more patient and intimate than male telemarketers. That indicates females may be better at Telemarketing.

Q9. What would be your response if you received a Telemarketing phone call?

This response is from people who have never received a Telemarketing phone call. 50% of the people said "I would end the call without listening," 33% of people said "I would be open to hearing caller," and 17% of people said "I would probably find the call intrusive." Because 50% of the people do not like to listen to callers, the telemarketers should improve their strategy of keeping the conversation going to achieve their selling purpose.

From the results of the field interviews by telephone, 90% of people have received Telemarketing phone calls, and most had received 5 or more calls in the past six months. This is not only to indicates that Telemarketing is very popular, but also that the sellers know the positive effects of Telemarketing and use it very frequently. On the other hand, 10% of people interviewed claim they have never received a Telemarketing phone call. Perhaps the reason they have never been called is because samples of field interviews were chosen randomly instead of by the methods used by telemarketers. It also indicates that telemarketers have an opportunity to develop their businesses further. It is possible that telemarketers should reach out to more buyers to get more effective selling.

According to the interview results, 54% of people have purchased from Telemarketers. No doubt, Telemarketing is becoming an effective tool of marketing. To promote sales by telephone is not an easy thing. Maybe traditional marketing methods are more easily accepted by customers. Fifty four percent of the interviewees have purchased products as a result of telemarketers, most were satisfied with their purchases. On the other hand, nearly half of people declined to buy anything. It is also clear from these results that the sincere attitude of telemarketers is the most important reason customers purchase. Of course, Telemarketing cannot allow customers to see the product and talk to them face to face, and people don't like strangers bothering them when they are at home. That results in one third of people not purchasing because of their concerns about fraud and the intrusion of privacy. However, it was surprising that only 20% of people were concerned about fraud, given the high rate of fraud in Telemarketing.

How can companies improve Telemarketing? Companies should teach telemarketers' skills about how to select the right time and to call the right person, keeping good attitude, professional knowledge, and controlling the time amount to let customers order their products. In addition, companies also cannot neglect their credit and reputations. Only good credit and reputations can make companies grow. Remember, 80% of customers come from 20% of customers.

Customer, satisfaction with products is also very important. More than three-quarter of the people were satisfied with their purchases, but nearly one quarter of the people weren't. If the customers weren't satisfied with the product, they will lose confidence to buy again, and the companies will lose their customers. Don't forget the most important reason that customers declined to purchase is their lack of interest in the product. So, attracting customers with an interesting presentation of products that will satisfy their needs is extremely important.

Most people don't care whether the sellers keep in touch with them by telephone or not. And, their feelings of good or bad are equal. Telemarketers should improve their selling abilities, change customers' bad feeling to good feeling, and keep in touch with them to extend their selling. Most people are also indifferent to the sex of telemarketers, but for those who had a preference, 40% of people preferred female telemarketers. Perhaps customers feel female telemarketers are much more patient and intimate than male telemarketers.

From all of the above responses of field interviews by telephone, it appears Telemarketing has already become a very popular and effective marketing method. Most people can accept it and give a positive response. If telemarketers can anticipate customers' needs, utilize Telemarketing well, and improve their skills and strategies, Telemarketing may have a better future.

REVIEW OF RELATED LITERATURE

Telemarketing is one part of Direct Marketing, Direct Marketing is one part of Non-Store Retailers. In this chapter, Non-Store Retailers and Direct Marketing are discussed. A full understanding of Telemarketing requires some knowledge of the more general subject of direct marketing, some of the aspects of direct marketing are discussed.

Non-Store Retailers

The definition of Non-store Retailers

Generally speaking, most people think that the focus of business activity is to build a store in a populous area in order to attract customers. But in recent years, a lot of businesses have gotten large revenues without shops or stores. That means that the epoch of Non-Store Retailers is coming.

Why Non-Store Retailers are Growing

Non-Store Retailers have existed for a long time. However, they have been growing rapidly in the recent years. Here are some reasons.

1. Increase in working women. Well over half the female adult population now works, and the number continues to grow, showing strength in all economic and educational levels. As a result, women have less time for traditional shopping. Convenience and time

become critical. Someday someone will come out with a catalog of timesaving products for busy people.

2. It is not easy to get a store. The population is growing but land is limited. As a result it is very difficult to find a location for a store to run a business.
3. Decrease in production profit. Too many intermediaries reduce profits.

According to the research data of International Management Technology Crop., the average growth rate of Non-Store Retailer is 17% in the most recent twenty years. It is higher than the overall retail trade's 10%. Japan has analyzed the motivation of Non-Store Retailers. Here is the result.

Direct Marketing

The Definition of Direct Marketing

The current "official" definition given by the Direct Marketing Association is:

Direct marketing is an interactive system of marketing which uses one or more advertising media to effect a measurable response and/or transaction at any location.

It is important to have a thorough understanding of the current official definition. Let's dissect the definition.

A: The expansion of new customers B: The various needs of customers C: The future attraction of non-store retailers D: The expansion of market place E: The growth of the operating earnings of retail store F: The counterplot for difficult to display merchandise G: The saving of investment H: The expansion of the limit for running retail store I: Others

- Interactive: Interaction one-on-one communication between marketer and prospect/customer is an important key.
- One or more advertising media: Direct marketing is not restricted to any one medium. Indeed, direct marketers have discovered there is synergism among

the media. A combination of media often is far more productive than any single medium, such as TV, radio, newspapers, magazines, and mailing.

- Measurable response: Measurability is a hallmark of direct marketing. Everything in the field, with rare exceptions, is measurable. Direct marketers know what they spend, and they know what they get back.
- Transaction at any location: The world is direct marketing's oyster - transactions can take place by telephone, at a kiosk, by mail, at home, at a store.

Direct marketing is accountable. It is advertising that can be justified and tracked. It is ideally suited for small business. Not only is direct marketing measurable, but it can be adapted to fit a budget and changing business goals. Like marketing, direct marketing involves analyzing the needs of a target audience and considering how best to design, package, and market a product or service that meets those needs. It means estimating the size of a market, thinking about the competitive environment, pinpointing customer preferences, establishing a customer profile, and devising a strategy to promote the product or service to that customer. But in direct marketing, the customer communication process is far different and so, often, is the way products actually reach the purchaser. In the traditional advertising, marketing, and sales process, a product is shipped to a distribution point such as a retail store. Advertising and promotion draw interested customers to the store, where salespeople can close the sale.

Direct marketing uses media to deliver a message that often asks the consumer to purchase through a separate, non-store distribution channel usually the mail or a private package delivery service like UPS. It may also direct the consumer to make a purchase through traditional channels.

Jim kobs, chairman and CEO of the direct marketing agency Kobs, Gregory & Passavant, describes direct marketing this way:

Direct marketing gets your ad message direct to the customer or prospect to produce some type of immediate action. It usually involves creating a database of respondents.

How Direct Marketing Started

There are historians who will argue that the roots of direct marketing are actually much older, but in the U.S. it is Mr. Ward and Mr. Sears who are credited with launching and refining the direct mail phenomenon. Both men, based in Chicago, used their "wish books" to market goods to farmers and small town citizens all across the country.

Aaron Montgomery Ward was a traveling salesperson who discovered that he could offer rural customers quality goods at up to 40 percent off if he purchased large quantities of goods for cash directly from manufacturers, and then sold them for cash directly to rural consumers. In 1872, he issued a single-page sheet listing items for sale and explaining how to order them. The single-page sheet quickly grew to 8 pages, and by 1884, Ward's catalog had 240 pages and listed ten thousand items.

As a railroad station agent, Richard Warren Sears took advantage of special freight rates to sell watches wholesale to other station agents, who marked them up and sold them again. When Sears, Roebuck & Company began in 1893, Sears branched out beyond railroad station agents, eventually serving the same largely rural audience developed by Ward. By 1897, Sears, Roebuck & Company had 318,000 catalogs in circulation; by 1907, 3 million.

When Ward's and Sears began, catalog distribution was problematic. The U.S. Postal System was still rudimentary in the late nineteenth century; while urban customers took home delivery of letters for granted, it wasn't until 1898 that "Rural Free Delivery" brought catalogs and first-class mail directly to farmers and small town residents.

Fulfillment – that is, how packages from Sears and Ward's actually reached rural patrons – was another challenge. Before 1913, the U.S. Postal Service delivered letters only. Packages were shipped via rail or by private carriers like American Express and Wells, Fargo. To receive a package, one had to go to the nearest railroad freight station. In 1913, the U.S. Postal Service introduced Parcel Post. Within a year, 300 million packages were shipped a boon to both companies. In the first year of Parcel Post, Sears received five times the number of orders it had the year before, and the increase at Ward's was almost as dramatic. That is about how direct marketing started.

How Direct Marketing Works

Getting a message "direct" to the customer or prospect means using a medium like direct mail or the telephone that can target a specific group of consumers with certain characteristics, instead of a medium like television that addresses millions of people at a time. In direct marketing, the message always requests a response the "immediate action" that it seeks to produce.

Responses can take a number of different forms. A catalog or a direct mail package asks recipients to purchase items by placing a mail or telephone order. But whether the response comes by mail or telephone, it can be measured. This means that the success of every direct marketing offer is evident as soon as all the responses are in. A lot of responses equals a successful offer, while less than was predicted means the offer failed.

The classic formula for direct marketing success is to build a list of satisfied customers, and then go back to them for repeat sales. That is why a database captures name and purchase information whenever a customer orders a book or a computer, sends in a check to a charity, or decides to go ahead with a security system installation. This "house file" is a direct marketing company's most important asset. It can be used to sell additional goods and services, or generate revenue by renting those names to noncompeting direct marketers. Even traditional marketers, such as package-goods manufacturers, are discovering that communicating with a customer database can boost in-store sales.

Direct marketing is sales, pure, and simple. Although some marketers are beginning to measure its results in terms of image, it is still radically different from traditional image advertising. Direct marketing is response advertising (through the mail, telephone, in a magazine, over the radio, or on TV, that is geared to making a sale.

The Media of Direct Marketing

Whether we use direct marketing for retail support, mail order, or business-to-business marketing, we need to define our market clearly, then select the appropriate media to carry our message to that market.

There are many kinds of media for direct marketing:

- Mailing
- Magazines
- Newspapers
- TV
- Radio
- Computer Networks
- Co-ops
- Telemarketing

Why Consumers Like Direct Marketing

Why consumer acceptance is growing so rapidly? Recent statistics from the Direct Marketing Association indicate that:

- Nearly 10 percent of consumers have spent over $300 on merchandise ordered by mail or phone.
- Among their purchases, 27.5 percent were for clothing, 16.8 percent for magazines, and 11.5 percent for books ordered by mail.
- 52.6 percent of the U.S. population ordered merchandise by phone or mail in 1991, spending almost $35 billion on catalog purchases alone.
- 16 percent bought items by mail or phone six or more times than in 1990.
- The total percentage of American adults shopping direct has increased nearly 70 percent since 1983.
- Annual sales of goods and services through direct marketing are over $200 billion.

Behind these impressive statistics are a number of factors. Understanding the causes and symptoms tells us what people want and why. Here are the major reasons.

1. Increase in the number of working women
2. Inbound telephone marketing
3. Debit card shopping
4. Wider selection
5. Central inventory
6. Shoplifting
7. Transfer of labour to the consumer
8. Improved graphic presentation
9. Mail order offers better customer service than do retailers
10. People basically don't like to shop

Why Businesses Like Direct Marketing

Businesses like direct marketing for its versatility. Time has demonstrated that there is almost nothing direct marketing cannot sell. It can be used to:

- Sell products directly to customers.
- Sell corporate season tickets for professional sports teams.
- Sell insurance and other financial services.
- Generate leads and convert them to sales.
- Generate traffic for retail stores.
- Launch new credit cards and attract new credit-card customers.
- Establish consumer demand for products that can be converted to retail.
- Get lower cost than other marketing methods.

"Traditional" direct marketing sales through catalogs and direct mail packages also run the gamut of possibilities.

Companies have discovered that they can use the direct-response media to sell a lot of commodities. Mail-order expert Maxwell Sroge estimates that more than 13,000 companies are involved in direct mail; it's estimated that hundreds of thousands are incorporating Telemarketing into their everyday sales and marketing efforts.

The purpose this research is to better understand what Telemarketing is, why companies choose Telemarketing, and how to do Telemarketing. Also it is to survey the responses and opinions of households on Telemarketing by means of field interviews conducted by telephone. The results show how frequently Telemarketing is used, the acceptance percentage of people on Telemarketing, the attractive factors that enticed the people to accept the Telemarketing, the reasons for rejecting offers, whether customers were satisfied with products purchased by Telemarketing, the responses if the people were to receive a Telemarketing phone call, their feelings about sellers keeping in touch with them by telephone, and the influence of sex on Telemarketing. According these responses, telemarketers can find a clear direction for effective Telemarketing and ways of improving it. This information will be good for Telemarketing in the future.

Telemarketing is a dynamic medium. When integrated into the total marketing process, it can increase sales efficiency and profits by qualifying leads, increasing response from catalogs, direct mail, print, and broadcast advertising, and maintaining contact with direct marketers' most priceless asset.

Telemarketing can be done on an ongoing basis or on an as needed basis, depending on the desire for new business. Telemarketing is an effective method of building business and it allows a firm to quickly assess customers' needs or interest in your business. However, not every business is appropriate for telemarketing.

Marketing is truly transition, and Telemarketing is becoming more and more an integral part of all successful marketing strategies. Information technology and database marketing have come of age in fact, it is these developments that have made Telemarketing possible and assured the need, acceptance, and dramatic benefits of this industry.

Whether the business involves selling, advertising, fundraising, market research, or customer service, Telemarketing will be a key to its success. Finally, it should be emphasized that Telemarketing is a terrific sales method. It is convenient, flexible, productive, and saves time and money. Use it correctly, and success is as close as telemarketer's nearest telephone.

Chapter 6

Internal Marketing and Sales

INTERNAL MARKETING

Internal marketing is an ongoing process that occurs strictly within a company or organization whereby the functional process aligns, motivates and empowers employees at all management levels to consistently deliver a satisfying customer experience. Relationship marketing stresses what it calls internal marketing. This refers to using marketing techniques within the organization itself. It is claimed that many of the traditional marketing concepts can be used to determine what the needs of "internal customers" are. According to this theory, every employee, team, or department in the company is simultaneously a supplier and a customer of services and products.

An employee obtains a service at a point in the value chain and then provides a service to another employee further along the value chain. If internal marketing is effective, every employee will both provide and receive exceptional service from and to other employees. It also helps employees understand the significance of their roles and how their roles relate to others'. If implemented well, it can also encourage every employee to see the process in terms of the customer's perception of value added, and the organization's strategic mission. Further it is claimed that an effective internal marketing Programme is a prerequisite for effective external marketing efforts. Key concepts of internal marketing include:

- IM functioning as a continual internal 'upskilling' process.
- Alignment of the organization's purpose with employee behaviour.
- Employees internalizing the core values of the organization.
- Motivation, reframing and empowerment of employee attitude.
- Inside-out management approach.
- Retaining a positive customer experience throughout the business objectives

Internal marketing used to be such a simple thing: an occasional product training day, a product launch at the annual sales conference, and a few memos to staff. Today's internal marketer faces a sterner, and much more crucial, task - driving and even changing organisational culture to ensure a business both survives and thrives. The Australian Marketing Institute's May webinar, 'Internal marketing', presented two case studies of internal marketing success, one which saved an Australian icon from oblivion and another that brought discipline and focus to a fragmented, uncoordinated recruitment operation.

The AMI webinar series is conducted through the online technology of Premier Global Services, which sponsors these professional development events. Members can participate in webinars from their home or work computer from any location in the world via the Internet and a standard telephone voice line. The first presenter was Maree Howard, head of HR, product manufacturing, AMP Financial Services (AFS), who told of how the company had recovered from a near-death experience that began in 2002. Its biggest business had breached its minimum regulatory solvency level, precipating a public crisis that quickly cost the jobs of the CEO, most of the senior management, the chairman, most of the board, and 500 employees.

"It was really quite a bewildering time for the employees," Howard said. "AMP was still basking in the glow from the

Olympics and they still thought everything was great. All the messages that had been given to them by senior management was that we were a company with a grand vision for global expansion. "The organisation had to change very quickly and the existing culture that we had just wasn't going to help the process. The new senior management team was passionate about tackling really deep-seated cultural issues."

Howard said AMP quickly had to become a nimble and commercial organisation. This started with job and cost cutting, and then moved into remaking the culture. "We got through this period largely thanks to our senior leaders displaying absolute passion and commitment and integrity for our company, and they took the rest of us with them for the ride," Howard said. AMP realised that its culture was not as performance focused as it needed to be, and that there were several strong internal beliefs that would inhibit the necessary changes. These were:

Inhibiting belief	Reframed belief
Big is safe	High performance is our only security
Low cost means low quality	Examples of where this is not so, such as Toyota
Low performance is tolerated	There are adverse consequences for low performance and higher performance gets higher rewards
Risk and control are boring	Risk management is about business survivaland high performance
I need to be involved in everything	I trust those with the accountability

Howard said that the key message was "only high performance will give us security". "That was a very confronting message for our employees," she said. "What it was really talking about was that nobody owes us a living and that our heritage counts for very little on its own. "It also gave us a very measurable goal for our employees. It allowed us to continually send a message to our staff that we need to raise the bar and that staying as we are, it's just not an option. We were trying to align our high performers and challenge our low performers, to say 'Is this still really the right place for you because this organisation is changing'."

AMP chose a 'back to basics' approach to communicate its cultural change. It eschewed the glossy brochures, coffee cups and abseiling-type options and instead relied on the passion and personal integrity of its senior leaders to transmit the messages, consistently and repeatedly. The message became 'The AFS story'. "We used story telling as our platform for delivering our message," Howard said. "It's quite a personal message, and we made our leaders use their own personal credibility and put their own reputations on the line for the way they delivered the story.

"Our leaders talk about what makes them get up and come to work each morning. Why they are staying with AMP. What do they see the future actually holding. The beauty of it was that it allowed the message to be personalised in a way from that leader and not as some glossy corporate message that was delivered without adequate content."

Reinforcing the New Messages

The AFS Story was launched at "town hall sessions", where the managing director talked about his belief in and passion for AMP and what could be achieved. Leaders in each part of the business supported and emphasised the core messages, making all employees think about how they could align with the new AMP. To reinforce the new cultural messages, AMP moved quickly to make changes to its structure, which was highly symbolic within AMP. "We moved our business to bring accountability closer to the individual, and not just held at a senior level," Howard said. "We tried to engage everybody into the new vision for the business."

AMP also reset the levers of its performance management systems. Misaligned benefits and handouts that sent the wrong messages were eliminated to get people thinking the new way. "We wanted to send the message that high performers in AMP will receive higher awards," Howard said. "We clearly focused on *how* people achieve the goals within their business line and their business strategy."

Howard said that one of the important lessons AMP learnt was that for messages to produce sustainable change, they had to be repeated continuously. "We repeat them on a number of levels and using a number of mediums," she said, from the managing director through to the local team leader. AMP has now moved its 'burning platform' from survival mode into 'burning ambition'. "So the goals are clearly aspirational; we are still on the journey," she said. "We have moved from 'high performance is our only security' to 'high performance is our best shot at winning'. We are trying to move people's mindsets around wanting to be part of a winning team, that AMP can actually be a winning team. Who is it that we aspire to be? What is it that AMP could be for Australia in the future?"

AMP conducted testing during the cultural change process to check that it was working, using direct staff polling via telephone contact. As the changes were realigning the staff to business results, financial indicators were also used a measure of success. "What our results tell us is that it does feel like quite a different place," Howard said. "We have moved on very much from 2002. People are choosing to stay with AMP in a very hot employment market, and we're finding that as people leave the business it's not because of the way that we have moved the culture, it's for other reasons."

Howard said the key message from the AMP journey was to "create a burning platform. That's always the most powerful driver of change, it just feels quite painful when you are going through it. Create really simple messages. And when you are in a time of crisis, I think the integrity and commitment of the leaders is the key way to deliver it".

The Search for Best Practice

The marketing team identified and reviewed the best practices among units to ensure they were in line with brand integrity and DFR outcomes, with the aim of building standardised procedures and processes for the recruitment of new ADF personnel. The result was the *Regional Marketing Guide*, which was tested with Tasmanian units in 2003, modified, and rolled out Australia wide during 2004 through launch workshops.

The Regional Marketing Guide is a paper-based manual that contains target marketing information: unit-specific demographic information; planners; activity guides; proven marketing and recruitment activities with step-by-step guidelines, artwork and tools; a full suite of advertising artwork and collateral; and reporting functions and evaluation tools.

"We were not talking about coming up with complex modelling or anything; we were just talking about standardising the simple approaches to local marketing, which include activity guides and how to run an information session, and so on," Crosbie said. The key part of the Regional Marketing Guide strategy was that it was not sent out to the units unsupported. A purpose-built call centre contacted every unit across Australia, once a fortnight, every fortnight – in the process discovering an additional 30-40 reserve units!

The call centre has accumulated a huge amount of information about the reserve units and has ended up being a key source of Army Reserve information. The call centre staff check how each unit is going with its marketing and advertising, and keys the units into the 'how to' resources available in the Regional Marketing Guide. The guide is also complemented by a bi-monthly, hard-copy newsletter, as many of the units do not have access to good-quality technology and downloading large PDFs is not possible.

Evaluation results were positive

The marketing team conducted an evaluation of the Regional Marketing Guide strategy.

The outcomes showed that:

- At the launch workshops, 98% of participants believed the guide would meet their objectives.

- The guide was adopted by 100% of Army Reserve units.
- A satisfaction survey achieved a 100% rating for the guide as meeting unit requirements.
- The achievement of the DFR's recruitment target rose from 66% to 90%.
- Relations between DFR and the reserve units improved considerably, as the units could see that DFR was adding to the value of their business.
- Awareness of national DFR marketing campaigns rose from 15% to 80%, as the units had media plans for across Australia and could see the creative that was being sent out nationally.
- There was more efficient allocation of budget and resources for marketing.
- There was more consistent brand execution at local levels.
- Units came to understand the importance of evaluating their campaigns, and to feel that they were actually part of a larger organisation.

RELATIONSHIP MARKETING

Relationship marketing is a form of marketing that evolved from direct response marketing in the 1960s and emerged in the 1980s, in which emphasis is placed on building longer term relationships with customers rather than on individual transactions. It involves understanding the customer's needs as they go through their life cycles. It emphasizes providing a range of products or services to existing customers as they need them.

Development of Relationship Marketing

The origins of relationship marketing observes: "What is surprising is that researchers and businessmen have concentrated far more on how to attract customers to products and services than on how to retain customers". The initial research was done by Leonard Berry at Texas A&M and Jag

Sheth at Emory, both of whom were early users of the term "Relationship Marketing", and by marketing theorist Theodore Levitt at Harvard who broadened the scope of marketing beyond individual transactions.

In practice, relationship marketing originated in industrial and B2B markets where long-term contracts have been quite common for many years. Academics like Barbara Bund Jackson at Harvard re-examined these industrial marketing practices and applied them to marketing proper. According to Leonard Berry, relationship marketing can be applied: when there are alternatives to choose from; when the customer makes the selection decision; and when there is an ongoing and periodic desire for the product or service.

Fornell and Wernerfet used the term "defensive marketing" to describe attempts to reduce customer turnover and increase customer loyalty. This customer-retention approach was contrasted with "offensive marketing" which involved obtaining new customers and increasing customers' purchase frequency. Defensive marketing focused on reducing or managing the dissatisfaction of your customers, while offensive marketing focused on "liberating" dissatisfied customers from your competition and generating new customers. There are two components to defensive marketing: increasing customer satisfaction and increasing switching barriers.

Traditional marketing originated in the 1960s and 1970s as companies found it more difficult to sell consumer products. Its consumer market origins molded traditional marketing into a system suitable for selling relatively low-value products to masses of customers. Over the decades, attempts have been made to broaden the scope of marketing, relationship marketing being one of these attempts. Marketing has been greatly enriched by these contributions.

The practice of relationship marketing has been greatly facilitated by several generations of customer relationship management software that allow tracking and analysing of each customer's preferences, activities, tastes, likes, dislikes, and complaints. This a powerful tool in any company's marketing strategy. For example, an automobile manufacturer maintaining a database of when and how repeat customers buy their products, the options they choose, the way they finance the purchase etc., is in a powerful position to custom target sales material. In return, the customer benefits from the company tracking service schedules and communicating directly on issues like product recalls.

Customer Retention

At the core of relationship marketing is the notion of customer retention. According to Gordon, relationship marketing involves the creation of new and mutual value between a supplier and individual customer. Novelty and mutuality deepen, extend and prolong relationships, creating yet more opportunities for customer and supplier to benefit one another. Studies in several industries have shown that the cost of retaining an existing customer is only about 10% of the cost of acquiring a new customer so it can often make economic sense to pay more attention to existing customers.

It is claimed by Reichheld and Sasser that a 5% improvement in customer retention can cause an increase in profitability of between 25 and 85 percent (in terms of net present value) depending on the industry. However Carrol, P. and Reichheld, F. dispute these calculations, claiming they result from faulty cross-sectional analysis.

According to Buchanan and Gilles, the increased profitability associated with customer retention efforts occurs because:

- The cost of acquisition occur only at the beginning of a relationship, so the longer the relationship, the lower the amortized cost.
- Account maintenance costs decline as a percentage of total costs (or as a percentage of revenue).

- Long-term customers tend to be less inclined to switch, and also tend to be less price sensitive. This can result in stable unit sales volume and increases in dollar-sales volume.
- Long-term customers may initiate free word of mouth promotions and referrals.
- Long-term customers are more likely to purchase ancillary products and high margin supplemental products.
- Customers that stay with you tend to be satisfied with the relationship and are less likely to switch to competitors, making it difficult for competitors to enter the market or gain market share.
- Regular customers tend to be less expensive to service because they are familiar with the process, require less "education", and are consistent in their order placement.
- Increased customer retention and loyalty makes the employees' jobs easier and more satisfying. In turn, happy employees feed back into better customer satisfaction in a virtuous circle.

Relationship marketers speak of the "relationship ladder of customer loyalty". It groups types of customers according to their level of loyalty. The ladder's first rung consists of "prospects", that is, people that have not purchased yet but are likely to in the future. This is followed by the successive rungs of "customer", "client", "supporter", "advocate", and "partner". The relationship marketer's objective is to "help" customers get as high up the ladder as possible. This usually involves providing more personalized service and providing service quality that exceeds expectations at each step.

Customer retention efforts involve considerations such as the following:

1. Customer valuation - Gordon (1999) describes how to value customers and categorize them according to their financial and strategic value so that

companies can decide where to invest for deeper relationships and which relationships need to be served differently or even terminated.

2. Customer retention measurement - Dawkins and Reichheld (1990) calculated a company's "customer retention rate". This is simply the percentage of customers at the beginning of the year that are still customers by the end of the year. In accordance with this statistic, an increase in retention rate from 80% to 90% is associated with a doubling of the average life of a customer relationship from 5 to 10 years. This ratio can be used to make comparisons between products, between market segments, and over time.
3. Determine reasons for defection - Look for the root causes, not mere symptoms. This involves probing for details when talking to former customers. Other techniques include the analysis of customers' complaints and competitive benchmarking.
4. Develop and implement a corrective plan - This could involve actions to improve employee practices, using benchmarking to determine best corrective practices, visible endorsement of top management, adjustments to the company's reward and recognition systems, and the use of "recovery teams" to eliminate the causes of defections.

A technique to calculate the value to a firm of a sustained customer relationship has been developed. This calculation is typically called customer lifetime value. Retention strategies also build barriers to customer switching. This can be done by product bundling (combining several products or services into one "package" and offering them at a single price), cross selling (selling related products to current customers), cross promotions (giving discounts or other promotional incentives to purchasers of related products), loyalty Programmes (giving incentives for frequent purchases), increasing switching costs (adding termination costs, such as mortgage termination fees), and integrating computer systems of multiple organizations (primarily in industrial marketing). Many relationship marketers use a team-based approach. The rationale is that the more points of contact between the organization and customer, the stronger will be the bond, and the more secure the relationship.

The Broad Scope of Relationship Marketing

Relationship marketing has been strongly influenced by reengineering. According to reengineering theory, organizations should be structured according to complete tasks and processes rather than functions. That is, cross-functional teams should be responsible for a whole process, from beginning to end, rather than having the work go from one functional department to another. Traditional marketing is said to use the functional department approach. This can be seen in the traditional four P's of the marketing mix. Pricing, product management, promotion, and placement are claimed to be functional silos that must be accessed by the marketer if she is going to perform her task. According to Gordon (1999), the marketing mix approach is too limited to provide a usable framework for assessing and developing customer relationships in many industries and should be replaced by an alternative model where the focus is on customers and relationships rather than markets and products.

In contrast, relationship marketing is cross-functional marketing. It is organized around processes that involve all aspects of the organization. In fact, some commentators prefer to call relationship marketing "relationship management" in recognition of the fact that it involves much more than that which is normally included in marketing.

Martin Christopher, Adrian Payne, and David Ballantyne at the Cranfield Graduate school of Management claim that relationship marketing has the potential to forge a new synthesis between quality management, customer service management, and marketing. They see marketing and customer service as inseparable.

In spite of this broad scope, relationship marketing has not lost its core marketing orientation though. It involves the application of the marketing philosophy to all parts of the organization. Every employee is said to be a "part-time marketer". The way Regis McKenna puts it:

"Marketing is not a function, it is a way of doing business marketing has to be all pervasive, part of everyone's job description, from the receptionist to the board of directors."

Because of this, it is claimed that relationship marketing is a more pure form of marketing than traditional marketing.

The Six Markets Model

Adrian Payne from Cranfield University goes further. He identifies six markets which he claims are central to relationship marketing. They are: internal markets, supplier markets, recruitment markets, referral markets, influence markets, and customer markets.

Referral marketing is developing and implementing a marketing plan to stimulate referrals. Although it may take months before you see the effect of referral marketing, this is often the most effective part of an overall marketing plan and the best use of resources.

Marketing to suppliers is aimed at ensuring a long-term conflict-free relationship in which all parties understand each other's needs and exceed each other's expectations. Such a strategy can reduce costs and improve quality.

Influence markets involve a wide range of sub-markets including: government regulators, standards bodies, lobbyists, stockholders, bankers, venture capitalists, financial analysts, stockbrokers, consumer associations, environmental associations, and labour associations. These activities are typically carried out by the public relations department, but relationship marketers feel that marketing to all six markets is the responsibility of everyone in the organization.

At times Payne sub-divides customer markets into existing customers and potential customer, yielding seven rather than six markets. He claims that each market will require its own strategies and recommends separate marketing mixes for each of the seven.

When to Use Relationship Marketing

Relationship marketing and transactional marketing are not mutually exclusive and there is no need for a conflict between them. However, one approach may be more suitable in some situations than in others. Transactional marketing is most appropriate when marketing relatively low value consumer products, when the product is a commodity, when switching costs are low, when customers prefer single transactions to relationships, and when customer involvement in production is low. When the reverse of all the above is true, as in typical industrial and service markets, then relationship marketing can be more appropriate. Most firms should be blending the two approaches to match their portfolio of products and services. Virtually all products have a service component to them and this service component has been getting larger in recent decades.

Criticisms of Relationship Marketing

Internal marketing and the six markets model has been criticised as not really being marketing at all. At the core of marketing is the marketing philosophy of first determining what the market wants, then providing it. It is doubtful that this is what is occurring in influence markets, supplier markets, recruitment markets, or internal markets. What is occurring is closer to public relations, persuasion, and management. It appears to be marketing because it uses some marketing techniques, but it would more accurately be described as salesmanship.

Relationship theorists tend to compare themselves to traditional marketing. In doing so they frequently present traditional marketing in an unfavourable light. For example, Adrian Payne claims that traditional marketing concentrates on product features, has minimal interest in customer service, limited customer contact, and quality is primarily a concern of production. Although there may still be some marketers that think this way, these statements have not reflected marketing best practices for more than three decades.

THE ROLE OF THE EMPLOYEES IN INTERNAL SALES

As an Internal Sales Executive, you will be responsible for generating new business for hospitality. New business will be generated via outgoing telephone calls only, on the back of product evaluations, marketing campaigns and general sales enquiries.

Main Duties

- Call on opportunities generated from specific marketing campaigns, procured databases, reseller databases and incoming evaluations
- Make 60 dials, with 20 contacts per day (to include cold calling from prospect list)
- Work with Channel Managers and their resellers in joint marketing campaigns, giving input into the creation of data lists, agreeing timescales/ dates of campaigns and agreeing on a mechanism for feedback of information to the account manager and the reseller
- Accurately update in-house database information
- Support other sales teams on specific campaigns and ensure that accurate and complete information is passed to the appropriate account manager on time
- Conduct both specific and general awareness campaigns to promote hotel facilities and products within targeted markets, as directed by Manager, Marketing or Channel Partners
- Develop and maintain detailed knowledge of both hotels and competitor products and services

EMPLOYEE EMPOWERMENT

People are firm's most underutilized resource. In the new knowledge economy, independent entrepreneurship and initiative is needed throughout the ranks of the organization.

Involvement in an organization is no longer a one-way street. In today's corporate environment a manager must work towards engaging organization forcefully enough to achieve its objectives. New knowledge-based enterprises are characterized by flat hierarchical structures and multi-skilled workforce. Managers assume more leadership and coaching tasks and work hard to provide employees with resources and working conditions they need to accomplish the goals they've agreed to. In brief, managers work for their staff, and not the reverse.

Empowerment is the oil that lubricates the exercise of learning. Talented and empowered human capital is becoming the prime ingredient of organizational success. A critical feature of successful teams, especially in knowledge-based enterprises, is that they are invested with a significant degree of empowerment, or decision-making authority. Equally important, employee empowerment changes the managers' mind-set and leaves them with more time to engage in broad-based thinking, visioning, and nurturing. This intelligent and productive division of duties between visionary leaders, focusing on emerging opportunities, and empowered employees, running the business unit day to day (with oversight on the leader's part) provides for a well-managed enterprise with strong growth potential.

Employee empowerment is a two sided coin. For employees to be empowered the management leadership must want and believe that employee empowerment makes good business sense and employees must act. Let us be clear about one thing immediately, employee empowerment does not mean that management no longer has the responsibility to lead the organization and is not responsible for performance. If anything the opposite is true. Stronger leadership and accountability is demanded in an organization that seeks to empower employees. This starts with the executive leadership, through all management levels and includes front line supervisors. It is only when the entire organization is willing to work as a team that the real benefits of employee empowerment are realized. For an organization to practice and foster employee empowerment the management must trust and communicate with employees. Employee communication is one of the strongest signs of employee empowerment. Honest and repeated communication from elements of the strategic plan, key performance indicators, financial performance, down to daily decision making.

If an organization has not be actively cultivating employee empowerment, it may take considerable time and effort before employees start to respond. Often the first efforts and communications are met with employee derision and mockery. Those who are only interested in trying the latest management fad will give up when met with this response. A good rule of thumb for communications to employees is to enumerate what management considers adequate and then multiple by a factor of ten. When considering employee understanding and acceptance of decisions consider how long it takes for the management team to discuss and then make a decision. Allow several multiples of this time for employees to think about the issue.

For management wanting employee empowerment the evidence will not come across the board with wide spread acceptance. A small number will accept the invitation to become more involved, say 3-5 per cent. The rest will be watching every move to see what happens. Every communication, decision and action by management will be viewed as either supporting a move to employee empowerment or not. Probably nothing demonstrates the commitment or lack of commitment to employee empowerment more than promotions and selection for leadership positions. Employees know those that attempt to "shine up while dumping down".

For an organization to enjoy the returns from employee empowerment the leadership must diligently work to create the work environment where it is obvious to all that employee empowerment is desired, wanted and cultivated. Management's responsibility is to create the environment for employee empowerment. When organizational leadership has started to take actions to encourage employee empowerment it is then up to the employees to decided if they wish to take advantage of the opportunity or not. It is not unusual for only a small minority to accept the challenge initially. Also it is very likely that some fraction will never respond. It is the large middle group that must be convinced to practice employee empowerment.

It is our conviction that most organizations have exactly the level of employee empowerment the management wants. This is demonstrated by the amount of communications, level of training provided employees, opportunities for personal growth, the solicitation and implementation of ideas, the recognition and reward system, promotion and advancement criteria, and uncountable little signals from management that demonstrate whether employees are valued or not. When Six Sigma is deployed in an organization employees have numerous opportunities to demonstrate that they are empowered. Unless there is employee motivation to accept and act on the opportunities little will change. Employee empowerment is evidenced by working with a six sigma project team to understand the changes coming out of the project. Being a participant using improvements found by others is a form of empowerment.

Employee can demonstrate empowerment by suggesting areas or processes that might be candidates for a six sigma project. Part of employee empowerment is the recognition by management that often people who most know of pressing needs for improvement are those who have to work in the process. Employee empowerment can take the form of being asked to bring expert knowledge to six sigma projects. Even if not a full time member of the project team the fact that competence and first hand experience are valued and an employee is willing to help demonstrates a level of empowerment.

The employee can volunteer to serve on a project team as a Green Belt. This usually means that the employee has some subject matter expertise in the process scoped for a project. By completing the Green Belt training the employees will learn the Fundamental Improvement tools and will learn how to use the Define Measure Analyze Improve and Control steps as part of problem solving. With this additional skill sets the empowerment of the employee is increased, they are able to work more effectively and efficiently in solving problems and providing potential solutions.

Employees can make it know that they would like to become Black Belts. This form of employee empowerment assumes that the employee has the necessary skills and ability to complete the Black Belt training. Usually this means a college level education with comfort in mathematics and if not some statistical understanding a willingness to learn.

One of the strongest signs from employees is when they take the lead to advance their skills and knowledge with education and training either provided by the organization or out side the organization. Management has the obligation to create the environment that fosters employee empowerment, employees have the duty to accept the opportunity and demonstrate they are willing and capable.

INTERNAL MERCHANDISING

Many marketing efforts that should be assigned to specific people for coordination sometimes fall between the cracks. The great majority of hotels have a basic problem that makes it difficult to be as successful as they could be. The problem is that many of the marketing responsibilities are ignored or not given the attention they require.

It all starts with the definition of marketing. To understand the problem, we must look at the definition of marketing. Here's one definition: Marketing is the blending and controlled supervision of all efforts that affect the sale of your product. What are these efforts? There are a number of separate but related efforts that affect the sale of a hotel product -

- Research
- Public relations, including relations with the community, prospects, present customers and employees
- Product design
- Pricing
- Selling
- Yield/revenue management
- Media advertising
- Packaging
- Direct mail
- Planning/evaluation
- Internet marketing
- Internet merchandising

So what's the problem? When hotel general managers are asked as to who is responsible for their marketing, they often say, "We have a director of sales who handles that." Then later, when the directors of sales are asked to define their responsibilities, they usually include the following: all groups requiring sleeping rooms, plus corporate and government transient business.

Going back to the list of marketing efforts, who then is handling such efforts as public relations, packaging, internal merchandising, pricing, Internet marketing, and food and beverage marketing? The conclusion is always the same. Many of the efforts that should be assigned to specific people for coordination have fallen between the cracks and are handled on a piecemeal basis as the need arises.

Even in large hotels, where marketing staffs are larger and the responsibilities a little better defined, some efforts still fall between the cracks. For example, seldom does one find a hotel that has a well-thought-out annual plan for internal merchandising. If you ask what tent card will be featured in the sleeping rooms next month, you get lots of blank stares.

Many hotels that are members of national brands leave it up to the brand to do all of the internal merchandising without thinking about how this medium can be used to promote local restaurants and packages that would benefit greatly from this simple marketing effort. As far as pricing is concerned, seldom does a marketing plan indicate that a specific package will go up in price by $10 on a specific date.

The reason usually is that no one person takes responsibility to give pricing the attention it deserves throughout the year, rather than just during the week that budgets are submitted for the coming year. A lot of money is left on the table because of last-minute decisions that deserve more thought.

How to Pull it Together

What is needed is that close looks is taken at all of the responsibilities and establish a marketing committee chaired by your general manager to coordinate all of these activities? Spread the responsibilities throughout the hotel so several of your people will be responsible to the marketing committee for every aspect of the plan.

This concept involves getting more employees involved in the marketing of the hotel and encourages advance planning to replace the old "next Sunday is Mother's Day and we have to get an ad in the paper by 2 this afternoon" concept of marketing, a practice that wastes money and drives us to complete frustration. Planning your marketing in an orderly fashion will build a positive team spirit that will motivate your people as never before.

Producing Effective Materials

Generally customers don't want to read a lot of information before they find something interesting. Customers need to be inspired to 'try and buy'. Use words that are descriptive and eye catching:

Describe the freshness of the product:

- Pure
- Natural
- Real
- Freshly squeezed

- Hand picked each day
- Fresh
- Describe the environment:
- Free range
- Corn fed
- A herd name
- From our local market
- Home grown
- 'Happy animals'

Describe the overall product:

- Local flavour
- Traditional
- Inventive use of ingredients
- House speciality
- Chilled
- Ask your supplier what words they would use!

MAJORITY MARKETING TO MINORITIES

With the explosion of ethnic and racial populations across the U.S., smart businesses of all sizes are discovering the buying power of the nation's minorities. Just consider these statistics from the 1990 census. The Asian-American population exploded by 107 percent in the 1980s; Hispanic-Americans, 53 percent; American Indians, 38 percent; and African-Americans by 13 percent. By comparison, non-Hispanic whites increased by only six percent in the last decade. Immigration is a key factor: America continues to take in more immigrants each year than all the rest of the countries in the world combined.

In California particularly, the growth of Hispanic and Asian populations has been enormous. Hispanics increased by 70 percent during the 1980s, to 25.8 percent of the population. Asians doubled in numbers and now represent 9.4 percent of California residents. In San Francisco, this figure is 30 percent. Around the year 2000, half of California's population will be Hispanic, Asian or black. In addition to their sheer numbers, these ethnic markets are increasingly prosperous. African-Americans earn $262 billion a year, twice the gross national product of Mexico. Hispanic buying power has grown from $54.4 billion in 1980 to $172 billion today. And Asian consumers have the highest average household income of any group, including whites. They earned $36,102 in 1988-89, while whites averaged just $30,400 in comparison.

Many experts say that minority consumers show a high degree of loyalty. As their interests have historically been neglected, when a small business addresses their needs directly, it can have an enormous impact. In fact, the success of many small businesses may well be determined in the coming decades by whether they find ways to attract minority consumers – especially in California. Experts agree that businesses do not need to do anything different with minority segments than with majority ones. The basics of any marketing Programme – product design, development, distribution, advertising and market analysis – remain essentially the same. And the foundation of all these is understanding your target group. Here are some issues to consider.

Don't make the mistake of thinking that all minorities are alike. Not only are each of the major ethnic markets vastly different from one another, but there is also a great deal of diversity within a specific ethnic segment based on country of origin, and linguistic and sociocultural adaptation to the United States. In terms of the Hispanic market, the four major sub-groups are Mexican, Cuban, Puerto Rican and "Other Hispanic" – a category that mainly includes Spanish-speaking people from Central and South America, the Caribbean and Spain. There's a tremendous difference between the preferences and buying patterns of Puerto Ricans living in New York, Cubans in Miami, and Mexicans and Central and South Americans living in the South-western states.

Within the Asian category, there are more than two dozen ethnic groups, each with a distinctive language, religion, culture and value system. Topping the list numerically nationwide are Chinese (who may speak Mandarin or Cantonese), Filipinos, Japanese, Asian Indians, Koreans and Vietnamese. And within the African-American segment, French-speaking Haitian-born Americans, for example, may have little in common with American-born blacks. Equally important are generational differences. The first generation represents a significant segment: 70 percent of today's Asian-Americans have arrived since 1970. And half of all Hispanic adults in this country spent their formative years in Latin America. Obviously, non-English speaking, newly-arrived immigrants have far different buying behaviors than do third-generation ethnic consumers who have adjusted far more completely to a new culture and language.

Consequently, it is virtually impossible to create generic advertising or promotional tools that appeal to all segments of this diverse ethnic market. The solution is to pick a very specific target – a particular ethnic group in a particular location – and tailor your message to that target. If you are trying to attract more than one ethnic group, you may have to create more than one message.

Learn as much as you can about your potential customer's traditions and beliefs. And show respect in your advertising and other promotional efforts for that particular culture's holidays, ceremonies, and the meanings of symbols, numbers and colors. Red, for example, connotes good luck in China, but signifies bad luck to many Koreans. In Western societies, black is the colour of mourning, yet Asians traditionally wear white to funerals because it is the colour of sadness.

One way to learn about cultural nuances is by making contacts within the target community, and using these contacts as an informal focus group. Most ethnic groups have business organizations and chambers of commerce. In addition, treat your store as a research site. For small business owners, surveying customers is a simple form of research, and the customer's word is often the most effective data available, particularly when trying to understand subtle cultural distinctions.

Be careful when translating English, especially slogans, into foreign languages. And don't make the mistake of thinking that one generic pitch will work for all cultural groups. After establishing a general marketing concept, figure out which aspects might attract the particular ethnic group you are targeting. Then hire someone who knows the language (ideally a native speaker when creating advertisements with voice-overs) to express your message properly. In appealing to Hispanics, use informal "spoken" Spanish rather than formal Spanish, and be sure to avoid dialects.

The importance of ensuring that your advertising messages are translated properly is borne out by numerous cases of communication mistakes which even large marketers have made. To give just one example, an ad for an American-brand shirt in a Mexican magazine should have read, "when I wore this shirt, I felt good." Instead, the words translated as "until I wore this shirt, I felt good."

Use the native language media of the group you want to attract – particularly in print media. Since minority groups tend to be geographically concentrated, narrowly segmented media outlets – such as foreign-language newspapers or broadcasting shows (which are proliferating nationwide) – effectively reach high percentages of consumers. Many of these outlets are less expensive and more effective than their mainstream counterparts. Another way to gain long-lasting impact is to place an ad in the foreign language Yellow Pages available in many urban communities. Paul Sladkus, president of a New York-based ethnic marketing company, claims these publications are "like a Bible to the community."

Have staff members who speak the language of the ethnic group or groups you are targeting, and make sure signs and fliers printed in the appropriate languages are displayed prominently in your establishment. These simple and logical cultural sensitivities are appreciated, and can help spread positive word of mouth. 6. Reject stereotypes and cliches. Create positive images (or nonverbal cultural symbols) that are meaningful to the customers you want to serve. For example, Hispanics see themselves as upbeat, colorful and lively, and enjoy being portrayed as such. They appreciate commercials that convey a sense of pride in pleasing and providing the best for their families. In general, they do not identify with overt materialistic displays of success. Themes that appeal to Asian consumers include family togetherness, security and respect for elders. They value education, literacy and musical culture, and have a strong sense of community.

In the same vein, sharpen your sensitivity to cultural slurs or taboos. One widely shown commercial featured a woman who asks television viewers not to hate her because she's beautiful. Because a woman stating that she's beautiful violates Hispanic cultural mores, the ad inadvertently alienated potential Hispanic consumers. Another example of a cultural gaffe is an ad run several years ago by a large insurance company in a Korean magazine showing a family in traditional dress – Chinese dress, that is. Or take the full-page newspaper ads once run by Playboy magazine, famous for its rabbit-eared logo, wishing Chinese-American readers a happy "Year of the Rabbit." Unfortunately, the Chinese characters were out of order and made no sense. Such cultural taboos can be tricky for most non-minorities to grasp. No matter how good your intentions, you run the risk of accidentally offending the group you're trying to reach. That's why successful marketers have their promotional materials reviewed by members of the minority group or groups being targeted.

If you can afford to hire a specialty advertising agency or marketing consultant, the money will be well spent. They will be able to keep tabs on not only the language used, but the customs and traditions with which you may not be familiar. If your budget does not allow this, assistance is generally available from the advertising department of local ethnic newspapers, radio or television stations. Don't forget to also draw on the ethnic expertise of your own staff.

Be prepared to "educate" your audience. Understand that many are extremely skeptical of "official" proclamations and messages. Point out what's "good" or what works about your product or service. Product demonstrations or free samples are particularly effective in this regard, especially for new immigrants who may not be accustomed to selecting from a wide range of choices. If you and your product or service represent the high end of your field, don't be afraid to project an image of quality.

Finally, get involved with the minority community. Sponsor or help promote a cultural event such as an ethnic festival or holiday celebration honoring the consumers you want to reach. This will build name recognition at the grass-roots level and distinguish you from competitors, while at the same time help to build customer loyalty. This involvement is particularly important because many ethnic groups, especially those who have recently arrived in this country, attach high value to their local community. Underlying all these points is the fact that marketing will always be marketing. The bottom line to success – whatever your target group – is thoroughly knowing these customers and their specific needs. Be patient, for long-term goals have to be approached with long-term strategies. It will take time and a steady stream of communications to establish – and strengthen – new business relationships. But the effort is bound to pay off. The economic influence of ethnic groups will increase exponentially in the coming years, as those once considered the "minority" emerge as a new majority. Tapping into this vast potential only makes good business success.

A PRIMER ON PROTOCOL

Doing business in America today means working with a wide cultural range of individuals and companies – each marked by a distinctive style. There are, of course, some universals: wearing conservative clothing, the code of delivering on promises, business socializing, business lunches, and making new contacts are part of everyone's business life. Despite these common denominators, however, the styles represented in this increasingly multicultural marketplace reflect different business traditions and social values. And they're differences anyone conducting business across ethnic groups needs to understand to avoid problems that may stand in the way of bottom-line success.

Retail Relations

The byword of customer relations in any culture is always prompt, courteous service. Yet the requirements of courtesy may differ among various ethnic groups. Asian-Americans, for example, place great value on respect for elders, whom salespeople should treat with honor and greet specifically, if not first, when they come to the store with younger generations of their family.

Asian-Americans differ, however, in their behaviour as customers. "Chinese-Americans ask many questions," says David Hsu, co-owner of Huan Yuan restaurant in Oakland, California, "and they are very picky." Japanese-Americans also ask many questions – "a lot more than most Americans," comments Hiroyasu Kitagawa, San Francisco manager of Matsuzakaya department store. And they want informed answers without high-pressure selling, which they find impolite.

Korean- and Filipino-Americans, in contrast, ask few if any questions. "Koreans are very sensitive about loss of face," says Harry Kim, chairman of the San Francisco-Seoul Sister City Committee, so they are uncomfortable showing they don't know. The same is true of Filipinos, according to management consultant Rex Drilon of Fremont, California, who notes that brand-conscious Filipino-Americans, representing a $13 billion market, respond best when allowed to decide on their own. Latinos also ask few questions and are highly brand-conscious, preferring U.S.-made goods when they first come to this country and, later on, European ones. In addition, Latinos are turned off by sales pressure.

"They won't fold," warns Roberto Barragan, executive director of San Francisco's Mission Economic Development Association. "They'll walk away." Caucasian and African-American customers, on the other hand, may ask numerous questions. Caucasians are "very careful about details," comments John Goldeen, manager of H. John's clothiers in Oakland, California. "They need to feel sure an item is exactly right." Business Etiquette "We make a friendship, then do business with friends," emphasizes Kim in describing the Korean style of business. "We respect age, seniority and position," says Kitagawa of the Japanese style. But both could be speaking of Asian-American business etiquette in general, which calls for sincerity, politeness, modesty, tough but quiet strength, and deference to the decisions of the person who is in charge. Asian-American etiquette also calls for the patience to build a business friendship over time. For no transaction can ever be concluded until this friendship develops sufficiently, through social conversations and activities, to support the business negotiations that are proceeding simultaneously.

In Japanese, Korean- and Filipino-American companies, people are greeted by a handshake (a bow, for Japanese and older Koreans) and addressed by last names and professional titles. Punctuality is important – more so for Japanese, less so for Filipinos. And giving gifts such as liquor or tasteful logo-imprinted items is an established part of building business rapport. Chinese-Americans depart from this style in that they may wrap up a transaction in a single meeting ("There's no time to `develop a relationship,'" explains Hsu). More Americanized Chinese often use first names, except for elders, while traditional Chinese are not only more formal, but may speak little or no English. This is why non-Chinese companies should have a Chinese associate from a good family as their representative.

Similarly, Spanish is the preferred or only language in many Hispanic businesses, making Latino associates advisable for non-Hispanic firms. Respect for age and authority is extremely important, and deals may require that a top officer or sales supervisor from the firm that's selling pay a courtesy call on the decision-maker of the firm that's buying. Socializing is also part of Hispanic business relationships, and politeness toward all is essential because the decision-maker – the only one whose approval counts – may be a less-than-obvious person, such as the president's father. As for etiquette, last names and handshakes or abrazos (hugs) are used. And punctuality is required not of the buyer but of the seller – who should allow leeway for late-starting meetings.

In predominantly African-American and Caucasian companies, first names are most often used, handshakes (firm ones) are the gesture of greeting, and punctuality is appreciated. Decisions can be finalized in a first meeting. Participants in meetings are admired for the ability to expedite decisions through quick understanding, persuasiveness and articulate statements of opinion.

Business Meetings

Business meetings vary among ethnic groups in the way they channel conflict and accord power to the person in charge. For example, Latino companies operate on the word of one person, often the owner, whose decisions – sealed with a handshake – are not disputed. But, claims Daly City, California, business owner Alejandro Anaya, conflict is fully aired in lower-level meetings to "discuss alternatives for the person in charge to consider." Caucasian firms may "tolerate and even encourage conflict," notes Rosemary Muller, owner of Muller & Associates in Oakland, California. "The person running the meeting usually doesn't control who speaks, and there's a lot of give-and-take." The same is true in African-American companies. As Aurea Luis-Carnes of the Northern California Black Business Association points out, "We're all majority-trained from the cradle to the grave."

Among Asian-Americans, who strive for "consensus and harmcny," as Drillon puts it, decisions are made at the top, respected for their origin, and never publicly questioned. Among Chinese-Americans, however, strong disagreements are acceptable. "It's business," remarks Josephine Hui of the Oakland (California) Chinatown Chamber of Commerce, "and the bottom line is making money."

"We really care about you. We're here to help." These words, part of the recorded phone message at A Woman's Way Driving School in Valley Stream, New York, sum up the philosophy of owner Lynn Fuchs, a certified driver education and traffic safety specialist since 1979. Fuchs, whose copyrighted methods are being incorporated into the state drivers manual, offers very individualized instruction so students can proceed at their own pace. "We work as a team," she stresses. To accommodate increasing ethnic diversity, Fuchs hired a female office manager born in South America who teaches and tutors Spanish-speaking students on how to interpret the drivers manual. Fuchs, who has also taught non-English speaking students by diagram and nonverbal communication, finds that foreign-born men are more comfortable having their wives taught by a woman. "And women tend to prefer female teachers as well because they find them more patient and understanding." Fuchs' hard work and dedication in her field, together with efforts to reach out to minorities, brought her the recognition of being named 1988 Business Woman of the Year by the American Business Women's Association.

Kim Hunter Urges Sensitivity to Cultural Nuance

"If you're going to play in the African-American market, you must be sensitive to its nuances," emphasizes Kim Hunter, president and chief executive officer of LAGRANT Communications. This full service advertising and public relations firm in Los Angeles specializes in social marketing issues such as HIV/AIDS, infant mortality, teenage pregnancy, recycling and transportation, as well as health care, public affairs and banking. "While African-Americans are not separated from the mainstream by linguistic differences, as is the case with Hispanics or Asians, cultural differences definitely exist in how we communicate, dress and family values.

Businesses interested in reaching African-Americans need to get in tune with that audience to get them to respond." Hunter suggests contacting a local black chamber of commerce to obtain the right "sense of direction," and also strongly advocates radio as the most effective advertising avenue. "Whether rich or poor, African-Americans are brought up listening to radio, and are historically and culturally adaptable to that medium." Hunter warns against making stereotypical assumptions such as "all African-Americans play sports," and further advises that "people want to be treated with respect and portrayed in a positive light." Appliance Sales & Service Targets Ethnically Diverse Communities "Our staff is like the United Nations," explains Mike Hanika, vice president of Appliance Sales & Service Co. in San Francisco.

"Together, our employees speak 16 languages – including Arabic, Armenian and Cantonese." The company, which specializes in small electric housewares and personal care items, carries 80 product lines and stocks 14,000 parts. "Our database gives us acçess to one million parts in all to handle our wholesale, retail and mail order business, and we have three 800 lines to take care of long-distance requests. We also have four technicians on site who repair 1,000 units per month, both in and out of warranty." Hanika, who advertises statewide in the Yellow Pages, says that he targets market areas according to specific needs not being met by local competition. "In ethnically diverse communities such as San Francisco, we are able to provide shavers and clippers for African Americans, pressure cooker parts for Filipinos and Latinos, and ricers for Asians. And no matter what language customers speak, we can handle it." The firm currently has 17 employees, including Hanika's wife Carol, who serves as president.

Chapter 7

Restaurant and Lounge

RESTAURANT, LOUNGE AND BAR

The law concerning the placement of video lottery machines has been amended several times since the initial passage of the video lottery legislation in 1989. The law has always required that the placement of video lottery machines be restricted to no more than ten in number in businesses with an on-sale alcoholic beverage license. However, the initial legislation imposed no other restrictions on the placement of machines within those locations nor did it attempt to define the primary business activity of a business licensed as a video lottery establishment.

In an attempt to restrict the placement of video lottery machines, the legislature in 1991 amended the law to prohibit machine placement in general access areas. The law required all licensed video lottery establishments holding a malt-beverage or wine license to place machines in an area restricted to persons 21 years of age or older. This could be accomplished by either constructing a permanent wall separation at least four-feet high between the general access area and the restricted area of the machine placement or by restricting the entire business premises to persons 21 years or older. The 1991 legislation also limited the types of on-sale businesses that could be video lottery establishments to restaurants, bars, lounges, and lodging establishments. A restaurant, bar or lounge was defined as a business where "seating, food preparation or other activities directly related to the sale of malt beverages for consumption on the premises constitutes at least 75% of the square footage of the business premises where alcoholic beverages are served in the ordinary course of business."

The requirement that a licensed establishment be a restaurant, bar, lounge or lodging establishment only applied to businesses making application for a license after January 1, 1991. In 1992, the legislature again amended the statutory provisions restricting machine placement. Deleted from the definition of a licensed establishment were restaurants and lodging establishments. A licensed establishment is now defined as a "bar or lounge owned or managed by an individual, partnership, corporation, or association licensed to sell alcoholic beverages for consumption upon the premises where sold."

The 1992 amendment also deleted the 75% square footage space requirements for associated on-sale business activities. Bar or lounge is now defined as "an enterprise primarily maintained and operated for the selling, dispensing, and consumption of alcoholic beverages on the premises and may also include the sale and service of food." The new law provisions also struck down the minimum four-foot wall requirements between general and restricted areas. It does allow for a bar or lounge to be connected to another enterprise or business within the same building. While there may be interior access between a bar or lounge and a connected enterprise, the two businesses must be separated by a floor-to-ceiling opaque wall separation.

Policy

The history of amendments defining a video lottery establishment reveals the difficulty in establishing a consistent standard for the approval and renewal of such licenses. The legislature did not attempt to set minimum space requirements that a business would have to meet in order for it to qualify as a bar or lounge. Accordingly, nor should the Commission attempt to impose a minimum standard size for a video lottery establishment. However, it is the responsibility of the Lottery Commission to establish a policy setting forth licensing criteria to serve as a guideline for the renewal and approval of video lottery establishment licenses that is in keeping with the legislative intent.

The law requires that video lottery machines must be located in bars or lounges where access is restricted to persons 21 years of age or older. The law states that a bar or lounge, if connected to another business where general access is permitted, must be separated by a floor to ceiling opaque wall separation. Interior access is allowed between the bar or lounge licensed as a video lottery establishment and the other business enterprise. A sign must be posted at the entrance of the video lottery establishment that the premises are restricted to persons 21 years or older.

The legislature defined a bar or lounge as "an enterprise primarily maintained and operated for the selling, dispensing and consumption of alcoholic beverages on the premises and may also include the sale and service of food." For purposes of licensing a business location as a video lottery establishment, it must first meet the definitional requirement of a bar or lounge. It must include within the premises an area where malt beverages or wine are sold, dispensed and consumed in the ordinary course of business. The rules adopted by the Commission state that all video lottery machines in licensed establishments must be physically located in an area where alcoholic beverages are regularly dispensed and consumed in the ordinary and usual course of business.

For purposes of meeting the statutory and regulatory requirements, alcoholic beverages may be dispensed from an area contiguous to a licensed video lottery establishment.

While video lottery machine placement and play may be an integral business component of the bar or lounge, the premises cannot be designed solely for video lottery machine placement and play. The bar or lounge, in order to qualify for a video lottery establishment license, must also provide service and seating for the on-sale consumption of alcoholic beverages for patrons. Such seating within the bar or lounge must be available other than at video lottery machines and in relative proportion to the area reserved for machine placement.

The interior access between the bar and lounge and other business activity must sufficiently segregate the two businesses as being separate and distinct. The requirement that the wall separations be opaque means building materials used may not allow for activities in the bar and lounge to be viewed from the general access area. Windows or vents may be installed near the ceiling in the wall between the general access area and bar and lounge for light and ventilation purposes. The bar or lounge licensed as a video lottery establishment must be adequately monitored by management and employees at all times.

This may be accomplished by the full-time presence of management or employees in the video lottery establishment during business hours or by means of mirrors or cameras approved by the Lottery with periodic physical inspections by employees of a contiguous business enterprise to avoid machine tampering and under age play.

POINT OF SALE SYSTEM FOR RESTAURANTS AND BARS

Below is just some of the features and reasons why this is top of the line:

Wireless Waitress Restaurant Point - of - Sale

Wireless Waitress the foremost leading edge point of sale system for restaurants and lounges. The system features are near limitless, everything from back-office accounting and time management to customer tracking. The system has layered password protection to allow for quality and limited access controls. (For instance, a waitress could mark a percentage down for something that was what the customer wanted but only the manager could actually delete the item from the guest check)

Why Go Wireless?

Mobility- Allowing the server to go from customer to customer without leaving the table area, thereby cutting both the order-taking process and allowing for more time with the customer.

Line and Table Management

Improves table turnover and allows for pre-order by customer name, thereby reducing time it takes to serve the customer's requests.

Table Ordering- With a touch of a pen, a customer's order is entered by simply tapping on the screen, making the computerized printout easy for the cook staff to understand and consistent from server to server. When the order is entered, a touch of the pen sends it to the appropriate printer (kitchen, bar, etc.)

Why Computerize With Wireless Waitress?

While any cash register can tell you how much money that you took in for the day, perhaps even by shift, it cannot tell you how many of any one type of beverage at that price. By computerizing with Wireless Waitress, not only can you tell how much your gross sales was by the day, you can even see the sales breakdown if you prefer. Also, you will know how many beverages were sold, what type they were, and how many you have left in your inventory. Beyond that it can produce daily reports on such things as gross sales, inventory shortages, and employee scheduling/labour hours.

In addition, Other Things to Consider

- Reduce Theft
- Reduce Inventory Shrinkage
- Increased Control of Inventory Ordering Process
- See your Margins Daily
- Speed Customer Checkout
- Greater Accuracy

- Create a Customer Database
- Wireless Waitress costs under $3 a day to Operate but saves over $70 a day on average (based on $500k gross sales)

What's Included

- Touch Screen Monitor w/ all in ones point of sale software system
- Cash Drawer
- 2 Palm Pilots (for remote table ordering) w/ charging base
- 3 Thermal Printers
- 1 Wireless Router. All Associated Cables, Power Supply, & Manuals

THE BAR CODE

A bar may be a perfect place to socialise, but managing it is no easy matter. A pub or a public house, as it was known in the 18th century, like all catering ventures is risky business. Only here, the scope to lose money is much higher.

There is a lot that goes in the making of an efficient, well-managed and cost-effective bar. Spills, waste, over-pouring, free drinks or unrecorded sales, disputes, and theft are just a few of the inherent challenges that are present wherever liquor, beer and wine are served. The core of any bar management technique is to control the liquor inventory effectively. Every bar owner or club manager knows the difficulty - rather the impossibility - involved in this task because every place has at least one bartender with a heavy hand, or worse still, one who gives away the house.

The core of any bar management technique is to control the liquor inventory effectively. Every bar owner or club manager knows the difficulty - rather the impossibility - involved in this task because every pub has at least one bartender with a heavy hand.

Control is Key

Monitoring a bar's finances involves many activities including keeping tabs on its inventory, having a foolproof payment system in place, etc. The most constant aspect in the business that every operator would like to achieve is to control costs by preventing losses.

Every management ensures that the number of guests never exceeds a certain limit, which would otherwise make it difficult to serve or keep tabs on the payment. In some bars that normally accommodate 450 guests, the number sometimes exceeds even 700 during peak hours. Samir Jilani, manager at Insomnia at the Taj Mahal Palace & Tower, informs, "Luckily our nightclub is designed with three bars so the crowd gets distributed. Also, we don't allow the numbers to exceed a point where we can't manage either the entry or the crowd inside the place."

While the count of guests pouring in is important, of equal concern is the staff strength. Normally, the number of employees required depends on the number of bars in a pub or a nightclub and their size. On an average, four to five bartenders are enough. The floor waiters who take orders outside the bar generally number five besides one cashier and one manager who supervises the overall operation of the outlet. This does not include other hands required for clearing glassware, etc.

Many times mistakes in billing or overcharging causes a lot of unpleasantness hence care should be taken when dealing with bills. Often it is the duty of the floor waiters to either maintain a record of the consumption of a particular guest or collect their credit cards and hand them to the cashier, who maintains the record. There are people who get drunk and create problems for us. But a pub manager has to maintain his cool and handle the situation with tact. People do dispute the billings. At the bar the chances of dispute are less than on the floor. So the floor waiter has to remember what he is serving, when and to whom. We try our best to give beverages to the guest on time, but because the place is always crowded, it does take time for a floor waiter to serve.

The situation can get tricky where there is no proper seating arrangement, unlike restaurants where the table number is punched in the system making it easier for staff to track charges. In pubs or nightclubs with limited seating, guests tend to ramble. At times when the place is packed with liquor consumption exceeding normal limits, it becomes almost impossible to keep tabs with the result that guests walk out without settling their bill.

Payment Getaway

There can be other problems too. If the Point of Sale (PoS) software cannot keep pace with the guest inflow, pubs usually switch over to manual operations. Some bars find it convenient to switch over to coupons. But then there is always the chance of someone faking the stamp. Insomnia at Taj or Enigma at J W Marriott in Mumbai collect an entry fee and issue coupons in exchange for that value which can be used for buying food or beverages. But Czar takes cash or credit cards upfront at the bar, keeps tabs on the consumption and then charges the total amount when the guests leave. Shetty says, "At times guests do not give their own credit card, or give a stolen or an expired one and succeed in walking out without making the payment. That is when we suffer a lot."

Deepak Jethi, restaurant manager of Bandra-based Purple Haze, says, "A practice that is gaining popularity is the system of debit cards where guests pay a certain amount of cash at the counter and buy a debit card worth that amount. The remaining amount is refunded when they leave. Such cards are transferable as there is no bearer's name on it."

Some international bars have gotten even more innovative, like Bar Soba in Glasgow - a Scottish nightclub - that has found an ingenious method of collecting payment. It employs a microchip the size of a rice grain called 'digital wallet' which is implanted in the customer's arm. This guarantees entry to the club and allows them to buy drinks on account. The VeriChip is inserted by a medical professional and then scanned for its unique ID number as and when the customer enters or leaves the bar. There are a number of advantages to this VeriChip from instant access, to not having to carry money or credit cards, to letting bar staff know a customer's name and favourite drink. By the time they walk to the bar, they are greeted by the bartender by name with their favourite drink in hand. These are ideas whose time is yet to come. But until such a time, pub managers would do good to start from the ground up.

A bar is a business that sells alcoholic beverages for immediate on-premises consumption. (By contrast, a liquor store sells alcohol for off-premises consumption.) Some bars serve food or may be parts of restaurants. Bars that are part of hotels may be known in some areas as *long bars*. Alternatively, "bar" can refer to the specialized counter on which the drinks are served, and it is from this term that the establishment itself as a whole gets its name. The "back bar" or "gantry" is a (sometimes ornate) set of shelves of glasses and bottles behind that counter. Frequently when food is served elsewhere in the establishment, it may also be ordered and consumed at the bar.

Kinds of Bars

A topless bar is a bar, where, as an attraction, personnel (usually female) are topless. A biker bar is a bar marketed to and frequented by bikers, often sharing the "outlaw" reputation. A sports bar is where sports fans go to watch sports games and possibly meet other sports fans. A gay bar is where gay men and lesbians go to meet other gay men and lesbians. A cop bar is a bar known for being frequented by off-duty law enforcement agents.

United States

In the United States, legal distinctions often exist between restaurants, bars, and even types of bars. These distinctions vary from state to state, and even among municipalities. *Beer bars* (sometimes called taverns or pubs) may be legally restricted to only selling beer or possibly wine, cider and other low-proof beverages. *Liquor bars* sell everything from beer to hard liquor.

Bars are sometimes exempt from smoking bans that restaurants are subject to, even if those restaurants have liquor licenses. The distinction between a restaurant that serves liquor and a bar is usually made by the percentage of revenue earned from selling liquor, although increasingly, smoking bans include bars too. In most places, bars are prohibited from selling alcoholic beverages *to go*. There are few exceptions. Usually brewpubs and wineries can serve alcohol *to go*, but under the rules applied to a liquor store. In some areas, such as New Orleans and parts of Las Vegas, alcohol may be prepared *to go*. This kind of restriction is usually dependent on open container law.

Historically, the western United States featured saloons. Many saloons survive in the western United States, though their services and features have changed with the times. Newer establishments have been built in the saloon style to duplicate the feeling of the older establishments. Since the late 1970s, many Irish or British themed "pubs" have opened in the U.S.

United Kingdom

In the UK bars are either areas that serve alcoholic drinks within establishments such as hotels, restaurants, universities, or are a particular type of establishment which serves alcoholic drinks such as wine bars, "style bars", private membership only bars. However the main type of establishment selling alcohol for consumption on the premises is the public house or *pub*. Some bars are similar to nightclubs in that they feature loud music, subdued lighting, or operate a dress code and admissions policy and have bouncers at the entrance.

Australia

In Australia, traditionally the 'public bar' was where only men drank, while the 'lounge bar' or 'saloon bar' was where women or men could drink (ie mixed drinking). This distinction is not seen now as anti-discrimination legislation and women's rights activism has broken down the concept of a public drinking area accessible to only one sex. Where two bars still exist in the one establishment, one (that derived from the 'public bar') will be more downmarket while the other (deriving from the 'lounge bar') will be more upmarket. Over time, with the introduction of pokies into hotels, many 'lounge bars' have or are being converted into gaming rooms.

Italy

In Italy, a 'bar' is a place more similar to a Café, where people go during the morning or the afternoon, usually to take a coffee, a cappuccino, a hot chocolate and eat some kind of snack like pastries and sandwiches (panini or tramezzini). However, any kind of alcoholic beverages are served. Opening hours vary: some establishments are open since very early in the morning and close relatively early in the evening; others, especially if next to a theatre or a cinema, may be open until late at night. In larger cities like Milan, Rome, Turin or Genoa, many larger bars are also restaurants and disco clubs. Many Italian bars have introduced a 'so called' "aperitivo" time in the evening: everyone who purchases an alcoholic drink then has free access to an usually abundant buffet of cold dishes like pasta salads, vegetables and various types of appetizers.

Spain

Bars in Spain are very common and form an important part in Spanish culture. In Spain it is common for towns to have multiple bars and it is not uncommon to see two or more of them in the same street. Spanish bars are also known for freely serving snacks called "tapas". Due to a recent law being introduced, some bars ban smoking thought their number is comparatively small with the bars that allow it. Bigger bars must have always a smoke-free zone. Spain is the country with the highest ratio of bars/population and it alone has double the number of bars than the oldest 15-members of the European Union.

Elsewhere

In most major cities of the world there is at least one Irish pub. Some capitals such as Brussels have more than twenty. Bars range from down-and-dirty "dives" which are little more than a dark room with a counter and some bottles of liquor, to elegant places of entertainment for the elite. Many bars set a happy hour to encourage off-peak patronage. Contrastingly, bars that fill to capacity typically implement a cover charge, often similar in price to one or two cocktails, during their peak hours. Such bars often feature entertainment, which may be a live band (often of the blues variety), a popular D.J., or a variety (female impersonation) show.

CATERING SALES

Integrated sales and catering systems help property managers closely track room availability, monitor sales person productivity, and maximize profitability through the ability to set flexible rates and fees. Sales and catering system solutions let managers effectively communicate and coordinate activities throughout a property. The systems centralize event orders for greater visibility and help to simplify billing through the integration of point-of-sale and accounting systems. Guest histories are maintained for analysis and ranking. Using a sales and catering system, a manager can tell within seconds if all the rooms set aside for a wedding party have been reserved, if a corporate customer has placed a convention deposit, or if the restaurant can accommodate a 50-member dinner party sometime next week.

With an integrated sales and catering solution, properties can:

- Increase occupancy through focused management of room and meeting space inventory.
- Adjust rates to match current market conditions.
- Provide employees and management with quick access to information to help improve company productivity.

- Delight guests by providing quicker response times to queries and requests.
- Integrate legacy systems to help increase revenue and guest satisfaction.
- Use customer information to drive sales between multiple properties.

The Catering Sales Manager will be responsible for

- Solicit new and existing accounts to meet/exceed revenue goals through telephone solicitation, outside sales calls, site inspections and written communication
- Prepare correspondence to customers, internal booking reports and file maintenance
- Participate in daily business review meeting, pre-convention meetings, training and other catering sales related meetings as required.
- Work with other departments within the hotel to provide quality service to customers.
- Attend community/social events and industry meetings.
- Develop/maintain knowledge of market trends, competition and customers.
- Professionally represent the hotel at all industry/community functions.
- Participate as a team player with all departments.
- Assist with reports and/or competition data collection.

The Challenge

One of the biggest challenges in small hotels is to clearly define catering responsibilities. Does it belong with Food and Beverage or does it belong with Sales? Is it an operations function or a direct sales function? Over the years, customer needs and tastes have evolved, and new competition has emerged with demand for free standing restaurants, lofts and penthouses, and tourist attractions. With the many venue choices for customers, it is important to understand how to drive business into your venue. And with the impact on GOP, it is critical to maximize those revenues generated. Therefore, in order to drive market share and maximize revenues, it is necessary to:

- Identify and understand all of the components which create awareness in the market place.
- Generate the best and highest revenues on any given day.
- And successfully integrate and revise each component based on specific needs and market conditions.

The first step is to clearly define the "sales" and "operations" responsibilities" of the staff, to maximize performance. Then, understand and work with the components. The components, which are: direct sales, operations, marketing, pricing, and yield management.

The Components

Direct Sales

Many times, we refer to "Catering Sales Managers" as sales people, when in reality the catering sales manager handles only inquiries that come into the property, sends out contracts and event orders, and oversees the functions in an operations capacity. "Sales" is really just order taking and takes a back seat to operations.

1. Establish a Strategic Plan : By definition, "sales" is the proactive approach to identify and solicit business person to person. If "sales" is the goal, it is important to establish an action plan based on an overall strategic plan. A well established foundation will provide the confidence to "stay the course" and avoid rushing into short term strategies. The strategic plan should include targeted market segments, market position in competitive set, and demand/need periods. The action plan should be very specific and targeted, addressing in great detail, how to achieve the targeted revenues.

2. Training : If "sales" is the operative function, then also ensure that proper sales training takes place, as "sales" is a skill. Good looks and personality may open doors, but they don't replace professional skills to identify customers, understand their needs, and close the business.
3. Set Goals: Even with good skills, goals are critical to ensure success. Top athletes will tell us that they are much more competitive with score-keeping. Therefore, establish specific goals into two criteria:
   - New business booked
   - Business consumed

Breaking it down into the two goals provides a balanced way to achieve the goals. If new business booked is not tracked, it is easy to fall behind in the consumed business goals.

Additionally, effective booking goals are based on specific targets such as food, beverage, and other revenues, or based on specific market segments. Revenue goals should match or exceed the budgeted goals. A rolling 12-month advanced sales report will assist in maximizing revenues and in identifying need periods.

Operations

Small hotels, in particular, tend to have limited staff. Therefore, it is typical to have one catering position with sales and operations functions combined. But, it is wise to analyze the pros and cons of having two positions vs. one position which have two responsibilities. Sometimes, a direct sales function can generate substantially more revenues than the cost of the two positions of sales and operations. But that analysis can only be done effectively if a strategic plan and specific goals and have been established.

Lastly, it is important to have a clear understanding of roles and responsibilities, regardless of the number of positions.

Marketing

Once the position in the market place has been established, then all standards, operating and pricing philosophies are established. The quality and look of all collateral, web site, and in-house signage establishes an identity. Once that identity is in place, a plan should be devised and implemented to cost effectively reach the targeted markets. The marketing efforts will support the direct sales effort as well as reach other segments such as weddings and social functions cannot be solicited through direct sales. Demand from these segments is generated through targeted marketing Programmes and initiatives.

The Web is rapidly becoming the most cost effective means to reach potential customers, and is the great equalizer. High profile hotels, large, small, independent, or chain-affiliated hotels, all have the same opportunity on the Web when done with expert planning and implementation.

Pricing

Pricing is established based on the product offered and an understanding of the marketplace. Those responsible for booking business should have information on costs in order to negotiate. For example room rental could represent 75% profitability whereas, food could represent 33% profitability. The catering sales person will understand where discounting is less likely to impact profitability.

Knowledge of demand periods is key for negotiating effectively as well. Understanding these two elements places the catering person in a position of strength and confidence when dealing with customers, ensuring that the best financial interests of the hotel are met as well as inspiring customer confidence.

Yield Management

As in rooms, each segment for catering sales has its own booking trend and demand period. Therefore, by understanding each segment's patterns, the hotel can proactively establish selling guidelines to ensure that the space is sold effectively. For example, if wedding demand is high for weekends in June, it is important keep the space available for that lucrative business, rather than selling out to low rated business prematurely. Or if October is high demand for corporate meetings, monitor the selling of the space so that by capturing the natural demand, space is sold effectively. Booking a one-day group meeting on a Wednesday in peak periods would displace the potential revenues of a four-day meeting, which would be in high demand.

Additionally, it is critical to budget and forecast catering revenues on a daily basis, broken by meal period, and/or by market segments. Many times, owners and managers will project increases based on percentages, without looking on a daily basis. This can lead to faulty projections. For example, there could be greater revenue opportunities from weddings because of an additional weekend in June from the previous year. Or a mid-week holiday could decrease the corporate group business potential, compared to the previous year.

Even though there is software available for yield management, in my opinion, nothing replaces the good judgment of an experienced, competent professional.

A thorough understanding of where the business falls will lead to booking business which gives the highest return. And a proactive plan to generate business for low demand periods will create financial success. Having an in-depth understanding of each component and how to successfully integrate each one into a strategic plan, will ensure that an owner/manager will cost effectively drive catering revenues, and ensures profitability regardless of market conditions.

FOOD & BEVERAGES SALES

While U.S. hotels have enjoyed a strong increase in room revenue during the current recovery period, growth in hotel food and beverage sales, while improving, lacked the same kind of sizzle, according to an recent study by a leading hospitality consultant. Fortunately, tight cost controls by management have enabled food and beverage profitability to keep pace with the profit growth of other operating departments.

In 2004, hotel food and beverage (F&B) revenues grew 6.7 percent, the result of a 6.9 percent increase in food sales and a 5.5 percent bump in beverage sales. The 6.7 percent growth rate is certainly very healthy, but it does fall short of the 8.6 percent growth in rooms revenue, and 7.6 percent increase in total hotel revenues achieved during the same time period.

Mix of Food and Beverage Revenues 2004

Banquet Food	38.2%
Food Outlets / In Room	25.0%
Other	15.5%
Beverage Outlets / In Room	11.1%
Banquet Beverage	6.1%
Banquet Meeting Room Rental	4.1%

"While the magnitude of the increase in food and beverage revenue may have fallen short, the pace of profit growth equaled that of the other operated departments within a hotel. This can be attributed to good expense control practiced by F&B management," Woodworth concluded. In 2004, food and beverage departmental expenses grew 6.2 percent versus and an average of 6.9 percent for all other operated departments. The bottom- line was an 8.1 percent growth in food and beverage profits for 2004. This equals the increase in total Operated Department Income for all hotels.

Food and beverage revenues and expenses are just some of the 200 discrete hotel revenue and expense items captured in 2005 Trends in the Hotel Industry report. The 2005 report marks the 69 th annual review of U.S. hotel operations conducted by PKF. This year's sample draws upon year-end 2004 financial statements received from more than 5,000 hotels across the country. Hotel managers use the PKF Trends report to benchmark the performance of their hotel's revenues, expenses, and profits.

Volume Drives Revenue Gains

The growth in food and beverage revenues appears to be driven more by increased guest and customer counts, as opposed to increases in pricing. While food and beverage revenues measured on a per-available-room basis grew 6.7 percent in 2004, food and beverage revenue measured on a per-occupied-room basis grew 2.3 percent. "The implication from these two statistics is that the increase in F&B revenue was more attributable to the fact that there were 4.3 percent more rooms occupied, as opposed to any substantial increase in the F&B expenditures per occupied room. Of course, another reason could be a boost in food and beverage patronage from local residents.

When looking at the sources of food and beverage business for the typical hotel in PKF's sample, revenues from banquet events account for 44.3 percent of the total sales. This compares to 36.1 percent of the total sales volume that comes from the restaurants, lounges, and room service. The remaining 19.6 percent is derived from the rental of meeting and banquet rooms, as well as other miscellaneous sources. When looking at growth by the revenue source, we found sales emanating from restaurants and lounges increased 6.1 percent in 2004, while banquet and catering related revenues grew 7.0 percent.

Tight Expense Controls

For hotel food and beverage departments, the "prime costs" are labour and cost of goods sold. In 2004, the cost of food and liquor purchased for re-sale averaged 25.6 percent of total food and beverage revenue. Salaries, wages, and employee benefits combined for another 56.1 percent of the dollars spent in the department. Like most other departments in a hotel, labour costs are the biggest expense item. In 2004, F&B labour costs rose 6.1 percent. This compares favorably to the 6.3 percent overall growth rate in labour costs throughout the hotel. It also looks like the chefs and bartenders did a good job in the back-of-the- house limiting food and beverage cost increases to only 4.9 percent."

As a result of the tight cost controls, food and beverage department profit margins improved from 30.4 percent in 2003 to 31.0 percent in 2004. While food and beverage sales accounted for 26.2 percent of total hotel revenues in 2004, F&B department profits were only 11.1 percent of total Operated Department Income for the year.

More Free Food

Since the proliferation of limited-service and all-suite hotels, a growing percentage of travelers have grown accustomed to complimentary breakfast and/or cocktail receptions. These expectations have become so prevalent that an increasing number of full-service, resort, and convention hotels are now offering complimentary food and beverages as part of special packages, preferred guest Programmes, or corporate rate contracts. The amount of money U.S. hotels spent on complimentary food and beverage increased 13.1 percent from 2003 to 2004.

For the industry segments that have traditionally offered complimentary breakfast, growing competition and evolving social patterns have resulted in an increase in both the quantity and healthiness of the food offered. "When measured on a dollar per-occupied-room basis, limited-service and all-suite hotels increased their spending on complimentary food and beverage by 5.0 percent. Clearly, these segments are making an effort to upgrade the quality and quantity of the food and beverages they offer to their guests. Stale doughnuts just don't cut it anymore," Woodworth said.

Food and beverage serving and related workers are the front line of customer service in restaurants, coffee shops, and other food service establishments. These workers greet customers, escort them to seats and hand them menus, take food and drink orders, and serve food and beverages. They also answer questions, explain menu items and specials, and keep tables and dining areas clean and set for new diners. Most work as part of a team, helping coworkers to improve workflow and customer service.

Waiters and waitresses, the largest group of these workers, take customers' orders, serve food and beverages, prepare itemized checks, and sometimes accept payment. Their specific duties vary considerably, depending on the establishment. In coffee shops serving routine, straightforward fare, such as salads, soups, and sandwiches, servers are expected to provide fast, efficient, and courteous service. In fine dining restaurants, where more complicated meals are prepared and often served over several courses, waiters and waitresses provide more formal service emphasizing personal, attentive treatment and a more leisurely pace. They may recommend certain dishes and identify ingredients or explain how various items on the menu are prepared. Some prepare salads, desserts, or other menu items tableside. Additionally, they may check the identification of patrons to ensure they meet the minimum age requirement for the purchase of alcohol and tobacco products.

Waiters and waitresses sometimes perform the duties of other food and beverage service workers. These tasks may include escorting guests to tables, serving customers seated at counters, clearing and setting up tables, or operating a cash register. However, full-service restaurants frequently hire other staff, such as hosts and hostesses, cashiers, or dining room attendants, to perform these duties.

Bartenders fill drink orders either taken directly from patrons at the bar or through waiters and waitresses who place drink orders for dining room customers. Bartenders check identification of customers seated at the bar, to ensure they meet the minimum age requirement for the purchase of alcohol and tobacco products. They prepare mixed drinks, serve bottled or draught beer, and pour wine or other beverages. Bartenders must know a wide range of drink recipes and be able to mix drinks accurately, quickly, and without waste. Besides mixing and serving drinks, bartenders stock and prepare garnishes for drinks; maintain an adequate supply of ice, glasses, and other bar supplies; and keep the bar area clean for customers. They also may collect payment, operate the cash register, wash glassware and utensils, and serve food to customers seated at the bar. Bartenders usually are responsible for ordering and maintaining an inventory of liquor, mixes, and other bar supplies.

The majority of bartenders directly serve and interact with patrons. Bartenders should be friendly and enjoy talking with customers. Bartenders at service bars, on the other hand, have less contact with customers. They work in small bars often located off the kitchen in restaurants, hotels, and clubs where only waiters and waitresses place drink orders. Some establishments, especially larger, higher volume ones, use equipment that automatically measures, pours and mixes drinks at the push of a button. Bartenders who use this equipment, however, still must work quickly to handle a large volume of drink orders and be familiar with the ingredients for special drink requests. Much of a bartender's work still must be done by hand to fill each individual order.

Hosts and hostesses welcome guests and maintain reservation or waiting lists. They may direct patrons to coatrooms, restrooms, or to a place to wait until their table is ready. Hosts and hostesses assign guests to tables suitable for the size of their group, escort patrons to their seats, and provide menus. They also schedule dining reservations, arrange parties, and organize any special services that are required. In some restaurants, they act as cashiers.

Dining room and cafeteria attendants and bartender helpers assist waiters, waitresses, and bartenders by cleaning tables, removing dirty dishes, and keeping serving areas stocked with supplies. Sometimes called backwaiters or runners, they bring meals out of the kitchen and assist waiters and waitresses by distributing dishes to individual diners. They also replenish the supply of clean linens, dishes, silverware, and glasses in the dining room and keep the bar stocked with glasses, liquor, ice, and drink garnishes. Dining room attendants set tables with clean tablecloths, napkins, silverware, glasses, and dishes and serve ice water, rolls, and butter. At the conclusion of meals, they remove dirty dishes and soiled linens from tables. Cafeteria attendants stock serving tables with food, trays, dishes, and silverware and may carry trays to dining tables for patrons. *Bartender helpers* keep bar equipment clean and wash glasses. *Dishwashers* clean dishes, cutlery, and kitchen utensils and equipment.

Counter attendants take orders and serve food in cafeterias, coffee shops, and carryout eateries. In cafeterias, they serve food displayed on steam tables, carve meat, dish out vegetables, ladle sauces and soups, and fill beverage glasses. In lunchrooms and coffee shops, counter attendants take orders from customers seated at the counter, transmit orders to the kitchen, and pick up and serve food. They also fill cups with coffee, soda, and other beverages and prepare fountain specialties, such as milkshakes and ice cream sundaes. Counter attendants also take carryout orders from diners and wrap or place items in containers. They clean counters, write itemized checks, and sometimes accept payment. Some counter attendants may prepare short-order items, such as sandwiches and salads.

Some food and beverage serving workers take orders from customers at counters or drive-through windows at fast-food restaurants. They assemble orders, hand them to customers, and accept payment. Many of these are combined food preparation and serving workers who also cook and package food, make coffee, and fill beverage cups using drink-dispensing machines.

OFF PREMISES CATERING.

Off-premise catering is serving food at a location away from the caterer's food production facility. One example of a food production facility is a freestanding commissary, which is a kitchen facility used exclusively for the preparation of foods to be served at other locations. Other examples of production facilities include, but are not limited to, hotel, restaurant, and club kitchens. In most cases there is no existing kitchen facility at the location where the food is served. Caterers provide single-event foodservice, but not all caterers are created equal. They generally fall into one of three categories:

Party food caterers supply only the food for an event. They drop off cold foods and leave any last-minute preparation, plus service and cleanup, to others.

Hot buffet caterers provide hot foods that are delivered from their commissaries in insulated containers. They sometimes provide serving personnel at an additional charge. Full-service caterers not only provide food, but frequently cook it to order on-site. They also provide service personnel at the event, plus all the necessary food-related equipment—china, glassware, flatware, tables and chairs, tents, and so forth. They can arrange for other services, like décor and music, as well. In short, a full-service caterer can plan an entire event, not just the food for it.

Off-premise catering can mean serving thousands of box lunches to a group of conventioneers; barbecuing chicken and ribs for fans before a big college game, serving an elegant dinner for two aboard a luxury yacht, or providing food, staff, and equipment for an upscale fundraiser with hundreds of guests. On a "degree of difficulty" scale from one to ten—one meaning "easy" and ten meaning "most challenging"—on-premise catering is a two, and off-premise would rank a ten! G Off-premise caterers meet the needs of all market segments, from the low-budget customer who looks for the greatest quantity and quality for the least amount of money, to the upscale client with an unlimited budget who wants the highest level of service, the ultimate in food quality, and the finest in appointments—crystal stemware, silver-plated flatware, and luxurious linens. Between these two extremes is the mid scale market segment, which requires more quality than the low-budget sector, but less than the upscale. Off-premise catering is an art and a science. The art is creating foods and moods, as the caterer and client together turn a vision into reality. The science is the business of measuring money, manpower, and material.

Successful off-premise caterers recognize the importance of both aspects—art and science—and are able to work at both the creative and the financial levels. In off-premise catering, there is only one chance to get it right. Many events, such as wedding receptions, occur only once in a lifetime. Other events are scheduled annually, quarterly, or on a regular basis, and the caterer who fails to execute all details of such an event to the satisfaction of the client will seldom have another chance. Unfortunately for some, off-premise catering can be like living on the brink of disaster unless they are experienced. Uninitiated amateurs may not recognize a volatile situation until it becomes a problem, later realizing they should have recognized it earlier. Catering off-premise is very similar to a sports team playing all of its games away from home, in unfamiliar surroundings, with none of the comforts of home to ease the way. There is no home field advantage, but there is a minefield disadvantage!

As caterers plod their way toward the completion of a catered event, there are thousands of potential "land mines" that can ruin an otherwise successful affair.

Some examples follow:

- Already running late for a catering delivery, the catering van driver discovers that all vehicle traffic around the party site is in gridlock. The traffic has been at a standstill for more than an hour, the police say it will be hours before the congestion can be eliminated, and the clients and their guests are anxiously awaiting dinner.
- The only freight elevator in a high-rise office building has been commandeered for the evening by moving and cleaning people, thus preventing access to the floor where a caterer is to stage an event scheduled to start in two hours.
- The wrong hot food truck is dispatched to a wedding reception. The error is not discovered until the truck has reached the reception and the bride and groom are ready for their guests to be served. It will take more than an hour to send the correct truck with the food that was ordered.

- A cook wheels a container filled with cooked prime ribs down a pier toward a yacht where the meat will be served to a group of 80 conventioneers in half an hour. Suddenly, the cook is distracted, and the prime rib container tumbles over the edge of the pier into 40 feet of water.
- The table numbers have vanished, and the guests are ready to be seated for dinner.
- The fire marshal arrives at a party site 20 minutes before a catered event and refuses to allow guests access to the party site because the space had not been authorized for party use.
- The catering crew arrives at the party site with a van full of food, cooked to order—exactly one week early.
- A new customer places an order and asks that the caterer deliver to a home where family members and guests will have gathered prior to a funeral service. The caterer sends the food and, upon arrival, is told that the person with the checkbook is at the funeral home and is asked to please stop back in an hour for the money. The delivery person leaves without obtaining a signature. Upon returning, there is no one home and no one from whom to collect payment.
- While using a garbage disposal in a client's home, the caterer suddenly hears a terrible noise and watches in horror as water and garbage spew from the disposal all over the floor. The irate customer refuses to pay the caterer and threatens to sue for the cost of replacing the garbage disposal that was ruined because of (in the customer's words) the caterer's "negligence."
- After catering a flawless party at a client's home and loading the catering truck to capacity, the caterer is shocked to learn from the client that all 15 bags of trash must be removed from the client's property because of the neighborhood's zoning ordinances.

– The caterer's rental company representative calls the caterer the morning after an event and advises the caterer that the $600 rented chafing dish is missing. It was there the night before, when the caterer left the client's home. Get the picture? We could tell horror stories all day!

Seasoned off-premise caterers agree, these are only a few of the thousands of obstacles that stand in the way of completing a catered event. This book addresses the various ways to professionally and successfully deal with difficult situations. With all of these very real potential problems, why are there more than 50,000 off-premise caterers in the United States? Why are more young people studying catering at two-year and four-year colleges and universities? Why are thousands of people starting their own catering companies, risking their savings on their dreams of future success? The reasons are numerous. They may love the adventure of working in new and exciting places. They look forward to the peaks and valleys of the business cycle. They love the intense feeling of satisfaction that comes after successfully catering a spectacular party. They love the myriad challenges of this very difficult profession. Many are their own bosses, with no one to answer to but the client. Many pick and choose the parties they wish to cater. Many make six-figure incomes each year, and others cater occasionally, just for the fun of it. What are the differences between off-premise catering and on-premise catering? Let's examine these differences, from both the client's and the caterer's viewpoints.

From the Client's Viewpoint

Most clients fail to consider the cost of the rental equipment such as tables, chairs, linens, china, glassware, and flatware when they consider engaging an off-premise caterer. They think it will be less expensive to entertain in their homes, or at unique off-premise sites, than in hotels. In fact, it can be more expensive, considering not only the cost of the rental equipment, but also other costs such as transportation of food and supplies to the site, the costs of special labour and décor, the need for tenting, air-conditioning and/or heating, and other expenses. Clients may save some money by buying their own liquor, but this can be insignificant as compared with the added costs. For many clients, the additional costs are far outweighed by the benefits of entertaining in the privacy of their own homes or the uniqueness of a special off-premise location such as a museum, state-of-the-art aquarium, antique car dealership, or historical site.

From the Caterer's Viewpoint

Off-premise caterers must plan menus that can be prepared successfully at the client's location. For example, foods to be fried should not be cooked in unventilated spaces, like small kitchens in high-rise office buildings. On-premise caterers are not as limited in this regard, and they are generally supported by built-in equipment that can support a wider variety of menus. On-premise party personnel are more familiar with the party facilities than those who work at a variety of unfamiliar locations. Off-premise catering generally has greater seasonal and day-to-day swings in personnel needs, which can create a greater challenge for the off-premise caterer, who is constantly recruiting and training staff; turnover is usually high because such work is on an "as-needed basis." There is definitely a greater potential for oversights in off-premise catering.

Backup supplies, food, and equipment can be miles away or even inaccessible when catering, for instance, aboard a yacht miles from shore. In spite of the uncertainties, off-premise catering offers the opportunity to work in a greater variety of interesting locations. The work is more likely to be different each day, resulting in less boredom and more excitement. For those looking for unlimited challenges and rewards, off-premise catering may be the answer. Advantages and Disadvantages of Off-Premise Catering In his book How to Manage a Successful Catering Business, Manfred Ketterer mentions the numerous advantages of catering.

Advance deposits Limited start-up investment Limited inventories Controllable costs G Additional revenues Business by contract Direct payment Advance forecasting Free word-of-mouth advertising Selectivity Let's discuss a few of these items in more detail. First, most off-premise caterers require some form of advance deposit prior to an event. This deposit provides the caterer with some security if the event is canceled and also can be used to purchase some or all of the food and supplies for the party. There is no need for large amounts of capital to get started, since most off premise catering operations begin by using the existing kitchen facilities of a restaurant, club, hotel, church, or other licensed foodservice business. (It is common knowledge that many start their catering businesses in their home kitchens, but it is imperative to state that this is in direct violation of most local zoning ordinances.) In addition, all of the necessary catering foodservice equipment such as china, glassware, flatware, tables, chairs, and linens can usually be rented, thus avoiding having to invest in expensive equipment inventories.

Food and supply inventories, as well as operating costs, are much more easily controlled, because clients must advise the caterer in advance as to the number of guests that are expected. Off-premise caterers need buy only the amounts necessary to serve the event, unlike a restaurant where there is a large variation from day to day regarding the number of patrons and their menu selections. Off-premise catering generates additional revenues for existing operations like hotels, clubs, and restaurants. They can generate even more profit by providing other services—rental equipment, flowers, décor, music, entertainment, and other accessory services. Both the client and the caterer have expectations regarding the outcome of the party. These expectations should be clearly spelled out in a written contract.

Payment for an event is normally made directly to a manager or owner, eliminating a middleman, whether it's a wedding planner, on-site food and beverage director, or one of the caterer's own staff members. This form of direct payment provides for better cash control and fewer folks to share the profit. Advance forecasting is more accurate for off-premise caterers, because parties are generally booked weeks, months, or years in advance. Moreover, each part of the country has seasonal swings, which make revenue forecasting somewhat easier. For example, in the South the summer months are generally less busy, but in the North these are the busy months. Off-premise events generate tremendous amounts of free word-of-mouth advertising, which can produce future business without the necessity of advertising. Many off-premise caterers feel that satisfied guests at one party will either directly or indirectly book another party by speaking favorably to friends and co-workers about the event and the caterer. In other words, one party can create future parties. Caterers also have the advantage of being somewhat selective about their clients. There are no laws that require you to accept every request to cater.

If the job doesn't Advantages and Disadvantages of Off-Premise Catering % 5 meet your standards, politely decline. In sticky situations where you've already begun to work with a client but find that your communication styles just don't mesh— or, as sometimes happens with weddings, the client is not heeding your advice and you can't even decide who's really in charge—you can walk away, as long as you do so within the terms of your written agreement. Off-premise catering does have some disadvantages too: Catering managers, owners, and staff undergo periods of high stress during very busy periods. Deadlines must be met. There are no excuses for missing a catering deadline. Stress is compounded because the workload is not evenly spread throughout the year. For most off-premise caterers, 80 percent of the events are scheduled in 20 percent of the time. For most, weekends are generally busier than weekdays. Certain seasons, including Christmas, are normally busier than others. Of course, caterers must maintain general business hours too! Many have left the catering field, burned out by the constant stress and high energy demands.

]The seasonality of the business makes it difficult to find staff at certain times. Revenues are inconsistent, making cash management very difficult, particularly during the slower periods when expenses continue yet revenues do not. For those caterers who operate hotels, restaurants, clubs, and other businesses, the time away from the main business—spent on the off-premise business—can hurt. It is difficult for even the most well-organized person to be in two places at the same time. Many hoteliers and restaurateurs find the rigors of off-premise catering too great. Some quit after realizing the difficulty of catering away from their operations.

They feel that the financial benefits are insufficient compared with the effort required to cater off-premise events. Elements of Successful Off-Premise Catering What does it take to become a successful off-premise caterer? What experience is necessary, and what personality traits are desirable? Work Experience. Prior experience in the catering profession or the foodservice industry is important. Experience in food preparation and foodservice (both backof- the-house and front-of-the-house) helps caterers understand the procedures and problems in both areas and how the two areas interface. Those with a strong kitchen background, for example, would be wise to gain some front-of-house experience, and front-of-house personnel should learn the kitchen routine.

Many successful off-premise caterers began by working as accommodators. Accommodators are private chefs who are hired to prepare food for parties. Many assist the client with planning the menu, purchasing the food, and even arranging for kitchen and service staff. The food is prepared and served in the client's home or facility, eliminating the need for a catering commissary. Accommodators receive a fee for their services. The party staff is paid directly by the client.

Passion

Successful professionals are passionate about their work, and caterers are no exception. They love what they do! Clients and staff members will quickly detect a lack of passion, and it will cost you business and good workers. If you don't love what you do, move on and try something else.

An Entrepreneurial Nature

The desire to be an entrepreneur is a trait that is highly desirable for off-premise caterers. An entrepreneur must be willing to spend extraordinary amounts of time and energy to make the off-premise catering business successful, possess an inherent sense of what is right for the business, have the ability to view all aspects of the business at once rather than focusing only on one or two parts, and demonstrate a strong, incessant desire to be his or her own boss and become financially independent.

Basic Business Knowledge :

- Accounting and bookkeeping skills are necessary to understand the financial aspects of operating a catering business. The ability to prepare and interpret financial statements is essential.
- Learn as much about computers as you can. You'll be amazed at how much you can accomplish by using e-mail, having a website, and using specialized Programmes for everything from budgeting to menu planning.
- It's also important to understand the legal aspects of catering. Laws that affect caterers include regulation of licensing, contracts, liability, labour, and alcoholic beverage service. A caterer, like any other businessperson, must have some human resource skills. Knowing how to recruit, train, motivate, and manage personnel is critical.
- Off-premise caterers should be knowledgeable about how to develop and implement a marketing plan.

Ability to Plan, Organize, Execute, and Control

These are the four basic functions of management. To plan, a caterer must visualize in advance all of the aspects of a catered event and document the plans so they are readily understood by the client and easily executed by the staff. Organizing is simply breaking down the party plans into groups of functions that can be executed in an efficient manner. Execution is the implementation of the organized plans by the party staff. Controlling is the supervisory aspect of the event. All well-organized and well-executed plans require control and supervision. The adage is, "It is not what you expect, but what you inspect." The premier off-premise catering firms in the United States insist on excellent supervision at each event.

Ability to Communicate with Clients and Staff

Listening is the key to good communication with clients and prospective clients. Off-premise caterers must listen carefully and attentively to determine what the client needs. A client who calls and asks, "Are you able to cater a party next Friday?" should be dealt with differently from one who calls and asks, "How much will it cost for a wedding reception?" The first caller is ready to buy your services, whereas the second caller is shopping. Astute caterers must be able to respond to client requests in such a manner that the client will immediately gain confidence in the caterer. Communicating with staff is a complex issue. In simple terms, it can be reduced to the ability to tell staff what is expected so that they understand, and the ability to receive their feedback regarding problems, both actual and potential. The result of effective communication is an off-premise catering staff that professionally executes a well-planned party that meets or exceeds the client's expectations.

Willingness to Take Calculated Risks

Off-premise catering is a very risky business. It is not for the fainthearted who are afraid of the unknown. For example, it is more risky catering a corporate fund-raiser at the local zoo under a tent than serving the same group in a hotel ballroom. Off-premise caterers must know when the risk outweighs the gain. In this particular example, catering the event at the zoo without adequate cover in case of rain would probably be too risky. The event could be ruined. The tent makes the risk of rain a calculated one.

Sound Body and Mind

Off-premise catering requires working long hours without rest or sleep, lifting and moving heavy objects, intense pressure as deadlines near, and even long periods of little or no business, which can cause concern. Successful caterers should be in good physical shape, have a high energy level, and be able to mentally deal with seasonal business cycles that range from nonstop activity to slow periods with little or no business. Off-premise caterers must be self-confident, but at the same time realize that they must always find ways to improve the quality of their food and services. In this profession a fondness for people and feeling comfortable in crowds is important. A "cool head" when under pressure, will keep both staff and client calm while potential problems are resolved professionally and efficiently.

Creativity

This is the benchmark of all outstanding caterers. Creative caterers are able to turn a client's vision into reality by creating the appropriate look, feel, menu, service, and ambiance. Those who are not very creative can learn to be, or they can employ those who are creative.

Dependability

Dependability is a major cornerstone of success in off-premise catering. When a caterer fails to deliver what was promised, the negative word of mouth travels fast among clients and potential clients. Even in those situations where circumstances change, making it more difficult to perform as promised, the outstanding caterer will find a way to deliver rather than use the changed circumstances as an excuse not to deliver.

Open-Mindedness

Open-minded caterers read up on catering trends and try new recipes and menus. They are willing to prepare unfamiliar dishes requested by clients, after thoroughly testing and understanding the recipes. They discover and try new dishes. They are always learning better ways to run their businesses.

Ability to Meet the Needs of Clients

The needs of the client must always come first. Success in this business comes from identifying these needs and satisfying them. Unsuccessful off-premise caterers are those who get lost in trying to satisfy their own needs for money, equipment, and greater self-esteem. They forget that the primary goal is to serve the needs of the client. When a client's needs are met, the caterer's needs for revenues, profits, and positive feedback will automatically be met.

Ability to Project a Favorable Image

Prospective clients hire caterers based on their perceived image of the caterer and what the caterer will provide. In some sense, then, caterers are selling themselves more than their food. Off-premise caterers must be able to project a favorable image to the client, one that is in accord with the client's expectations. For example, a caterer whose image is sophisticated and upscale will be hard-pressed to sell a Little League banquet with a low budget. Successful caterers understand their projected images and target their marketing efforts at those clients who desire that image.

Sense of Humour

In this pressure-packed, deadline-oriented, and stressful business, it is easy to get carried away with the magnitude of the undertakings and become so tense and uptight that work ceases to be fun. Laughter at the right time can relieve that tension and stress, putting a renewed sense of fun into the work at hand. How do caterers serve shrimps? They bend down! Managing an Off-Premise Catering Operation Even those who possess the qualities that indicate off-premise catering success must know how to put these talents to use effectively.

Off-premise caterers should be hands-on managers who are constantly customer focused. They must be able to lead staff and clients alike, while conducting business in a professional manner. They must be able to make timely, ethical decisions, while understanding what makes for a successful event. They must also avoid those situations that cause a business to fail. Developing a Strategic Plan Yogi Berra, the zany former New York Yankee catcher, is famous for his many witticisms, such as, "Nobody goes there anymore—it's too crowded." But his best quote may be this one: "If you don't know where you're going, you will wind up somewhere else." That's the reason you need a strategic plan—a roadmap to help you determine the direction in which you wish to go, and the specific goals you'll need to accomplish to get there. A strategic plan starts with a statement of core values, which may include things like client satisfaction; ethical business practices; staff satisfaction, training, and motivation; community service; and operating an environmentally conscious business.

From these core values, a caterer can develop a Mission Statement—a succinct sentence that sums up the company's mission. Here's an example: "To meet the catering needs of the corporate community, providing high levels of service and food quality that result in repeat business and vital growth." After the Mission Statement comes the Vision Statement—a concise summary of where you want to be in the future. Again, an example: "Within five years, our company will be the top-ranked catering firm in our area, with continuing sales and profit growth, while giving back to our community." It's not enough to brainstorm about these statements. Writing them down is the first step to making a commitment—to make them a reality. Only after they are put in writing can you develop more specific objectives to increase sales and profits, measure customer satisfaction, size up your competitors, and plan the ways in which you will give back to the community.

Your Mission and Vision Statements lead naturally to the next step—to establish goals for the operation. You may have heard time management experts use the term "SMART" when describing goals.

The acronym stands for:

Specific: The goals to be accomplished must be easily understood, concise, and unambiguous.

Measurable: There should be no question about whether one attains, or falls short of, a goal. It may be measured in terms of quality, cost, quantity, or time.

Attainable: The goals may be just out of reach, but they're not out of sight! The best goal challenges and motivates you and your team. If it's practically impossible, it may be too frustrating.

Relevant: The goals must fit well with your long-term mission and vision, your objectives, and the results you expect.

Time-bound: There must be a specific deadline for completion of each goal. An example of a SMART goal might be to increase sales and profits by 20 percent each year for the next five years.

Once a caterer has set goals, there must be certain trade-offs. To increase sales, for instance, may require raising prices, hiring more staff to be able to cater more events, or spending money on advertising. The major goals can be broken into smaller, intermediate steps, with a time line to keep the company on track. And remember, goals are not just for the owner of a company. The staff and other professionals employed by the company—tax preparer, banker, attorney—should also be well aware of the goals. You'll need their help to achieve them, and you want them on your side, committed to your goals. Too often, caterers believe they can do everything themselves. They fail to ask for or accept advice from outside consultants and colleagues. It is far more intelligent to ask for assistance when you need it. Someone familiar with your plans and your passion for them is far more likely to be helpful. Finally, as soon as a goal is set, take some action on it. The last part of a strategic management process is to reevaluate your mission, vision, and goals periodically. Times change, trends change, and you become aware of new information. Let's say a caterer's sales year showed a 50 percent increase, when he or she had set a 20 percent annual goal. In this case, the next year's goal might be more realistically revised to a 30 percent increase.

Hands-on Attention to Detail Management

The devil is in the details. Have you ever heard that old saying? Another way to put it: We've all been bitten by a mosquito or stung by a bee, but how many of us have been bitten by an elephant? It's always the little things that get us! In catering, the details are virtually endless, a stream of tiny elements that might go wrong and result in a catastrophe. One thing forgotten, misheard, or misplaced can ruin an event. So it's important to check and recheck and to be prepared for last-minute emergencies. It is simply not possible to run this kind of business from behind a desk, reading computer printouts and delegating all tasks. Off-premise catering companies must be managed from the center of the action, whether that is with the guests or preparing foods in the kitchen. It comes from checking and rechecking every detail to ensure that it meets the highest of standards. It comes from inspecting for the best and expecting the best. Some call this management style "management by walking around." In one sense that is true, but there is more to it than walking around.

Astute offpremise caterers must:

- Obtain feedback from clients and guests regarding the food and service.
- Oversee the catering staff to ensure they are performing as directed and as expected.
- Help out when a table needs to be cleared or when the bar suddenly becomes very busy. Help in the kitchen during critical times such as hot food dish-up, and even help scrape, stack, and wash dirty dishes if that's what is necessary. It's a roll-up-your-sleeves kind of profession, and you should never be totally satisfied with the way things are. Always look for new ways to present food and make it more flavorful, and for better and more efficient ways to do things.

Customer-Focused Management

An off-premise caterer's full-time mission must be to satisfy the needs of clients. Mike DeLuca, editor of *Restaurant Hospitality* magazine, puts it this way: Companies that are 100% customer focused make the customer's satisfaction their only goal. They do not have as goals, increasing sales by a certain percentage, raising a profit margin, or reducing debt. They believe that if you strive to sell only the highest quality product and strive to please every customer, sales, profit and success will follow. This is a difficult concept for many of us to grasp. It means letting go of a financial accounting structure passed down from generation to generation of Harvard MBAs who've instilled in us that the only way to build your bottom line is to raise your top line and squeeze the middle. That can work ut wouldn't you rather make the quality of your food, the dining experience and your customer's satisfaction your primary concern?2 The moral is simple: If you satisfy your customers while charging a fair price and controlling costs, profits will follow.

Managerial Decision Making

Off-premise catering managers must make decisions that keep their operations running smoothly. They realize that some decisions will be better than others, that there is no perfect solution to every problem, and that the best decision-making goal is to find the best possible solution with the least number of drawbacks. Connie Sitterly, a management consultant and author, states that to be a good decision maker you should "plan ahead so when problems crop up, you're prepared to act, not react. Control circumstances, instead of allowing them to control you. Take the initiative by anticipating and solving business problems." Although hundreds of books have been written about decision making, the following tips from Ms. Sitterly should be helpful. They're paraphrased from an article she wrote back in 1990 in *The Meeting Manager*, but they are still up-to-the-minute when it comes to making tough decisions successfully.

- Remember that there's seldom only one acceptable solution to the problem. Choose the best alternative.
- Make decisions that help achieve the company objectives.
- You need to consider feelings whenever people are involved. Even if you must make an unpopular decision, you can minimize repercussions if workers know you have taken their feelings into account.
- Allow quality time for planning and decision making pick a time when you are energetic and your mind is fresh.
- Realize that you'll never please everyone. Few decisions meet with unanimous approval he appointed authority, not the majority, rules.
- Make time for making decisions in business, delaying a decision can cost thousands of dollars.
- Put decision making in perspective. Every executive feels overwhelmed at times by either the enormity or the number of decisions made during a business day. For peace of mind accept that you are doing the best job you can with the time, talent, and resources you have.
- Don't wait for a popular vote. Rallying your colleagues around your decision before you take action or waiting for their vote of confidence before deciding anything may cost too much in time. There are times when you just have to *do* something.3 Leadership

There are major differences between those who lead and those who manage. Catering companies need both types of executives, and some who can do both. If a catering company is earning seven- and eight-figure annual revenues, it is most definitely being led by people with leadership skills. Leaders are able to get people to do things they don't necessarily like to do, but they do them and even enjoy them. You might say: Maintains Develops Administers Innovates Relies on systems

Relies on people Counts on controls Counts on trust Does things right Does the right things Works within the system Works on the system Manages things Leads people A leader is more like a thermostat than a thermometer. A thermostat sets the standard temperature for the space it's in. A thermometer simply records the temperature; it can't change anything. And one more important trait:

Leaders take a little more than their share of the blame and a little less than their share of the credit. Professionalism and Common Business Courtesy Off-premise caterers who are not professional in their business practices will never reach the pinnacle of success in the field. Before we address the technical aspects of catering in the succeeding chapters, it is of utmost importance that we define professionalism.

The following guidelines are adapted from an article by Carol McKibben in *Special Events* magazine:

- Become known for doing what you say you are going to do.
- Give price quotes and commitments only when you know everything about the event.
- Treat clients and staff members with respect.
- Build relationships with clients. Do not look at them as accounts or projects.
- Be on time, or a bit early, for appointments. Be prepared for an appointment.
- Be honest; don't play games.
- Stand behind your work. If it is wrong, make it right.
- In the face of abuse from others, don't respond by becoming abusive. Try to detach yourself from it emotionally and handle it logically. Of course, do not use your position of power to abuse others.
- Dress professionally.
- Enjoy your work as an off-premise caterer. When work ceases to be enjoyable, it is time to quit and find a new career.

Index